EGYPT
IN THE AGE
OF
CLEOPATRA

MICHEL CHAUVEAU

EGYPT
IN THE AGE OF
CLEOPATRA

HISTORY AND SOCIETY UNDER THE PTOLEMIES

translated from the French by David Lorton

CORNELL UNIVERSITY PRESS   *Ithaca & London*

The publisher gratefully acknowledges the assistance of the French Ministry of Culture - Centre national du livre.

Original French edition, *L'Egypte au temps de Cléopâtre,* copyright © 1997 by Hachette Littératures, Paris. All rights reserved.

English translation copyright © 2000 by Cornell University

English translation first published 2000 by Cornell University Press
First printing, Cornell Paperbacks, 2000

Printed in the United States of America

Cornell University Press strives to use environ-mentally responsible suppliers and materials to the fullest extent possible in the publishing of its books. Such materials include vegetable-based, low-VOC inks, and acid-free papers that are recycled, totally chlorine-free, or partly composed of nonwood fibers. Books that bear the logo of the FSC (Forest Stewardship Council) use paper taken from forests that have been inspected and certified as meeting the highest standards for environmental and social responsibility. For further information, visit our website at www.cornellpress.cornell.edu.

Library of Congress Cataloging-in-Publication Data

Chauveau, Michel.
[Egypte au temps de Cléopâtre. English]
Egypt in the age of Cleopatra : history and society under the Ptolemies / by Michel Chauveau; translated from the French by David Lorton.
p. cm
Includes bibliographical references and index.
ISBN 0-8014-3597-8 (cloth)—
ISBN 0-8014-8576-2 (pbk.)
1. Egypt—Civilization—332 B.C.–638 A.D.
2. Ptolemaic dynasty, 305–30 B.C. I. Title.

DT61.C4613 2000

99-049898

Cloth printing
10 9 8 7 6 5 4 3 2 1
Paperback printing
10 9 8 7 6 5 4 3 2 1

® GCU

FSC FSC Trademark © 1996 Forest Stewardship Council A.C.
SW-COC-098

CONTENTS

TRANSLATOR'S NOTE   IX

GENEALOGICAL TABLE OF THE PTOLEMAIC DYNASTY   X

MAP OF EGYPT   XII

INTRODUCTION   1

1 HISTORICAL PERSPECTIVE   6

The Heritage of Alexander the Great   6
Crisis in the Kingdom under Philopator and Epiphanes   11
Ptolemy VI Philometor and the Recovery of Egypt   13
The Fat King and His Wives   15
Physkon's Children   16
Ptolemy the Flutist   18
The Flight and Return of Auletes   20
Auletes's Children   22
Cleopatra, Ally of Rome   24
Cleopatra and Antony   26

2 GREEK PHARAOHS AND THEIR SUBJECTS   29

Kings, Queens, and Royal Children   29
A King for the Greeks   33
The Deified King   34
A Pharaoh for the Egyptians   37
A Pharaoh for the Gods   39
Protection of the Temples   40
Royal "Philanthropy"   41
Visits to the Provinces   43
A Regal Life   44
The Program of the Royal Titularies   45
The Allegiance of the Clergy   46
The Ideology of Resistance   49

3 CITIES AND COUNTRYSIDE   52

A Unique Land   52
A Multitudinous Population   55
The Lagide Capital   56
The Center of the Hellenistic World   58
The Delta   63
Memphis and the Faiyum   65
Map of the Faiyum area   67
Upper Egypt   67
Architecture and Urbanism   69

4 ECONOMY AND SOCIETY 72

The Weight of Bureaucracy 72
The *Strategos* 73
The Official Scribes 76
The Burden of Taxation 78
Resistance and Contraband 80
A Cash Economy 82
The Ravages of Inflation 84
The Misery of the Peasants 87
Autopsy of a Village: Kerkeosiris 90
Artisans and Shopkeepers 93
Greeks and Egyptians before the Law 95
Slavery 98

5 PRIESTS AND TEMPLES 100

The Most Religious of Peoples 100
New Sanctuaries 102
Sacred Animals 106
The Prestige of the Priests 108
Piety outside the Temples 109
Greek Priests 113
Temple Economy 115
Oracles and Oaths 117
Strange Slaves 117
The Deities of Memphis 118
The Life and Dreams of Ptolemaios the Recluse 123
Coveted Virgins 127
The Woes of an Egyptian Mendicant Friar 129
To Be Greek in an Egyptian Temple 131
An Informer in the Temple 133

6 LIVING ON THE DEATH OF OTHERS 135

The Land of the Dead 135
The Greeks and the Egyptian Afterlife 136
Specialists in the Service of the Dead 137
The *Choachytai* at Work 139
A Professional Association 141
"Saints" Sometimes Disturbed 143
Division of Labor in the Other Corporations 143
A Disputed House 145
Cadavers in the City 147
An Embalmer Complains to the King 149

7 SOLDIERS AND PEASANTS 151

A Military State 151
Soldiers in the Countryside 152
The Hazards of Cohabitation 154
Independent Income from Real Estate 155
A Soldier-Speculator: Dionysios, Son of Kephalas 156

A Curious "Persian"   158
A Military Colony in the South of Egypt: Pathyris   160
A Cretan in Egypt: The Cavalryman Dryton   160
The Solidarity of an Egyptian Family   164
The Sudden Disappearance of a Garrison   166
The End of the Lagide Army   167

8   TWO LANGUAGES, TWO CULTURES,
     THREE WRITING SYSTEMS   170

A Multicultural Society   170
The New Athens   171
Decline and Rebirth of Alexandrianism   173
Medicine in the Reign of Cleopatra   176
Greek Culture in the Countryside   177
Poems in the Midst of Accounts   178
Hellenizing Distractions at the Serapeum   180
Apollonios and the Last Pharaoh   182
The Native Temples as Guardians of Religious Culture   183
Demotic: Living Language and New Literature   185
Egyptian Stories and Romances   186
Wisdom and Satire   187
Hellenism at Edfu   189

CONCLUSION   191

ABBREVIATIONS   197

NOTES   199

GLOSSARY   214

INDEX   217

TRANSLATOR'S NOTE

In this book, the following conventions have been followed in the citations from ancient texts:

Parentheses ( ) enclose words or brief explanations that have been added for clarity.

Square brackets [ ] enclose words that have been restored in a lacuna.

An ellipsis . . . indicates that a word or words in the original text have been omitted in the citation.

An ellipsis in square brackets [. . .] indicates the presence of a lacuna for which no restoration has been attempted.

English-speaking Egyptologists have no single set of conventions for the rendering of ancient Egyptian and modern Arabic personal and place names. Most of the names mentioned in this book occur in a standard reference work, John Baines and Jaromír Málek, *Atlas of Ancient Egypt* (New York, 1980), and the renderings here follow those in that volume. The only exception is the omission of the typographical sign for *ayin;* this consonant does not exist in English, and it was felt that its inclusion would serve only as a distraction to the reader.

There is also no single set of conventions for rendering ancient Greek words and names in the Roman alphabet. The system followed here is essentially that used by Dorothy J. Thomson in *Memphis under the Ptolemies* (Princeton, 1988), the principal exception being the name of Cleopatra herself, for which the more familiar spelling has been retained here.

For decades, there has been no fresh history of the Ptolemaic period in English, and Michel Chauveau's book will be all the more welcome for its focus on social and economic history. I thank Cornell University Press for asking me to serve as its translator, and I wish to express my thanks to the author and to Mrs. Marinette Rosenfeld for their help while this project was in preparation.

GENEALOGICAL TABLE OF THE PTOLEMAIK DYNASTY

(Except as otherwise noted, the dates of the reigns are indicated; d. = "died.")

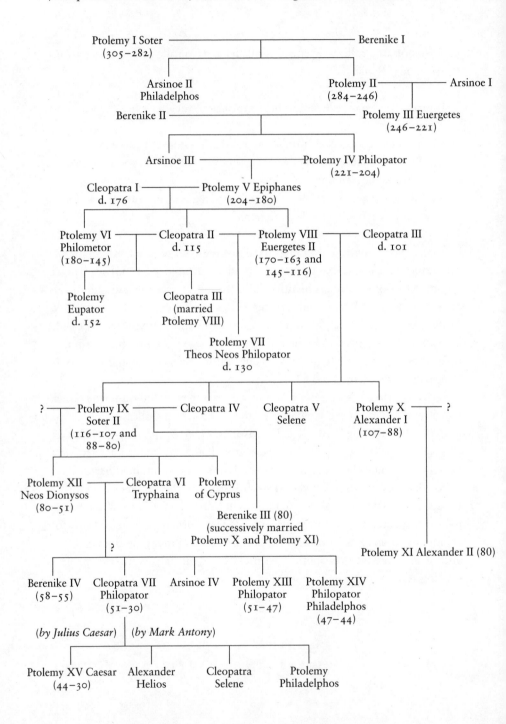

EGYPT
IN THE AGE
OF
CLEOPATRA

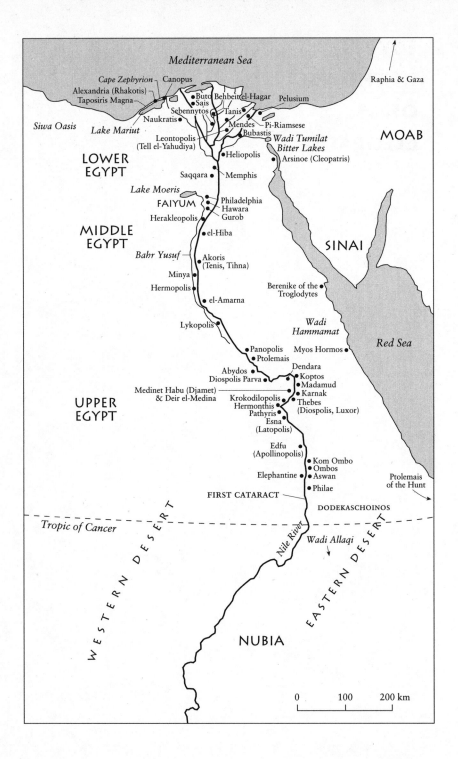

INTRODUCTION

Though it is one of the most familiar episodes in ancient history, the reign of Cleopatra is generally recounted from only one point of view: that of Rome. Like literature and film, classical history has in fact focused only on the role played by this Egyptian queen at just that crucial and dramatic moment when the unstable republican state, which had yet to learn how to rule the immense, disparate, and dispersed territories it dominated, and which was torn moreover by incessant civil wars, was transforming itself into the autocratic empire with universal pretensions that would, with its conversion to Christianity, prove to be the founder of our Western civilization. By way of contrast, Egypt—the very territory from which Cleopatra derived her wealth and power—seems like nothing more than an exotic backdrop devoid of substance, whose only function was to supply the queen with the material means and the charms and attraction she needed in her quest to seduce the crude Roman generals. It must be noted that ancient historiography is in large part responsible for this point of view. The Greek and Roman historians who created this image of Cleopatra were interested only in her interventions in Roman affairs, for the most part to stigmatize their pernicious effects; their portrayals of this period are stamped in large part by the intense and of course negative propaganda campaign unleashed by Augustus against the Lagide queen both before and after Actium.[1] Egypt itself played virtually no role in this propaganda except as a facile cliché: a society corrupt at its top, backward at its bottom, and ever slave to ridiculous superstitions. But historians and geographers who were contemporaries of Cleopatra, and whose interests were focused on her land and its inhabitants, in fact described a country that was above all unchanging and atemporal, a pharaonic Egypt capable of captivating readers eager for the exotic and the paradoxical, one evidently indifferent to the changes that three centuries of Macedonian occupation had imposed on it.[2]

This unbalanced perception of Cleopatra and her times is also manifest in most of the modern biographies devoted to her:[3] Roman affairs are by far their primary concern, while matters internal to Egypt are practically ignored. This imbalance is due to the near silence of the classical authors, to be sure, but also to the relative lack of other kinds of sources. Yet for students of ancient history, Egypt is unique in the abundance and variety of documentary evidence it supplies. Everywhere else in the Mediterranean world, almost without exception, researchers have only an epigraphic record at their disposal, that is to say, inscriptions on stone, for only these could survive the damage inevitable in the case of organic materials. But the special nature of Egypt's arid climate permitted the survival, in its sands, of thousands of papyri and *ostraca* (texts written in ink on potsherds or pieces of limestone) of all periods, from the Old Kingdom to the Islamic Middle Ages, written in the various scripts of the Egyptian language (hieroglyphs, hieratic, Demotic, Coptic) as well as those of occupiers and immigrants (Aramaic, Greek, Latin, Pahlavi, Arabic). The documents from Graeco-Roman Egypt, composed most often in Greek or in the Demotic stage of the Egyptian language, represent perhaps the most important portion of this profusion of texts.[4]

It is only in the last two centuries that the scholarly world has been aware of the existence and importance of the papyri discovered in Egypt, and it was only in the second half of the nineteenth century that the first scholarly publications of the Greek and Demotic papyri began to appear. Beginning in 1877, fortuitous discoveries in the Faiyum and in Middle Egypt placed a significant number of Greek papyri on the antiquities market. The systematic excavations undertaken by British scholars—William Matthew Flinders Petrie at Hawara and Gurob from 1888 to 1890, and Bernard P. Grenfell and Arthur S. Hunt around 1900, in various sites in the Faiyum (Tebtunis) and later at el-Hiba—and then by the French archaeologist Pierre Jouguet at Ghoran and Magdola in 1901–2, led to the accumulation of an especially rich and homogeneous collection of documents.[5] To date, nearly thirty thousand Greek papyri and more than a thousand in Demotic have been published. Many unedited papyri remain hidden in museum collections, while the soil of Egypt has scarcely ceased yielding its secrets, for ongoing excavations continue to discover new texts in appreciable numbers.[6] If we add the thousands of *ostraca* from Thebes, Edfu, Saqqara, and elsewhere, and the many stelae and inscriptions in Greek, Demotic, and hieroglyphs, and the numismatic sources—not to mention the unique corpus of inscriptions furnished by all the temples and chapels constructed or rebuilt in the Ptolemaic period and covered with hieroglyphic inscriptions—we can begin to take measure of the abundance of sources available to the historian who wishes to touch on Egyptian society in the Ptolemaic era.

The highly uneven distribution of this documentation, both in time and in space, is evidently the result of the hazards of the preservation of evidence. But while certain texts have survived in isolation, others—fortunately, the greater number—comprise dossiers or archives that bring to life before our very eyes an individual, a family, a professional group, or an entire administration. Thus, while the image of Graeco-Roman Egypt furnished by the papyri is highly discontinuous in space, in time, and in the social milieux on which they touch, each collection of documents is like a lantern shedding light on its immediate environment while leaving the vast expanses beyond it in darkness. Thus, we might indeed know a certain village at a given time or be able to follow a whole group of professionals through several generations, while the next village and the other professions remain in the shadows. From a strictly chronological point of view, the hazards of preservation have made the age of the great Cleopatra one of those less blessed with papyrus archives: only about fifty Greek papyri can be dated with certainty to her reign. Most of these are from the official archives of the *strategos* of Herakleopolis, with a mere handful of Demotic papyri originating in the Faiyum.[7] Thus, paradoxically, the Egypt of the most famous of its queens is less well known than that of her less illustrious predecessors.

Because of this lack of documentation, the initial aim of this work, which was to present a picture of Egypt in the approximately twenty years when the last Lagide queen was in power, seemed to be a challenge indeed. Although the Roman occupation constituted a major turning point in the history of this land, one that had profound repercussions on all aspects of social and cultural life, the same was not true of Cleopatra's accession to the throne, which was but one more incident in a turbulent dynastic history rich in highly colorful personalities. Prior to Octavian's victory at Actium, the only comparable event was none other than the conquest by Alexander the Great. But to choose such a point of departure would bring us back to the treatment of all of Hellenistic Egypt, and the abundance of sources for this period would have necessitated limiting this treatment to far too brief a summary of a number of fascinating problems.

The reign of Ptolemy V Epiphanes, the great-great-grandfather of Cleopatra VII, represents an important discontinuity in the history of Ptolemaic Egypt. It was a period of crisis marked by a violent reaction of the native population to Macedonian occupation, a revolt that was suppressed only with great difficulty by a regime that was also weakened in its foreign relations. The consequences, which were profound, led to an evolution in social relations between the autochthonous population and the descendants of the Greek-speaking immigrants, an evolution favored by the near-complete halt in immigration from the Greek world. A certain Egyptianizing of succeeding generations of Greeks and a relative Hellenization of a privileged minority of Egyptians roughed out a society that, if not fully integrated, was at least more harmonious while at the same time more diversified.

In 195 B.C.E., Ptolemy V married a princess Cleopatra, the first Lagide queen to bear that name. Daughter of the Seleucid king Antiochus III, who had just inflicted a defeat fraught with consequences on his future son-in-law, she compensated by bringing new blood to the family line of her husband, who was himself the fruit of an incestuous union. Other women had already played an important role in the Ptolemaic dynasty. Arsinoe II and Berenike II had been strong personalities who in large part inspired the political decisions of their respective husbands, but Cleopatra I had the privilege of being the first to exercise sole power, upon the death of her husband in 180, in the name of her minor son. In inaugurating her short period of regency, Cleopatra I established women's right and qualifications to rule as fundamental givens for the future of the country. From that time on, most of the queens would take the name Cleopatra, thus recognizing their dynasty's debt to the woman who had assured both her lineage and the political transition at an especially dangerous moment. Indeed, a number of princesses who had received another name at birth ended by adopting that of Cleopatra when they arrived at the apogee of power, such as Berenike III,[8] wife of Ptolemy Alexander, and undoubtedly also Berenike IV,[9] daughter of Ptolemy XII. One can speak of a veritable dynasty of Cleopatras, parallel to that of the Ptolemies, one often in conflict with the latter, one possessed of its own political vision, and the personification incarnate of the attempt to harmonize the diaparate components of the land which characterized this entire epoch.

We shall thus treat only briefly the early years of Ptolemaic Egypt, which witnessed the installation and organization of a foreign power through colonization by immigrants from all parts of the Greek world and its barbarian margins. The most important archive bequeathed to us by all antiquity is that of the Carian Zenon of Kaunos, the superintendent of a domain in the Faiyum ceded by Ptolemy II to Apollonios, his minister of finance. It constitutes the basis for our knowledge of the economy, administration, and society of Egypt in the third century B.C.E., and it has been admirably treated elsewhere in recent works in the French language.[10] We shall therefore refer to these archives, as well as other important sources of this same period, only to the extent that they shed light on the general framework of Egyptian society during the two centuries before our own era, the society of the Cleopatras.

1 HISTORICAL PERSPECTIVE

THE HERITAGE OF ALEXANDER THE GREAT

The three centuries separating the invasion of the Persian satrapy of Egypt by the troops of Alexander in 332 B.C.E. and the taking of Alexandria by Octavian's Roman soldiers on August 1, 30 B.C.E. constituted a paradoxical interval in the history of Egypt. In the hands of a dynasty foreign to its traditions, its language, and its religion, Egypt was nevertheless to experience a period of economic prosperity, political power, and intense intellectual and artistic activity. For the first time in their history, however, the Egyptian people were now confronted by a genuine social and cultural challenge: the settlement on their soil of a large number of immigrants, heirs to a different and highly advanced civilization, who would try to impose their own way of life and modes of organization as the dominant model.

Alexander (Figures 1 and 2) found a nation that, after about sixty years of independence (404–342 B.C.E.), had fallen once again, ten years earlier, under the yoke of the Great King. This second Persian occupation was borne with difficulty by the Egyptians, who were subjected to ferocious repression, and they seem to have welcomed the Macedonian king as a liberator. The "conquest" thus went smoothly, once the Persian satrapy accepted the terms of an honorable surrender. With his visit to the sanctuaries of Memphis, his eventual coronation as pharaoh in the temple of Ptah, and finally his consultation with the oracle of Ammon at Siwa Oasis, the ruling classes of Egypt made it known that Alexander was heir to the ancient native dynasties. Moreover, he placed the satrapy in the hands of a Greek born in Egypt, Kleomenes of Naukratis, who was assisted by two Egyptian

FIGURE 1. Bronze statuette of Alexander the Great, reputedly found in Egypt. Walters Art Gallery 54.1045. Photo courtesy of The Walters Art Gallery, Baltimore.

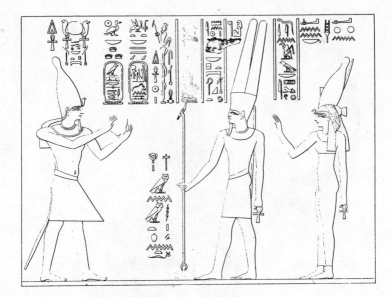

FIGURE 2. Alexander the Great presenting an offering to Amun and Mut. Temple of Luxor. After J.-F. Champollion, *Monuments de l'Égypte et de la Nubie,* Vol. IV (Paris, 1845), Pl. CCCXLVII.

nomarchs, Petiese and Doloaspis; the occupying troops were entrusted to two Macedonian officers. But Alexander's most enduring achievement was the founding of a new Greek city in the western delta, on the Mediterranean coast, one that less than twenty years later would become the capital of the land. The administration of Kleomenes nearly alienated the Egyptian population from their new masters. The exorbitant sums extorted from the priests under threat of closing their temples, the arbitrary taxes on trade in grain, and various other exactions nearly made them nostalgic for the time of the Persians.

After Alexander died at Babylon in June of 323 B.C.E., and while the succession was being settled in at least a temporary fashion, the Macedonian generals proceeded to divide up the provinces that had recently been conquered. One of the oldest and most capable, Ptolemy son of Lagos, a distant cousin of Alexander, took Egypt for himself. After easily doing away with Kleomenes, he had to face the threats that his contemporaries' aspirations to hegemony brought to bear on his newly acquired possession.

As a result of the extinction of the Argead dynasty with the death of Alexander's posthumous son in 310 B.C.E., and after an interregnum caused by the rivalries and the indecisiveness of the various satraps, Ptolemy (Figure 3) assumed the royal title in 305–304, following the example of the

FIGURE 3. Portrait of Ptolemy I on a bronze fulcrum (armrest) applique. Walters Art Gallery 54.599. Photo courtesy of The Walters Art Gallery, Baltimore.

other *diadochoi.* Soon rid of his most formidable enemies, he was able to devote himself entirely to the organization of his kingdom and the embellishment of his new capital, Alexandria.

Ptolemy left his heirs a state characterized by stability and a relative balance between the two principal population groups, the Graeco-

FIGURE 4. Ring depicting Arsinoe II. Walters Art Gallery 71.608. Photo courtesy of The Walters Art Gallery, Baltimore.

FIGURE 5. Obverse of a gold octodrachm depicting Ptolemy III. From the Ottilia Buerger Collection of Ancient and Byzantine Coins, photograph © 1995 courtesy of Lawrence University, Appleton, Wisconsin.

Macedonian and the Egyptian, and with the embryo of a Mediterranean empire that could assure political security and commercial prosperity for the land and its capital. At the end of several wars, not all of them equally successful, his son Ptolemy II managed to add considerably to the possessions his father had left him. Moreover, he managed a propaganda coup on behalf of his dynasty by marrying his own sister, Arsinoe II (Figure 4), and by treating her death as an opportune apotheosis: the cult of the new goddess Philadelphos made it possible to unite Greeks and Egyptians in a common loyalistic fervor, thus assuring the long-term attachment of his subjects to his line. Ptolemy III (Figure 5), who became king in January 246 B.C.E., took advantage of a domestic crisis in the Seleucid kingdom, whose domination of western Asia was quite precarious, to wrest fresh concessions at the conclusion of the Laodicean War, extending to the acquisition of Seleucia in Pieria, the very port of Antioch, the enemy capital!

CRISIS IN THE KINGDOM
UNDER PHILOPATOR AND EPIPHANES

The third century marked the apogee of the Lagide monarchy. Efficient administration of the country permitted investment in a foreign trade that was mostly profitable. These profits could be used to maintain a powerful army, to intervene in the affairs of all the coastal lands of the eastern Mediterranean, and to make Alexandria the beacon of Hellenism. But it was a fragile edifice that, in the end, could not resist the tensions provoked in Egypt itself by overexploitation of the land, tensions that could only be aggravated by the classic manifestations of corruption on the part of a bloated and overzealous administration and by the sociocultural antagonisms that divided the dominant class of foreign origin and the indigenous masses burdened by taxes and corvée labor. Only the danger of external aggression was needed to unleash these latent destructive forces. This menace took form in the person of the young Antiochus III, an ambitious and energetic monarch who was eager for revenge on his Lagide enemy. After succeeding brilliantly in redressing the domestic situation in his own kingdom, he attempted a first large-scale campaign intended to wrest the Syro-Palestinian provinces from Egyptian domination. Contrary to all expectations, he was beaten at the very gates of Egypt by an otherwise indolent and hedonistic Ptolemy IV in the battle of Raphia in June 217 B.C.E..

But the coin had its other side: this heaven-sent victory had in fact been made possible only by the en masse enrollment and arming of Egyptian combatants. These became conscious of their strength and were not slow to rise up against a power they found less and less acceptable in the context of an economic crisis provoked by the war effort. At the death of Ptolemy IV in 205 B.C.E., this unrest ended in the secession of the south of the country under the rule of a native dynasty that succeeded in winning the support of a good part of the priestly class, while at Alexandria, the rule of a minor sovereign was disputed with the help of the masses, who were manipulated by various rival cliques. For his part, Antiochus III was able to take advantage of this unexpected opportunity; he launched a lightning offensive and vanquished the Ptolemaic army at the battle of Panion, thus gaining all the Asiatic possessions of the Ptolemaic empire. Peace between the two kingdoms was nevertheless concluded with the marriage of the young Ptolemy V Epiphanes (Figure 6) to the daughter of Antiochus III, the first of the Cleopatras. The young sovereign was then able to occupy himself with putting down the native rebellion, which was accomplished in 186 with the final defeat of the rebel king Ankhwennofre. In the meanwhile, Antiochus III,

FIGURE 6. Allegorical bronze statuette depicting a triumphant Egyptian king (what remains of the royal uraeus on the diadem cannot be seen in the photograph), probably Ptolemy V. Walters Art Gallery 54.1050. Photo courtesy of The Walters Art Gallery, Baltimore.

who had been vanquished by Rome, was obliged to accept the disastrous peace of Apamea, which inaugurated the weakening of the Seleucids and had the result of freeing the Lagide state from a burdensome domination. Rome thus affirmed itself as the arbiter of the Hellenistic powers.

PTOLEMY VI PHILOMETOR AND THE RECOVERY OF EGYPT

Ptolemy V died prematurely in 180 B.C.E., leaving three minor children. Fortunately, the regency was exercised in the name of the young Ptolemy VI by Queen Cleopatra, and she conducted a cautious foreign policy toward her neighbor, who was gradually recovering from his humiliating defeat. After her death in 176, power fell into the hands of less sensible courtiers who increasingly provoked the new king of Syria, Antiochus IV Epiphanes. Believing they had the means to recover by force the territories lost in 200, they plunged Egypt into a new Syrian war. It turned rapidly into a catastrophe. For the first time since the invasion of Perdiccas in 321, an enemy army penetrated deep into Egyptian territory. Antiochus IV was even so insolent as to have himself crowned pharaoh at Memphis, while discord reigned between Ptolemy VI and his brother, whom the inept regents had associated with him on the throne.

The Lagides would be saved by Roman intervention. In the course of talks at the gates of Alexandria, the Senate's envoy, Gaius Popilius Laenas, enclosed Antiochus IV in a circle that he traced in the sand with his stick and demanded that he choose between Egypt and the friendship of the Roman people. The king, taking correct measure of the danger to himself, chose to preserve amity with Rome and promptly returned to Syria with his army, leaving the brothers Ptolemy to face one another. These brothers could not succeed in getting along; instead, they involved members of various ethnic factions who were vying for government positions in their quarrels. Thus rose the specter of another civil war, this time initiated by the heads of state themselves. The younger Ptolemy prevailed temporarily, sending his brother into exile in the month of October 164 B.C.E. In a sign of the times, the latter found refuge at Rome, a development that served to confirm the city's role as guardian of the Ptolemaic monarchy. After several months, when the younger Ptolemy had sunk to the nadir of his popularity at Alexandria, the Senate of Rome succeeded in imposing its plan for a division of the realm: Ptolemy VI Philometor would reign over Egypt and Cyprus with his sister Cleopatra II, while his brother would content himself with sovereignty over Cyrenaica.

Though it constituted yet one more step in the debasement of Lagide power and, in the end, toward its dismemberment, this plan had the merit of gradually restoring calm to Egypt. There was a perceptible improvement in the condition of the country between 163 and 145 B.C.E., as witnessed by the many architectural and decorative programs in the temples of Egypt during this period. The aborted attempts of the king's younger brother—who would bear the sobriquet *Physkon* (Fatty) because of his grotesque obesity—to take control of Cyprus had no repercussion in Egypt itself. More disquieting was the death in 152 of the crown prince Ptolemy Eupator, which raised the threat of a dynastic interruption, in the absence of other male children born to the royal couple. The future of the country became all the more uncertain in 155 with the publication of Physkon's will, which left his kingdom to the Roman people. This created a dangerous precedent, for Rome had become the dominant power in the eastern Mediterranean after having crushed Macedonia and liberated Greece at the conclusion of the battle of Pydna in 168.

The situation in Syria, however, had evolved in such a way as to present an opportunity for revenge on the part of Egypt. In fact, the Seleucid kingdom had undergone a singular decline after the death of Antiochus IV in 164 B.C.E. It was not spared dynastic quarrels, which were deliberately fueled by Rome and by the rival states of Pergamon and Cappadocia; an impostor, Alexander Balas, the pretended son of Antiochus IV, succeeded in overthrowing Demetrios, the legitimate Seleucid. After a long war provoked by Antiochus IV's attempts at a forced Hellenization, the Jews had won their independence under the leadership of the Hasmonean Jonathan. Balas, in danger of being overthrown in turn by the son of his victim, who was also named Demetrios, made an appeal to Ptolemy VI, who had already given him his daughter Cleopatra Thea in marriage. The Egyptian sovereign was able to put together an army and penetrate victoriously into Syria. His success was such that it alarmed Balas; fearing he might be ousted from rule, he attempted to have his father-in-law assassinated. After the attempt failed, Ptolemy VI made an alliance with the young Demetrios and turned against his former protégé. The population of Antioch, weary of Seleucids both real and false, offered the crown to Ptolemy, who thus saw the prospect of realizing, to his own profit, Antiochus IV's dream of unifying the kingdoms of Egypt and Asia. Fear of a reaction on the part of Rome caused him to decline, however, and he had Demetrios II acclaimed in his stead. He concluded his enterprise by crushing Alexander Balas at the battle of Oinoparas. Gravely injured by a fall from his horse, however, Ptolemy VI died some days later.

At the news of his brother's death, Ptolemy Physkon hastened from Cyrene to Alexandria, where he married the widow of the deceased king—Cleopatra II, who was at the same time his own sister. His return, though it was imposed by circumstances, provoked the hostility of a part of the ruling classes and the population of Alexandria, no doubt because of the appalling recollection left behind by his ephemeral rule nineteen years earlier. Galaistes, one of the counselors and generals of Ptolemy VI, claimed that he had the true heir to the throne in his care, an infant the deceased king had entrusted to him, and he attempted to enlist the support of the army, which was on the brink of mutiny because of a delay in the receipt of their pay. The reaction of the new king, who had assumed the epithet "Euergetes" (Beneficent), was dreadful. A merciless repression descended upon his opponents in the capital: nearly all the intellectuals of the Museum were forced into exile, leading to a long-standing eclipse in the city's reputation as the sanctuary of lettered and learned Hellenism. Calm was restored, however; luckier than his brother, Ptolemy VIII quickly had a son whose birth during the pharaonic coronation rites at Memphis in 144 B.C.E. led to his epithet "Memphites."

Ptolemy VIII Euergetes II was a curious character who owed his accession to the Egyptian throne on two occasions, in 170 and 145, only to crises that imperiled the Lagide royal house. Intelligent and cultivated, he composed "Memoirs" of which we have some extracts displaying his taste for anecdotes that are erudite, refined, and scandalous.[1] Nevertheless, it was this artistic man who, in a matter of weeks, destroyed the work of his predecessors, who had made Alexandria the intellectual capital of the Greek world. Though he was occasionally the author of a sensible and well-advised piece of legislation, by his fault alone, he plunged the country into a fresh and formidable civil war. Less than three years after marrying his sister Cleopatra II, he decided to marry his stepdaughter and niece Cleopatra III, thus bringing to fruition an old plan his brother had once conceived of to compensate for the lack of a male heir. Cleopatra III would bear him at least two sons and three daughters. The rivalry between the two Cleopatras, mother and daughter, was predictable; each of them wished to see her offspring the heir to the throne. The festering quarrel degenerated into war toward the end of 132, when Cleopatra II expelled her husband and her daughter, who took refuge on Cyprus. Having succeeded in attracting the young Memphites there, Ptolemy VIII had him assassinated, and he sent the dismembered body of the adolescent to his mother in the guise of an anniversary present! Worse still, the country was torn between the partisans of Cleopatra II and those of Ptolemy VIII and Cleopatra III, along various lines that divided the nation: between Alexandria and the *Chora* (the provinces), between Egyptians and Greeks, between Greeks and Jews, and between neighboring towns estranged by old animosities. Ptolemy VIII gradually gained the upper hand, and in his own turn, he succeeded in expelling his sister in 124.

But the troubles persisted. Local antagonisms degenerated into an unending series of provocations and reprisals; peasants fled from their villages and organized themselves into gangs of brigands; the fiscal functionaries and tax farmers took to imposing all sorts of exactions and failed to respect even the right of asylum in temples; fields were no longer cultivated; the prices of basic staples soared; and the entire country was on the brink of economic and social collapse. Such being the situation, the king decided to recall his sister. He acknowledged his wrongs by according her assassinated son Memphites a place in the dynastic pantheon with the paradoxical title "New God Who Loves His Father" (Theos Neos Philopator). And finally, in March 118 B.C.E., he issued an amnesty decree of unprecedented scope. Realistic and generous, the amnesty covered all acts committed during the civil war, with the exception of homicide and sacrilege. All debts were forgiven, in the hope of inducing the peasants to return home and once again labor for the profit of the crown. Various other provisions were intended to correct the abuses that had aggravated the crisis and to clarify basic legal principles, such as those governing the relationships between Greeks and Egyptians. Contrary to all expectations, these measures were well received, and the general situation was quickly ameliorated. As peace was gradually restoring prosperity, the king died on June 24, 116, at the age of about sixty-eight, paradoxically older than any other Lagide, with the exception of Ptolemy I, and after having more than once, by his own misdeeds, imperiled the future of his dynasty.

PHYSKON'S CHILDREN

Physkon left the crown to his oldest son, Ptolemy Soter II, surnamed Lathyros (Chickpea), but the new pharaoh was under the burdensome guardianship of the two queen mothers, in whose company he visited the south of the country, Aswan, and Lower Nubia, thus strengthening the frontier against the encroachments of the kingdom of Meroe. Happily for the maintenance of peace, Cleopatra II disappeared some months later, which left power in the hands of her daughter and former rival, Cleopatra III. The latter chose not to share it with her son, the titular king, but rather left him with the meager compensation of exclusive sovereignty over Cyrenaica alone.² The king, who was already married to his older sister Cleopatra IV, was obliged by command of his mother to repudiate her in order to marry his other sister, Cleopatra Selene. Cleopatra III in fact preferred her other son, Alexander, and she managed to procure the title of king of Cyprus for him in 114 B.C.E. In this manner, family quarrels were breaking up what remained of the Lagide empire. The queen, who found her older son insufficiently docile for her taste, ended by dismissing him entirely and replacing him with his younger brother Alexander as king of Egypt in 107. From that time on, the power of Cleopatra III was absolute, as she demonstrated by assuming the eponymous priesthood of Alexander, a supreme honor not normally accorded to any woman!

In the meanwhile, Ptolemy Soter, after a critical period, succeeded in gaining control of Cyprus, with the intention of using it as a base for winning back his kingdom. He made an attempt in 103 B.C.E., though in a highly indirect manner, by responding to an appeal for help sent out by the citizens of Ptolemais (Acre) on the coast of Palestine, who had found themselves besieged by the new Jewish king Alexander Jannaeus. After making a successful landing, he found himself refused entry into the city, for its inhabitants had in the meanwhile had a change of heart. That did not, however, prevent him from inflicting a bloody defeat on Jannaeus, after which he and his army ravaged the Jewish kingdom. This strong comeback on the part of her hated son, who was now in the proximity of Egypt, was threatening to Cleopatra III, and she, in turn, mounted an expedition to push him back to the sea. The war that ensued was a particularly confused one, entailing half a dozen different protagonists, for the two Seleucid kings who were at that time contesting the power at Antioch also became involved. Soter made an incursion into Egypt, but his forces were insufficient and he was quickly beaten back. After spending the winter at Gaza, he was obliged to return to Cyprus. As for Ptolemy Alexander, he took advantage of the disorder to assassinate his mother, whose yoke he could no longer tolerate. Thus ended fifteen years of authoritarian rule by a Cleopatra, demonstrating that the kingdom could be managed effectively enough by a woman, a lesson that would be remembered half a century later by her great-granddaughter, Cleopatra the Great.

Alexander reigned with his wife, Berenike III, who was curiously enough the daughter of his inimical brother Ptolemy Soter, so that her matrimonial circumstances reproduced those of her grandmother Cleopatra III with

Ptolemy VIII. Conditions in Egypt deteriorated considerably during the twelve years of this new reign, with unrest becoming endemic in Upper Egypt. The ever more frequent posting of royal decrees of asylum at the temples indicates either that the right of asylum was no longer respected or that it was being abused because of the general poverty and lack of public safety. Meanwhile, Egypt lost all control over Cyrenaica; it was ceded to a bastard son of Ptolemy VIII, Ptolemy Apion, who bequeathed it to Rome in 96 B.C.E. In 89–88, the garrison at Alexandria rose up against the king and demanded the recall of his brother, who was still ruling over Cyprus. Alexander was obliged to take flight and was killed during a battle at sea. Soter II was reinstalled in the capital, but he had to take steps to crush Upper Egypt, which was once again in revolt. Moreover, when he departed from Alexandria, Ptolemy Alexander had left a time bomb in the form of a testament designating the Roman people as his heir, a step taken in the vain hope of preventing the return of Soter to the throne. From that time on, the various factions struggling for power at Rome would have legal grounds for demanding the annexation of Egypt. Soter II survived his brother by a scant eight years. He was the last Lagide who was able to treat autonomously with Rome, for the latter, torn apart by the Social War and bogged down in an interminable conflict in the east with Mithridates, the king of Pontos, was scarcely in a position to concern itself any longer with Egypt.

PTOLEMY THE FLUTIST

Upon the death of Soter, his sister Berenike III, who was already the widow of Alexander, assured the succession. Since she had neither a husband nor a son with whom she could reign, she found it necessary to decide, after hesitating for some months, upon marriage to a bastard of her late husband, also named Alexander, who was at that time living in Italy. The new king was a protégé of Sulla, the newly uncontested master of Rome, who could thus easily impose his will on the royal court of Egypt. Just after the wedding, Ptolemy XI Alexander II, in too great a haste to assume sole power, instigated the murder of his new bride and former mother-in-law. But things turned against him, for like most of the queens of the dynasty, she was popular with the common people of Alexandria. In one of the violent riots that periodically shook the capital, an unbridled mob invaded the palace and lynched the young assassin before he had reigned a whole eighteen days.

After this interval, there was almost no one to inherit the throne of Egypt. Happily, no one at Rome had the resolve to demand the execution of the will of Ptolemy X, so the court at Alexandria was free to confer royal offices on the last illegitimate children of Soter II—two Ptolemies and a Cleopatra. The elder brother was married to his sister, according to the dynastic tradition, and the couple were placed on the throne of Egypt. To avoid any quarrel between the two brothers, the younger one became king of Cyprus. Thus began the unfortunate reign of Ptolemy XII and Cleopatra VI, who were pompously styled the two "Divine Lovers of Their Father and One Another." But the new Ptolemy, who was driven by his devotion to the patron god of ecstasy and the arts to the point of taking the epithet "New Dionysos," is better known to us by his sobriquet of "Auletes" (Flutist). This crowned artist saw his dynasty abased to the point of becoming a mere pawn in the hands of the leaders of the various factions at Rome. His situation, it must be said, was less than comfortable: he owed his throne to the uncontrollable caprice of the mob at Alexandria, while at the same time, he was menaced by possible intervention from Rome at any moment if he did not obtain the formal recognition of the great protector of the kingdoms and cities of the East. Ptolemy thus did his best to win the title of "ally and friend of the Roman People," without which his legitimacy would not have been recognized by Rome. To this end, he undertook to corrupt the politicians at Rome, dispensing lavish bribes that swallowed up a good part of his revenues.

There was scarcely any urgency until Pompey arrived in the East in 64 B.C.E. At that time, Mithridates was decisively beaten, and Pompey was eager to reorganize the political geography of the entire region to suit himself. Once he had put an end to what remained of the Seleucid kingdom by reducing Syria to a Roman province, had imposed an authoritarian resolution of the internal problems of the Jewish kingdom, and had undertaken to settle a score with the Arab kingdom of the Nabataeans, there was in fact scarcely anything left for him to do but involve himself in the affairs of Egypt. Auletes did not delay in sending an embassy to him, but Pompey chose to return to Asia Minor, for Mithridates had just taken his own life. At Rome itself, the Lagide's greatest ally was the fear aroused by the formidable power that a possible annexation of Egypt would confer on whoever might accomplish it. All attempts to authorize annexation were foiled by opponents of the project. Moreover, Ptolemy's largesse obtained the support of the triumvirate formed by Caesar, Pompey, and Crassus, and in 59, Ptolemy was officially recognized by the Senate. But in the complicated political game going on in Rome at that time, it was necessary to replace one prey with another, and Cyprus paid the price. In 58, Cato the Younger, who had been opposed to the project, was charged with taking possession of the island in the name of the Republic. Arbitrarily dispossessed, Auletes's brother committed suicide.

THE FLIGHT AND RETURN OF AULETES

When news of his death arrived, riots broke out once again in Alexandria. Auletes, already detested for having squandered the riches of the land, found himself blamed for the surrender of an island whose fate had for so long been linked to that of his dynasty. Unable to deal with the situation and fearing lest he suffer the fate of his ephemeral predecessor, Auletes abandoned his capital; taking his treasure with him but leaving his family behind, he set sail for Rhodes. Disconcerted by his sudden departure, the leaders of the insurrection decided to confer the throne jointly on Queen Cleopatra Tryphaina, whom Auletes had removed from power in 69 B.C.E., and the king's eldest daughter, Berenike IV. This was an emergency measure intended to assure continuity of power in a country that had been cast into poverty and constant unrest by the fiscal demands of the king and the exactions of officials and tax collectors. A papyrus from Herakleopolis dating to precisely this time recounts a violent demonstration against one of these corrupt officials:

> The next day, an even larger crowd gathered . . . and demanded the assistance of the queens (Cleopatra VI and Berenike IV) and their troops. The *strategos* . . . met with these people and learned again of many other misdeeds committed against each one of them by Hermaïskos's people. The complainants insisted that they would refuse to take on any work unless the *strategos* made a report to the queens and the Minister of Finance such that the people of Hermaïskos would be excluded from the nome.[3]

Cleopatra VI Tryphaina died shortly after her return to power, leaving Berenike IV the sole queen. Her counselors desperately sought a husband worthy of assuming the royal office. Various candidates were approached. One of them, an adventurer who was passing himself off as a Seleucid, nearly succeeded, but he was unmasked and killed immediately after the wedding ceremony. They finally turned to a certain Archelaos, son of an important general of Mithridates, the former king of Pontos, in the hope he had inherited the military skills of his father, which would be useful, considering the situation in the country. Meanwhile, Ptolemy, who had been quite rudely received at Rhodes by a Cato who was readying himself to take over Cyprus and advised him to return home, went instead to Rome, where he was warmly welcomed by Pompey. Using bribery, he attempted to induce the Senate to grant him military assistance for his return to Alexandria, but the political situation at Rome was such that no agreement could be reached on the question. As far as the Alexandrian court was concerned, the king had abdicated of his own accord, and they sent an embassy of a hundred men to Italy to defend their point of view. The king used his money to effect the assassination of most of these ambassadors, including the chief of the delegation, the philosopher Dio, before they could even be heard by the Senate. He gained scant profit from these crimes, for in the meanwhile, a consultation of the Sibylline Books, or rather a tendentious interpretation of them, had revealed that the deities themselves were opposed to the reestablishment of the king of Egypt by the Roman army.

Faced with so many opposing forces, Auletes decided to leave Italy in the autumn of 57 B.C.E. He took up residence in the famous temple of Artemis at Ephesos, one of the Seven Wonders of the World, while at Rome, Pompey endeavored with little success to sway his enemies and to have the mission of returning Auletes to Alexandria entrusted to him. The king had more luck with the governor of the new Roman province of Syria, Aulus Gabinius, who allowed himself to be persuaded by a commission of ten thousand talents. Abandoning his projected war against the Parthians, he gathered all his available troops and made his way into Egypt after easily taking Pelusium. Archelaos, Berenike's husband, set off courageously to meet the invader, but he perished in the battle, in which the Egyptian army was crushed. Ptolemy returned in all haste to Alexandria, where he had no need more pressing than to see to the death of his daughter Berenike. The second reign of Ptolemy XII thus began under sinister auspices, with the capital in the hands of the Gallic and German soldiers whom Gabinius had left behind for the protection of the king and the interests of Rome. Not only was his treasury depleted, but Auletes was obliged to repay the enormous sums he had borrowed from Roman bankers to fuel his attempts at bribery. Unable to meet his obligations, he devised the plan of conferring upon Rabirius Postumus, his principal creditor, the oversight of the finances of Egypt, with the title of *dioketes,* thus allowing him to help himself directly to the very source of Ptolemy's riches. This fateful expedient came to a sudden end, as Auletes had undoubtedly anticipated when he formed his Machiavellian plan. Under pressure from the rabble, the creditor turned minister was deposed from office and obliged to flee to save his own skin, while at Rome, an indictment on many counts of embezzlement awaited him.

In spite of everything, the financial problems of the kingdom were not resolved. The king was forced to resort to a drastic devaluation of the silver currency that had remained virtually stable since Ptolemy I adopted the Phoenician monetary standard. The most common coin—the *stater* or *tetradrachm*—saw its content in precious metal drop from ninety to thirty-three percent, marking the financial collapse of Lagide power and the prelude to its political death throes. To these difficulties were added the uncertainties caused by the lack of preparation for the succession to the throne. The king was prematurely old and sensed that his death was near; four surviving children were left to him, two sons and two daughters, but the latter were the older, which did not bode well for the future peace of the dynasty. To exorcise the dangers, he placed all his offspring into the hands of a college of the "New Gods Philadelphos," thus signaling a program of peace that was as much desired as it was improbable. Above all, however, it betrayed his inability to make a viable settlement of the Lagide inheritance.

AULETES'S CHILDREN

We do not have much information regarding the circumstances of the succession or the twists and turns of the power struggle that saw a conflict between the older daughter, Cleopatra VII (Figure 7), and her brother Ptolemy XIII—or, rather, the Alexandrian factions that supported each of them.[4] The sequence of events finally becomes somewhat clearer with the arrival of Julius Caesar at Alexandria in the autumn of 48 B.C.E. A curious mystery hangs over the last months of the reign of Ptolemy XII, between February and July 51. Either the king was already dead and it proved possible to conceal the news, or illness had rendered him incapable of governing; in either case, the situation was taken advantage of so as to arrange the succession in favor of one of his heirs, Cleopatra. Such a result was in fact plainly contrary to the last wishes of the king, who had anticipated an association of his elder daughter and his elder son. The execution of his will had been entrusted in principle to the Roman Senate, that is to say, to Pompey, who considered himself the patron of the Lagide dynasty. The latter found himself faced with a fait accompli, for Cleopatra, after a period of fictive coregency with her father, soon made her appearance as sole ruler.

a   b

FIGURE 7. Bronze eighty drachma coin of Cleopatra VII depicting Cleopatra on the obverse (a) and an eagle with a cornucopia in front of it on the reverse (b). American Numismatic Society 1941.131.1158. Photo courtesy of The American Numismatic Society, New York.

Though she was about eighteen years of age and doubtless already driven by the inflexible will to power that she would display on many occasions later, it is probable that she had the benefit of solid support within the dying king's circle of friends. But we know nothing at all about her supporters, though we have information about the opposing faction. The latter, in fact, did not remain passive and took effective steps to see that the supposed wish of the deceased king was respected. During the year 50, Cleopatra was obliged to accept the older boy, who was about twelve years of age, as junior coregent, after which she in turn was relegated to second place, leaving the field open to the guardians of her brother.[5]

At that time, the country was experiencing an outbreak of poverty and unrest, for a series of bad harvests had added to the chronic ills of the preceding reign. In October, the sovereigns promulgated an edict providing that all available surplus wheat in Upper Egypt be requisitioned and that it be transported exclusively to Alexandria, under pain of death.[6] Only the threat of famine could have justified so exceptional a step. Was Cleopatra trying to exploit the general discontent to her own benefit? In any event, she fled from Alexandria to seek support in the provinces. Things reached the height of confusion: Cleopatra inaugurated an ephemeral new era that was adopted by her partisans in the dating of documents,[7] while otherwise, "King Ptolemy and Queen Cleopatra, the Gods Philopator"[8] continued to be invoked, as though the rupture had never occurred. We do not know how Cleopatra was expelled from Egypt; but she found herself in Palestine, supported by the citizens of Ashkelon, who struck coins bearing her effigy.[9] To bar the way to her dreaded return, the councilors of her brother had taken him to Pelusium at the head of an army. This Egyptian civil war was but a minor incident, however, compared to the grave events shaking the territories dominated by Rome at that very moment. The two former allies, Caesar and Pompey, were engaged in an implacable war with each other.

After Pompey's army was crushed at Pharsalos in Greece on August 9, 48 B.C.E., he sought refuge in Egypt, where he hoped to be favorably received on account of the good will he had manifested toward the previous king. Instead, he met a tragic end made famous by Plutarch's moving account. Pothinos and Achillas, aware that Caesar was hot on the fugitive's heels and hoping to please the victor, thought it best to assassinate the former triumvir when he had scarcely disembarked on the beach of Pelusium.[10]

The rest of the story is well known. Caesar's arrival at Alexandria, his displeasure when he learned the circumstances of his rival's death, the hatred he conceived for the clique comprising the king's ministers, and Cleopatra's sudden appearance under incredible circumstances—all this ended in a provisional settlement of the crisis by a return to the status quo ante imposed by the new master of Rome. Caesar in fact underestimated the dangers of the situation, which was more complex than it seemed, and he soon found himself caught in the trap of an actual urban war, the fateful "Alexandrian War," whose ups and downs need not be recounted here. The death of the young king Ptolemy XIII, who drowned in the port, and the arrival of reinforcements long awaited by Caesar put an end to this episode, which failed to ruin the city or bring a premature end to the career of the dictator. The latter decided to consolidate Cleopatra's position as queen of Egypt, though on a solely pro forma basis, for he associated the younger of her brothers, yet another Ptolemy, on the throne with her. In the spring of 47 B.C.E., the conqueror and the young queen, who was already pregnant, took a cruise on the Nile that reinforced her prestige among the Egyptian people while strengthening the bonds that united the two lovers. Immediately after this pleasant interlude, Caesar left Egypt for good, though he took the precaution of leaving three legions behind to discourage any new unrest.

CLEOPATRA, ALLY OF ROME

From 47 to 30 B.C.E., Cleopatra ruled alone, unencumbered by any guardian or associate aside from her nominal one and without any limitations except for those imposed by a Roman protectorate whose benevolence she enjoyed. We would like to know more about the improvement in the domestic situation of the land that this favorable combination of circumstances enabled, but unfortunately, the age of Cleopatra is especially poor in documents: papyri are few in number, and inscriptions, whether Greek or Egyptian, are rare. The ancient authors are relatively eloquent, though, regarding the queen's interference in the affairs of Rome, in which her importance continued to grow until her ultimate fall.

On July 23, 47 B.C.E., Cleopatra gave birth to a son; he was named Ptolemy Caesar to dispel any doubts as to the union of which he was the fruit, notwithstanding its scandalous nature from both the Roman and the Egyptian point of view. Less than a year later, in May or June of 46, the queen, accompanied by her son and her brother-husband, set off on an official visit to Rome, whose avowed goal was to renew Auletes' treaty of friendship and alliance with the Senate and the Roman people. But it was a reunion with Caesar, who was preparing to celebrate no fewer than four triumphs in succession. One of these celebrations was devoted to his victory at Alexandria, and in it was displayed Cleopatra's own sister, the unfortunate Arsinoe, who had made the unpardonable mistake of taking the side of the insurgents. The Egyptian court prolonged its stay at Rome until the Ides of March, 44, which saw the assassination of the dictator. Caesar's will made no reference to the queen or her son; the young Octavian was named sole heir. Disappointed and bereft of her protector, Cleopatra returned in all haste to Alexandria, where she eliminated all possible risk of a challenge by effecting the disappearance of her brother, Ptolemy XIV. Ptolemy Caesar became her official coregent, even before his association with her on the throne was recognized by the Senate of Rome in 42.

During the two years that followed, the civil war touched off by Caesar's assassination plunged Cleopatra into a dangerous situation. Each camp sought her assistance, but taking the side of someone who might be defeated entailed the risk of bringing the wrath of the victor down on Egypt and, with it, the threat of annexation. She decided to rid herself of the legions Caesar had left behind and whose intentions she suspected; she sent them to the first of the belligerents who requested them, Dolabella, a partisan of Caesar who was quickly swept away. She hesitated to divest herself of her own forces, however, especially her fleet, which represented her trump card in any possible military engagement.

Having succeeded in avoiding the perils of war by delaying, Cleopatra approached the triumvirate formed in 43 B.C.E. by the Caesarians Octavian, Antony, and Lepidus in time to prevent the ambiguity of her conduct from seeming excessive. The two battles at Philippi in October, 42 left Octavian—the new Caesar—and Antony with virtually the upper hand. In the ensuing division of territories, all the East—the annexed provinces as well as the guardianship of the allied kingdoms—went to Antony. This faithful companion of Caesar knew Egypt well, for in 55, as Gabinius' chief of cavalry, he had defeated Archelaos on the road to Alexandria. When Antony summoned Cleopatra to a meeting with him at Tarsos in Cilicia to pledge Egypt's allegiance to him, the queen made her entrance as a dazzling apparition, the incarnation of Isis-Aphrodite, surrounded by special effects of the most theatrical sort. This encounter at Tarsos, which had been intended to humiliate Cleopatra, instead provided her an opportunity to display her uncommon talent for diplomatic persuasion—and it decisively settled the future of Egypt.

CLEOPATRA AND ANTONY

The details of the complicated relations between Cleopatra and Antony from 41 B.C.E. on are well known, even if the implications to be attributed to some of them are not always evident. This is due principally to the effectiveness of the propaganda unleashed beginning in 34 by the young Caesar, which was aimed principally at the queen of Egypt and only indirectly at Antony. This propaganda influenced nearly every source at our disposal for this period, impeding a clear conception of the actual motives and strategy of each of the protagonists.

Cleopatra, whose point of view is the only one of interest to us here, could at first have had no ambitions other than her own political survival and to retain her kingdom in the face of vague threats of annexation by Rome. She assured the former by eliminating her brothers and soon also her sister, whose head she demanded from Antony. The latter could only depend on the good will of the representative of Roman might in the East, that is to say, Antony. Gradually, Cleopatra assessed the influence she was able to have on Antony and caught sight of the possibility of reversing the course of history solely by means of her passionate sway. It is clear that she exploited Antony's immense military and political power with the aim of restoring the former Ptolemaic empire, but Antony had his own point of view. Up to that time and for many decades thereafter, Roman policy in the East in no way favored systematic annexations. Like Lucullus, Pompey, and then Caesar before him, Antony wanted to organize the East into a system of provinces administered directly by Rome, territories that were few in number and not too vast, but rich, well pacified, and easily defended. These provinces were to be surrounded by allied kingdoms in the hands of sovereigns of proven loyalty. In 37 B.C.E., when Antony once again met

Cleopatra after three years of separation and after having married Octavia, the sister of Octavian, he undertook a reallocation of these territories, as the *imperium* he held over the East legally permitted him to do. The substantial territorial enlargement he granted to Egypt was intended to reinforce the effectiveness of the system in the context of the ambitious expedition being planned against the Parthians. Cleopatra's propaganda trumpeted these concessions as a victory on the part of the queen; she thus inaugurated a new era and was hailed as the "Youngest Goddess" (*Thea Neotera*) by the Syrian cities over which she was now sovereign.[11]

The failure of Antony's campaign in Armenia and Media ruined his hopes of becoming a new Alexander and left him in a position of dependency vis-à-vis the queen. The latter induced him to develop an ever less Roman and more Hellenistic concept of power, to the point where he was forced to make a choice and repudiated Octavia, his legitimate wife, by the same stroke making a de facto break with his former associate. He had come to imagine a new organization of the East centered on Egypt and his association with Cleopatra. After a second campaign to Armenia, which saw that country annexed, he celebrated a triumph at Alexandria in the autumn of 34 B.C.E., thus making the city into a new Rome. This triumph, which was more like a Dionysiac procession than a Roman celebration, culminated in the extraordinary ceremony of the Donations. In solemn rites enacted before the crowd of Alexandria in the Great Gymnasium, the children of Cleopatra and Antony were crowned: the youngest, Ptolemy Philadelphos, born in 36, became king of Asia on the hither side of the Euphrates (Asia Minor and Syria), while Alexander Helios, born in 40, was made king of farther Asia (Armenia, Media, and all the Parthian domain yet to be conquered!); Cleopatra Selene, twin sister of the latter, became queen of Cyrenaica and Crete. Cleopatra was proclaimed "Queen of Kings" and Ptolemy Caesar, "King of Kings." One can easily imagine the disastrous impact of such a manifesto coming from the East. But despite everything, Antony still had staunch supporters at Rome and in the Senate itself, for the two consuls appointed for the year 32 were among those loyal to him. Only a long campaign of persuasion employing all the artifices of propaganda and venom finally enabled Octavian to obtain from the Senate a declaration of war against Cleopatra alone, with Antony deliberately left unmentioned.

It was not the balance of military forces that determined the outcome of the conflict but rather the strategic and tactical errors of Antony, whose indecisive attitude was the prime cause of his defeat. Against all logic, he chose a battle at sea, imprudently leaving a good part of the responsibility to Cleopatra, whose fleet was the cornerstone of his naval operation. Whatever the reasons for the queen's performance at Actium on September 2, 31 B.C.E., the ensuing disaster sealed her fate and that of Egypt. Less than eleven months later, the new Caesar made his victorious entry into Alexandria and paid homage to the mummified body of its founder. His arrogant indifference toward the tombs of the Lagides and the sacred animals of the pharaonic deities made it clear to the Egyptians that they had truly changed masters.

2 GREEK PHARAOHS AND THEIR SUBJECTS

KINGS, QUEENS, AND ROYAL CHILDREN

The Lagide family never established a solid principle of succession. In fact, two different traditions could be called upon in turn—that of the old Macedonian dynasty and that of the pharaohs—for the Ptolemies were in a position to claim they were heirs to both. Primogeniture should have prevailed in practice, but there was never a rule completely excluding daughters or younger sons. The sovereign's own choice was thus decisive, and Ptolemy I set a precedent by taking the son of his last wife as coregent, to the detriment of Ptolemy Keraunos, his eldest son by a previous marriage. His first three successors did not have a similar problem to resolve, for each of them left behind only one legitimate son. After 180 B.C.E., however, the descendants of Ptolemy V Epiphanes were repeatedly faced with family crises. Ptolemy VI Philometor was obliged to accept his younger brother as his associate on the throne after the first decade of his reign. Their relationship was so tumultuous that it proved necessary to decide, under the aegis of Rome, on a division of the Lagide possessions: Egypt and Cyprus went to the older brother, while the younger received Cyrenaica. The latter was not satisfied with his share, and he intrigued to add Cyprus to his kingdom until the accidental death of his brother enabled him to receive the entire inheritance. A similar situation occurred in the next generation, when Ptolemy Alexander disputed a diminished territorial domain with his older brother. The case of Ptolemy XII was somewhat different; a bastard child, he was able to pretend to the throne only upon the death of his half sister, Berenike III, who was the last legitimate representative of the Lagide family. He himself left behind four children, two boys and two girls, the daughters being the older, and their feuds constituted the last of the dynastic crises.

But the originality of the Ptolemaic dynasty lay in the ever-increasing importance assumed by its women, culminating of course in the great Cleopatra. In the first three reigns, the queens were chosen as a result of matrimonial alliances the kings thought it advantageous to contract with contemporary dynasties. Thus, Ptolemy II married Arsinoe I, the daughter of Lysimachos, king of Thrace, who was a natural ally for the Lagides against their Antigonid and Seleucid adversaries. In a similar vein, Ptolemy III took his cousin Berenike II (Figure 8), daughter of Magas, as his wife, which enabled him to add Cyrenaica to his own possessions. By way of reciprocity, princesses were given to foreign kings: Arsinoe II, daughter of Ptolemy I, to Lysimachos, and Berenike, a daughter of Ptolemy II, to Antiochus II. In the early part of the dynasty, the only exception—which was to have considerable repercussions—was the marriage of Ptolemy II around 276 B.C.E. to his own sister, Arsinoe II, who was at that point the widow of Lysimachos; to that end, he was obliged to repudiate Arsinoe I.

FIGURE 8. Ptolemy III and Berenike II with the falcon-headed god Khonsu. Temple of Karnak. After H. Rosellini, *Monumenti dell'Egitto e della Nubia*, Vol. I (Pisa, 1832), Pl. CLXIII.

This incestuous union, which was contrary to Greek customs, aroused considerable feelings, and instead of minimizing its import so as to contain the scandal, the king made it a major theme of his propaganda, stressing the divine nature of the couple, which could not be bound by the ordinary rules of humanity. In her own lifetime, Arsinoe became the goddess Philadelphos (She Who Loves Her Brother), and her cult was established in all the temples of Egypt, where she was associated with the various local deities.

Mythological precedents were not lacking: among the Greeks themselves, there was the marriage of Zeus to Hera, and the Egyptians had still others. The native priests could not have failed to be aware of the mystical significance of such a union, which was based on the original model of pharaonic royalty, with the incestuous couple Isis and Osiris. Aside from motives based on passion and other, less important considerations and contingencies, this marriage made it possible to establish an innovative basis for the dynastic cult, around which both Egyptians and Greeks could come together. But it was doubtless only progressively that the successors of Ptolemy II became conscious of the importance of this precedent. Ptolemy IV was the first to follow it by marrying his own sister, Arsinoe III (Figure 9), forming thus the couple known as "the gods Philopator." Ptolemy V undoubtedly had no sister, so he temporarily revived the more classic tradition of royal exogamy by marrying the daughter of the great Antiochus III, whose name Cleopatra would have a singular destiny in the Lagide dynasty. Upon the premature death of her husband, this Cleopatra would become the first woman since the New Kingdom to exercise sole power, in the name of her young son, Ptolemy VI, who took the epithet "Philometor" (He Who Loves His Mother). The latter also married his sister, Cleopatra II. Of their two daughters, the older, Cleopatra Thea, married three Seleucids in succession. There was a plan to marry the younger daughter, also named Cleopatra (III), to her uncle, who was at that time the king of Cyrene, undoubtedly in the hope of once again uniting all the Lagide territories under a single scepter. The unexpected death of Ptolemy VI prevented the realization of this scheme, for Ptolemy of Cyrene then judged it more politic to marry his sister, the widow of his brother, and thus become king of Egypt. The young Cleopatra did not give up hope, though, and some years later, she was quick to marry her uncle and stepfather! The sometimes open and sometimes latent conflict between the mother and the daughter, who had become rivals, would dominate the political history of Egypt for at least two decades.

With the death of Ptolemy Physkon, his widow Cleopatra III was able to exercise sole power in the name of her son from 116 to 101 B.C.E., after

FIGURE 9. Marble statue head of Arsinoe III. Walters Art Gallery 23.6. Photo courtesy of The Walters Art Gallery, Baltimore.

taking the precaution of getting rid of his older sister, Cleopatra IV, whose masculine ambition she feared. Later, at the death of Ptolemy IX Soter in 80, his daughter Berenike III represented the legitimacy of the royal line and received its inheritance. Though her assassination brought the bastard Ptolemy XII to the throne, the people of Alexandria entrusted the power once again to two women when Ptolemy shamelessly fled to Rome. As for his successors, we know how the last Cleopatra seized power to the detriment of her brothers.

The Ptolemaic dynasty was of nonroyal origin. Though its founder, the first Ptolemy, could boast of a distant relationship to the old Argead dynasty, nothing destined him a priori to claim the royal title. Only the political void created by the death of Alexander in a world thrown into upheaval by the Macedonian conquest can explain how such good fortune was possible. But his promotion was not accomplished at a single stroke. Like the other *diadochoi*, Ptolemy had to content himself for eighteen years with the title of *satrap*, that is, of one who governed a province in the name of the kings of Macedonia. After 310 B.C.E., this theoretically subaltern position became purely fictitious, because the dynasty died out with the assassination of Alexander's posthumous son. But it was not until 306, when the first step was taken by Antigonos the One-Eyed, the rashest of the satraps, that within the space of a year all the *diadochoi* adopted the royal title in their respective territories. Thus, in 305, Alexander's former general became King (*basileus*) Ptolemy for his Greek subjects and the new pharaoh of his Egyptian subjects.

Kingship was anything but a foreign concept to the Greeks living in Egypt and the other Lagide possessions. Though the majority of them were from cities with democratic or oligarchic constitutions, they knew that at some point in their histories, all the Greek city-states had been ruled by kings. Certain of them, especially the Macedonians, had known no other regime, and moreover, in the eyes of the Greeks, it was the Macedonian precedent that would serve as the model for the Lagide monarchy, as in the other kingdoms born of Alexander's conquest. But at the same time, in the Hellenic imagination, monarchy also conjured up the image of the hated regime of the Achaemenids, the Great Kings par excellence, that of the Persians against whom the Greek cities had valiantly and victoriously fought in the Persian Wars. Kingship was thus also the style of government of barbarian peoples incapable of governing themselves and living the lives of slaves—quite the opposite of the free citizens of the Greek cities. The new regimes of the Hellenistic monarchies thus found themselves in a delicate situation: they could not adopt the familiar forms of the former Macedonian sovereigns, for they were ill suited to the governance of vast territorial expanses inhabited by large and disparate populations, while at the same time they needed to distance themselves from the oriental despotisms that were, for the Greeks, synonymous with base servitude.

In result of this, the Lagide king would assume a double persona: accessible and familiar to his Greek subjects, for whom he was only "King

Ptolemy," and heir to the pharaohs in the eyes of his Egyptian subjects and, as such, of a quasi-divine essence. In fact, for the first generation of Greeks in Egypt—with the obvious exception of those who had established themselves there before the conquest, such as the Hellenomemphites—the ties that bound them to the king were those of employees to their employer rather than the dependence of subjects on their lord. Inevitably, the relationship between the king and the Greek colonists quickly evolved, in part along with their integration into the land of Egypt and their corollary distancing from their cities of origin, and in part because of the success of royal propaganda aimed at establishing the divine nature of the dynasty. But this development was never to reach its logical conclusion: the complete assimilation of the Greek population to the Egyptian masses and the consequent assimilation of the Lagide monarch to an autocrat of the oriental stamp. Though the Greeks living in the *Chora* or, more precisely, their descendants, found their recollections of their civic origins becoming ever hazier over time, to the point of disappearing entirely from their memory, their cultural identity at the same time affirmed itself, along with their awareness of belonging to a privileged minority of whom the king himself was but the most illustrious member. Though they succeeded in consolidating the legitimacy of their autocratic power, the Lagide monarchs would never succeed in winning from their Greek subjects the servile allegiance and mystical veneration that the peoples of the East had long been accustomed to display toward their divinely righted sovereigns.

THE DEIFIED KING

Nevertheless, the very nature of Greek conceptions of divinity left substantial possibilities for the creation and development of a royal cult. For the Greeks, quite unlike the Jews, transcendence was not the basic characteristic of the divine, and as a result, the boundary between the human realm and that of the gods was far from being impermeable. Just as deities could mingle as they pleased with mortals, so the latter, or at least certain ones, could accede to divinity. There was even an intermediate category, that of the heroes who, by dint of their prowess and their merits, had acquired certain attributes of divinity, such as immortality. But the ascription of heroic status was originally a purely cultural process reserved for mythical figures to whom were attributed the origin of cities and deeds that founded a certain social or political order. In historical times, it was possible to grant the status of hero to deceased persons because of their beneficent deeds on behalf of their city, which then wished to honor them in this manner. The divinization of the Lagide kings and queens, however, occurred through a different process, and Alexander himself furnished the basis for it. He had resorted to all sorts of artifices, wonders, revelations, accomplishments, and prophecies to convince at first his army, and then all the Macedonians and Greeks, of his divinity. The most famous exploit of this sort in Egypt was his expedition to Siwa Oasis, whose sole result was the alleged confirmation of his divine descent by the oracle of Ammon. This pretension aroused some resistance among his own officers, for such an idea was repugnant to Hellenes. The *diadochoi* were, by and large, more cautious and based their own propaganda on the apotheosis of Alexander, but they were often caught short by the initiatives taken by cities that accorded them divine honors, in some cases even before they had taken the royal title. It was thus that the citizens of Athens, in a well-known fervor of exuberant sycophancy, proclaimed Antigonos and Demetrios as the "Savior Gods" when the two drove the Macedonian garrison out of their city and restored its democratic government in 307 B.C.E.

The second generation, that of the epigones, did not have the same scruples, and in Egypt at least, the kings quickly understood the necessity of establishing the legitimacy of their power on a religious basis. We have seen how Ptolemy II took the initiative by marrying his own sister, Arsinoe, and deifying her, perhaps even during her lifetime, as the "goddess Philadelphos." His father, who had already received the epithet "Soter" (Savior) from the Rhodians, was also accorded divine status, along with his mother Berenike. The Savior Gods were matched by the Gods Philadelphos, as attested by coins on which the former are depicted on the obverse and the latter on the reverse (Figure 10).[1]

Ptolemy II took a whole series of measures to establish these new cults. Some concerned only the Greek population, such as the founding in 279–278 B.C.E. of the Isolympic Games (that is, the equivalent of the Olympic games), also called the *Ptolemaieia,* at Alexandria. Celebrated every four years in honor of Ptolemy Soter, these games included athletic events, horse races, and competitions in poetry and music, and they brought together delegates from most of the Greek cities of the eastern Mediterranean. Their third celebration in 271–270 was accompanied by an extraordinary triumphal procession intended to commemorate the Lagide victory at the end of the first Syrian war.[2] Of special interest to Alexandria was the creation in 269 of an eponymous priestess of the cult of Arsinoe Philadelphos called "*Kanephoros*" (Carrier of the Golden Basket) alongside the priest of

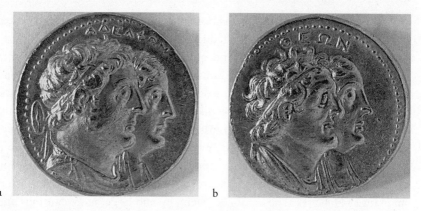

a   b

FIGURE 10. Gold octodrachm dating to 270–260 B.C.E. and depicting Ptolemy II (front) and Arsinoe II on one side (a) and Ptolemy I and Berenike I on the other side (b). From the Ottilia Buerger Collection of Ancient and Byzantine Coins, photograph © 1995 courtesy of Lawrence University, Appleton, Wisconsin.

Alexander instituted by Soter. The entire country, however, was affected by the establishment of a tax, the *apomoïra,* on the vineyards and orchards belonging to private persons, whose purpose was the maintenance of the cult of the new goddess Philadelphos in all the native temples. It was undoubtedly this last initiative that had the greatest effect. We may suppose that the queen was already quite popular during her lifetime and that everything possible was done to promote her image. She was thus the first queen to be depicted on coins.[3] Numerous epigraphic and iconographic remains, such as statuettes and stelae in a style that is sometimes unsophisticated and naïve, testify to a devotion to her that must have been sincere and widespread.[4]

The successors of Ptolemy II had only to follow the trail he blazed and add their own cults, one after another, to those of their ancestors. Thus, couple by couple, the dynastic pantheon was regularly enriched, amounting to a whole sacred genealogy that caused the roots of the Ptolemaic house to penetrate ever deeper into the soil of Egypt. The epithets adopted by each couple reveal the nature of the veneration of which the kings and queens claimed to be the object. Thus, the epithets *Soter,* "Savior" (Ptolemy I and IX), *Euergetes,* "Benefactor" (Ptolemy III and VIII), and *Eukharistos,* "Beneficent" (Ptolemy V) evoke the protection and prosperity the sovereigns were supposed to confer upon the land. *Epiphanes* (Ptolemy V) even more expressly identifies the king as a deity who was venerated on account of his miraculous appearance in the midst of mortals. The other epithets—*Philadelphos, Philopator, Philometor*—convey the bonds of love or mystical devotion that united various members of the dynasty, so that the royal family became an exemplary model, the terrestrial incarnation of divine genealogies. We can observe a certain progressive escalation in this royal theology as its value depreciated, to the point of a pure and simple identification of a sovereign with a divinity. Thus, Cleopatra III became "Isis, Great Mother of the Gods," while Ptolemy XII styled himself the "New God Dionysos." The last Cleopatra was not to be outdone: though her official protocol contained no such pretensions, literary texts and other documents more than once evoke her appearance in the finery of Isis-Aphrodite.[5]

A PHARAOH FOR THE EGYPTIANS

In the sacred context of this divine right monarchy, it was essential for the king to display his privileged relationship to the divine. In his capacity as king of Egypt, he had above all to be the elect of the gods and goddesses of the land, or he would have been nothing more than the chief of a foreign land in the eyes of his Egyptian subjects. Alexander had barely shown the way: his stop at Memphis, where he obligingly received the homage of Egyptian priests all too elated at the defeat of the Persians, was too brief to enable him to establish even the general outline of a program regarding his relations with the indigenous religion. His coronation as pharaoh, whose reality is, moreover, uncertain, was nothing more than a quick and formal affair expedited by a clergy delighted to submit this young foreigner to rituals he could have understood only with difficulty. The clergy had long been accustomed to registering changes in power by according a titulary in the traditional style to each new sovereign who exercised the office of pharaoh. Alexander's name was thus written in hieroglyphs on the walls of temples being decorated at that time, as was subsequently done with those of his successors, who never set foot in Egypt: his brother Philip Arrhidaios and his posthumous son Alexander.

The first Ptolemy understood that he could not be content with such a passive policy, and even before he assumed the royal title, he undertook a propaganda campaign intended to make his image conform to that of an ideal pharaoh. It is probable that he was induced to do this by certain Egyptians he had taken on as counselors. Several hieroglyphic texts inscribed on stelae or statues contain the biographies of Egyptians who held high administrative or military positions during the reign of Ptolemy Soter.[6] Some of these were even members of the last native royal family, that of the

Nectanebos.[7] But it is difficult to evaluate their precise role in the domestic policy of the first Lagide for lack of traces of them in the Greek sources. The latter acquaint us with only one of these high-ranking Egyptians at the court of Ptolemy Soter, specifically, a priest from Sebennytos named Manetho, who made his appearance toward the end of the reign. He exercised his role as an expert in Egyptian matters under Ptolemy II, who requested him to write a history of pharaonic Egypt in the Greek language.[8] We must suppose that Manetho had predecessors who informed the satrap regarding the usages and customs of Egypt and advised him in particular regarding the attitude he should assume toward the temples and their deities. The famous "Satrap Stela" most certainly bears the stamp of such an influence.[9] Commemorating a donation of lands made by a previous pharaoh to the temple of Buto, which was confirmed by Satrap Ptolemy, it includes a eulogy of the latter and a summary of his policies, both domestic (installation in his new capital of Alexandria) and foreign (expedition to Syria). It is clear that such a text, which is pure propaganda, must have emanated directly from the satrap's court. Nevertheless, its style and content, the models of which it makes use, and the themes it invokes betray an author who was of Egyptian origin but who was devoted to conveying faithfully the image of himself and his policies that the satrap wished to project to the native population.

One of the themes of this propaganda enjoyed great success, for it was repeated in other texts of the same genre during the century that followed. It had to do with the discovery and return to Egypt of divine statues and other cult objects that had been stolen and taken to Asia in the course of earlier invasions of the land, in particular by the Persians.[10] In the eyes of the clergy to whom these texts were addressed, such an act of piety would itself have justified the foreign expeditions undertaken by the Lagides. From this time on, these kings would become the protectors of the deities of Egypt, thus identifying themselves with Harsiese, the archetypical king who avenged his divine father Osiris, himself assassinated by Seth, a god easily identified with hostile foreigners.

It is difficult to assess the impact such proclamations were actually intended to have on the native ruling classes. We must surely reckon that stelae of this sort were set up in many temples besides this relatively minor one at Buto. If we consider the image the Egyptians might have had of their preceding pharaohs, the Ptolemaic propaganda must certainly have impressed them: in fact, not one king of the three last native dynasties had managed to mount an expedition outside Egypt. Even the Saite pharaohs, more than two centuries earlier, had enjoyed indifferent successes, in Asia at least, and these were often followed by bitter defeats. The characteristic genius of Lagide propaganda lay in its linking of military success to a display of loyalty to the deities of Egypt. To paraphrase a cliché from the pharaonic texts, "They did what no previous king had accomplished."

A PHARAOH FOR THE GODS

The Lagides were careful to establish close and frequent ties with the native clergy, allowing the temples considerable autonomy in their administration and internal organization, notwithstanding the de facto economic control imposed on the exploitation of their landed estates and the diversion by the state of certain taxes once administered directly by the priests. Because it was impossible for them to deal with each temple individually, they made it a custom to convoke general synods, bringing together delegates from all the temples of Egypt. These were annual in principle, but in practice were held at more or less regular intervals, at first at Alexandria itself or its outer suburbs (Canopus), and then more and more often at Memphis for reasons of convenience. We know of these synods only between the reigns of Ptolemy III and Ptolemy VI,[11] thanks to spectacular stelae that were theoretically supposed to be set up in every temple to commemorate the decisions made on the occasion of these solemn assemblies. Some of these stelae have come down to us in fairly good condition, and in certain instances, there are several preserved copies of the same synodic decree. These decrees, which normally included three versions—in Greek, in the current Egyptian language (Demotic), and in the sacred language (hieroglyphs)—rendered praises to the sovereigns for their beneficent deeds on behalf of the land and its deities and set forth a certain number of provisions expressing recognition of the clergy.

The beneficent deeds in question were generally real enough, for of the three best-known decrees, two commemorate military exploits: a memorable battle fought by Ptolemy IV with the Seleucid king (Raphia decree)[12] and the defeat of Egyptian rebels in the siege of Lykonpolis (Memphis decree).[13] The measures passed by the synods concerned statues, crowns, and priesthoods established in honor of the kings and their families, and also more general matters involving the organization of the temples and cults, undoubtedly under the direct influence of the king and his counselors. Thus, the Canopus decree provided for the creation of a fifth phyle consecrated to the "Gods Euergetes" in all the priestly colleges, as well as the introduction of the leap year into the calendar. It is improbable that all the synods gave occasion for setting up such epigraphic records, or more of them would have been found. Only some of them, exceptional because of the particular circumstances surrounding their convocation, such as the victory at Raphia, or because of the importance of the decisions made, were commemorated in this manner. It is impossible to tell whether the disappearance of such documents beginning with the reign of Ptolemy VI is due to the discontinuance of these synods or to their commonplace nature. In the latter case, the annual meeting of the pharaoh and the priests must have become a simple routine before falling, undoubtedly, into desuetude. Beginning with Ptolemy VI, the sovereigns were in the habit of making rather long and regular stays at Memphis, and delegates from the various temples probably took advantage of this to meet personally with the king, presenting him with their homage and their complaints.

PROTECTION OF THE TEMPLES

Like many a private person, the priests were led to complain of the exactions of the royal functionaries, which became ever more numerous as crises developed, and especially of the misplaced zeal of the tax farmers, who would try by any means possible to fulfill their commitments to the royal bank while maximizing their own profits from their activities. But the priests had their own particular brand of discontent, one linked to the many violations of the right of asylum. This temple privilege, which had been tacitly recognized since the time of the pharaohs, had been left to the discretion of the priests, who took care to limit its abuse. But abuse became common in times of unrest, with debtors seeking to escape their creditors or the tax officials, brigands fleeing royal justice, and so forth. As a result, local authorities or private individuals who had an interest in what was going on found themselves less and less able to resist the temptation to pay no heed and to seize the unfortunates and the malefactors who were taking refuge in the temple precincts. Toward the end of the dynasty, priests or an influential private person acting as patron of a temple frequently asked for and received an official decree from the king confirming the inviolability of a sacred perimeter around their sanctuary. These decrees, which were written in Greek but could be translated into Demotic, were posted around the enclosure they protected, usually in the form of stelae, a number of which have been recovered. By way of an example, here is the text of one of these stelae, which stems from the village of Theadelphia in the Faiyum and dates to February 19, 93 B.C.E.:

Place of asylum by (royal) ordinance. Access forbidden to undesirables—To king Ptolemy (X) Alexander, god Philometor, greetings (on the part) of the priests of Isis Sachypsis, the very great goddess who was the first to appear, of the temple in Theadelphia. . . . Oh very great king, given that the sanctuary in question has been sacred since the time of your ancestors, and that it has been venerated and placed in the highest rank in all times past, but that now, certain impious people, who are behaving contrary to convention, are not only driving out by force the suppliants who come to take refuge there, but also, by treating them roughly and using the most terrible violence, are committing sacrilegious acts, offending the piety you display toward the divine and especially toward the goddess Isis, oh most holy king, we therefore pray you, victory bearing god, if it pleases you, to ordain that the said sanctuary be a place of asylum, and that stelae of stone be erected towards the four winds, at a distance of fifty cubits (nearly 30 yards) around the temple, bearing the inscription: "access denied to undesirables." That, most great king, in your interest, . . . so that the sacrifices, the libations, and all the other ceremonies instituted for you, your children, and your ancestors in honor of Isis and Serapis might be better celebrated, and so that we might be blessed by your beneficent deeds. Good fortune. (Reply of the king:) To Lysanias (the *strategos* of the nome), execution (of the request of the priests). Year 21, Mekhir 7.[14]

Such "placards," which reassured the priests and enhanced the prestige of their temples, also served as royal propaganda, for they projected for all eyes to see the image of a sovereign who was touched by the sufferings of the weak and respectful of the prerogatives of the local gods, one who did not hesitate to crack down on the abuses of his subordinates.

ROYAL "PHILANTHROPY"

This same ideology is evident in the many royal decrees of amnesty issued on various occasions to put an end to the crises that grew numerous in the course of the last two centuries. The earliest of these decrees was promulgated by Ptolemy V Epiphanes in 186 B.C.E. to put an end to the after-effects of the great civil war that had ravaged the country during most of his reign. The most important and best known was issued by Ptolemy VIII and his two wives, once the latter were reconciled after the interminable dynastic war of 132–119. Here are the introduction and some extracts:

> King Ptolemy (VIII) and Queen Cleopatra (II) the sister and Queen Cleopatra (III) the wife proclaim amnesty for all their subjects from all errors, crimes, accusations, sentencings, and infractions of all sorts committed before Pharmouthi 9 of year 52 (April 28, 118 B.C.E.), with the exception of individuals guilty of murder and sacrilege.
>
> They also decree that individuals who have taken flight, being guilty of theft or other delicts, should return home and resume their former occupations, and they will be able to recover (any) goods of theirs which were seized by reason of these delicts, on condition that they have not been resold.

There follow numerous special measures concerning the remission of debts and taxes, and others suppressing the abuses of public office holders. Certain points have to do with the native temples, such as:

> And they have decreed that the sacred land and the other revenues that belong to the temples will remain theirs, and that the temples will continue to enjoy the benefit of the *apomoïra* they have been accustomed to receive from vineyards, gardens, and other (cultivated) lands. . . .
>
> And they have decreed that the expenses for the burial of the Apis (bull) and the Mnevis (bull) will be covered by the revenues of the Crown, as in the case of deified persons. . . .
>
> And they have decreed that the *strategoi* and other functionaries will not have power to constrain any inhabitant of the land to work in their own service or requisition their cattle for their private use. . . .
>
> Neither the *strategoi* nor any representative of the interests of the Crown, the cities, and the temples are, under any pretext, to arrest anyone for a debt, a quarrel, or a private matter or keep him prisoner in their houses or in any place whatsoever, but rather, if they accuse someone, they are to present him before the magistrates appointed in each nome, and they are to exact justice through decisions made according to the decrees and the regulations.[15]

The very designation of these measures, *philanthropa,* indicates the spirit in which they were drawn up. Above and beyond their practical interest aimed at restoring confidence by the discharging of accounts, these decrees above all afforded the sovereigns Euergetes a special opportunity to present themselves as benefactors of humanity and to display their piety through the concessions accorded to the temples.

VISITS TO THE PROVINCES

It was not rare for the royal couple to leave their palaces at Alexandria and travel into the *Chora,* like landowners visiting their domain, though they respected the old taboo that forbade the pharaoh to set sail on the Nile during the Inundation and allowed him to travel south only at certain specified times of the year.[16] These tours, which were announced in advance, were occasions for pomp and ostentation, though it is uncertain whether the sovereigns made use of the famed forty-bank ship built for Ptolemy IV, a veritable floating palace whose huge size and limited maneuverability confined its use to brief excursions on Lake Mariut or the canal leading to Canopus. The masses, whether native Egyptians or Greeks living in the provinces, had no other occasions to gaze on their pharaoh-king and his queen, veritable living deities whose appearance would arouse the hopes of many and the anguish of some. In fact, the popular enthusiasm was as much the result of naïve wonder at the pomp of the processions as of the conviction that the sovereigns came, as redressers of ill, to render all their due.

This faith in the royal sacrament translated itself into an avalanche of pleas and requests that were transmitted, after a summary examination and the addition of a brief notation, to the many secretaries who formed an ineluctable part of the royal baggage. These requests came from both individuals and established groups, professional associations or colleges of priests, such as the priests of Khnum at Elephantine on the occasion of Ptolemy IX's journey in 115 B.C.E. in the company of his mother and grandmother.[17] In like manner, the king enacted his pharaonic role by inaugurating temples whose construction was finished at the time of his journey, as when Ptolemy VIII consecrated the temple at Edfu on September 10, 142 B.C.E., or by default, inspecting construction works in progress, as Ptolemy II did at the temple of the ram of Mendes.[18] All such occasions served to demonstrate the king's interest in the native cults, even though the rites were conducted in a language he could not understand and must have left him as perplexed as a British monarch experiencing the welcoming ceremonies of a third-world tribe. We may similarly imagine Ptolemy VI at Thebes installing the new Buchis bull, the sacred animal of the god Montu, in the temple of Amun on the occasion of his excursion to Upper Egypt in 157.[19]

Notwithstanding his sudden fortune, the founder of the dynasty proba-bly did not live in an extravagant manner. His long service in the cam-paigns of Philip II and Alexander would scarcely have predisposed him to adopt a sumptuous mode of existence when he was master of Egypt, not even when he assumed the royal title. But it was quite different with his suc-cessors. In establishing the cult of the living sovereigns, his son Ptolemy II was obliged to distinguish himself from simple mortals by leading a differ-ent sort of life: hence the construction of palaces sumptuously decorated with the rarest of materials, marble, alabaster, and porphyry; and hence the progressive adoption of solemn and elaborate court rituals, in imitation of oriental usages, which regulated the life of the "friends," companions, and counselors of the king, as well as that of his numerous servants. At first, the king distinguished himself in his dress only by a diadem, the *tainia,* a simple cloth band around the forehead that was the traditional, sacred symbol of royalty in Macedonia. But soon, ever more costly robes became the rule at the many banquets that punctuated life at court and where the abundance and refinement of the dishes served formed part of the display of wealth the king was supposed to set before the eyes of visitors, ambassadors, and pres-tigious guests. Kings and queens even became physical incarnations of this abundance—whose symbol, the cornucopia, so often adorned their images and their coins—by means of a stoutness in which they took pride. When Egypt was weak externally, the Lagide sovereign laid all the more claim on this *tryphe* (magnificence), which did not fail to shock Romans, still guided by the austere code of their *mos maiorum* (custom of the ancestors). Thus, when Scipio Aemilianus, still basking in the glow of his victory over Carthage, disembarked at Alexandria in 139 B.C.E., he was greeted by a Ptolemy VIII so deformed by "the size and dimension of his belly that it was difficult to put one's arms around him. He was dressed in a robe that went down to his feet, with sleeves that reached his wrists." [20] Another au-thor adds, "He emphasized this deformity by the excessive thinness of his transparent clothing, as though he wanted to make a display of what any decent man would try to hide." [21] This long garment of transparent fabric lent the king the appearance of Dionysos himself, whose ivy garland he was also supposed to have worn. If the effect on the Romans was a disaster, this was not what the king was trying for: quite the contrary, he was attempt-ing to pay them honor by establishing his own *tryphe* and, in so doing, pre-senting them with a glimpse of the fabled riches of Egypt.[22]

Not all Romans, however, were impervious to the ethic peculiar to the court of Alexandria, and we are reminded, of course, of Mark Antony; many anecdotes exemplify the sort of sumptuous life he led with Cleopatra in the bosom of their highly exclusive club, "The Inimitables," whose unbridled luxury was grist for the mill of Octavian's propaganda. The proportions reached by their squandering are well illustrated by Plutarch's remarks[23] concerning the royal chef; when he was asked about the grandiose reception for which he had eight enormous wild boars roasting, he answered that no more than a dozen guests were expected and that they might want nothing more than a glass of wine to drink, yet he was required to have all sorts of dishes ready at all times, and in great quantity, just in case. True to her dynasty's ideal of *tryphe,* Cleopatra is supposed to have made her table the rival of those of the very gods and goddesses!

THE PROGRAM OF THE ROYAL TITULARIES

The Egyptian clergy fully recognized the pharaonic ritual status of the Lagide sovereigns, even though they did not personally participate in the traditional ceremonies, in which the king was believed to play an essential role. The hieroglyphic titularies conferred successively on each king and certain of the queens constitute striking examples of this recognition. This was not a new favor, for the first two Persian kings had also been endowed with pharaonic titularies, though reduced to two names.[24] Alexander, his two Macedonian successors, and the first two Ptolemies were treated to titularies of the normal length, though they were not very original. In its traditional form, the titulary comprised no fewer than five names arranged in a prescribed order, each preceded by a specific title. Each of the last two names was written in a cartouche. Taken together, they were supposed to evoke the theological personality of the king, which was established at his coronation and which determined the program of his relations with the gods and goddesses of Egypt. Thus, Ptolemy II was designated "*Horus* Sturdy Youth, *(He of) the Two Goddesses* Great of Valor, *Horus of Gold* Whose Father Made Him Appear (in Glory), *King of Upper and Lower Egypt* Power of the *Ka* of Re, Beloved of Amun, *Son of Re* Ptolemy." [25] All these names are purely conventional except for the third, which alludes to the king's coronation by his father Ptolemy I and thus establishes his legitimacy.

Beginning with Ptolemy III, these titularies were lengthened to a degree rarely attained even in the most glorious periods of pharaonic history, with the priests drawing on all the resources of their erudition to formulate a very specific royal ideology. The famous decree of Memphis, whose best-known version is the "Rosetta Stone," translates, exceptionally, the hieroglyphic titulary of Ptolemy V into Demotic and Greek: "*Horus* Youth Who Has Appeared (in Glory) on the Throne of His Father, *(He of) the Two Ladies* Great of Valor, Who Has Reestablished the Two Lands and Made Perfect the Beloved Land, Whose Heart Is Pious Toward the Gods, *Horus of Gold* Who Has Improved the Life of the People, Lord of Jubilee Feasts like Ptah and Sovereign like Re, *King of Upper and Lower Egypt* Heir of the Gods Who Love Their Father (= Ptolemy IV and Arsinoe III Philopator), Chosen of Ptah, Power of the *Ka* of Re, Living Image of Amun, *Son of Re* Ptolemy, Living Eternally, Beloved of Ptah, God Who Appears (= Epiphanes), Master of Kindness (= Eukharistos)."[26] The Greek version renders all these epithets faithfully enough, replacing Ptah with Hephaistos, Re with Helios, and Amun with Zeus!

From Ptolemy VI to Ptolemy XII, the royal titularies developed somewhat with the introduction of new themes, such as that of the king viewed as the twin brother of the living Apis, whose origin perhaps lay in the actual coincidence of the birth of Ptolemy VI with that of an Apis bull in 186 B.C.E. By way of contrast, Cleopatra VII herself was provided only with an incomplete titulary consisting of a Horus name and a single cartouche, like that of her ancestor Cleopatra I, which reveals the reticence of the clergy to admit that a woman could fully assume the theological role that devolved upon a pharaoh. Thus, at the temple of Dendara, Caesarion, the titular pharaoh, takes pride of place in front of his mother in the great relief on the southern exterior wall (Figure 11). The priests did not confer an original titulary on this infant king, however; his first cartouche was only a copy of that of his grandfather Ptolemy XII, a sign of the difficulties of justifying the legitimacy of Caesar's son from the Egyptian point of view.

THE ALLEGIANCE OF THE CLERGY

In the last analysis, the prestige of the Lagide monarchy, and even its authority throughout the land, were in essence founded on its recognition by the native clergy. We have seen the means and the mechanisms that were set in motion to assure this recognition, along with the loyalty that was its necessary corollary. At this point, we must ask whether they really worked. In fact, we may doubt the sincerity with which the priests rallied around a regime that represented a class of foreigners who had assumed a dominant position in the economy and administration of the land, perforce to the detri-

FIGURE 11. Temple of Dendara. Right: Ptolemy XV (Caesarion) and Cleopatra VII (far right) worshiping deities of the temple. Photo by Ragnhild Bjerre Finnestad.

ment of the old sacerdotal class. The very diversity of the Egyptian clergy, both in its geography and in its sociological makeup, affords a strong hint that unanimity, in one sense or another, could never have been achieved. Certainly, at one and the same time, there was a clergy of "collaborators" and one comprised of priests in rebellion. Unfortunately, though, there is rather less evidence for the latter in the surviving sources than for the former. It is thus easier to begin by citing some representative instances in which Egyptian priests consciously served the interests of the sovereign with the aim of obtaining benefits for themselves or their sanctuaries.

The Memphite priesthood represents a special case. The prestige of the cults of this city, especially that of the Apis bull, throughout all Egypt did not escape the notice of the central power, which displayed ever more signs of its regard for them. Thus, the coronation of the king in the temple of Ptah according to the ancient rites of the pharaohs was carried out regularly by the Lagides at least from the reign of Ptolemy V on, and perhaps earlier as well. The high priest of Ptah, the chief of this clergy, was thus a personage who was especially pampered by the sovereigns. It is surely no coincidence that this office, with its considerable importance, was handed down within a single family throughout the history of the Ptolemaic dynasty. It was, in fact, crucial that such responsibility not fall into less than certain hands, and in this case, inheritance constituted a relative guarantee of loyalty. Many of these high priests left behind funerary stelae with texts in hieroglyphs or Demotic, and sometimes with autobiographical texts that permit us to discern the nature of their relations with the Lagide kings:

> I went to the Residence of the Greek kings, which is located on the shore of the "Great Green" (the Mediterranean), on the west side of the Canopic branch, and whose name is Rhakotis. The king of Upper and Lower Egypt, the god Philopator Philadelphos, the young Osiris (Ptolemy XII) left his palace in life and vigor, went to the temple of Isis [. . .] and presented [the goddess] with numerous and profuse offerings. As he left the temple of Isis in his chariot, the king himself stopped his chariot and placed on my head a diadem of gold and all sorts of genuine precious stones, bearing the effigy of the king. I thus became his priest, and he promulgated a royal decree for all the cities and all the nomes, saying: "I have promoted Psenptaïs, the high priest of Ptah, to (be) priest of my cult, and I have accorded him revenues in the temples of Upper and Lower Egypt."[27]

The exchange of goods in this transaction is clear: the king publicly and solemnly installed the high priest of Ptah when the new candidate was only fourteen years of age, in return for which the latter was to carry out the rites of legitimation—that is to say, the coronation—on the person of the sovereign. In this case, the royal-sacerdotal relationship was founded on mutual support. Not all the priesthoods of Egypt could lay claim to such treatment. They could, to be sure, play a similar role on the strictly local level, but some of them, in the service of other venerable cults, such as the priests of Amun at Thebes, had legitimate reason to feel disappointed at the special favor enjoyed by their Memphite colleagues. It is therefore scarcely surprising that some priests employed particular stratagems to attract the attention of the kings. A group of *ostraca* discovered not long ago in the Memphite necropolis acquaints us with a certain Hor, son of Harendotes, a priest of Isis and Thoth from the nome of Sebennytos.[28] In 168 B.C.E., in the dramatic circumstances of Antiochus IV's invasion of Egypt, when the latter had assumed the pharaonic regalia at Memphis and was besieging Alexandria, Hor claimed that his deities had appeared to him in a dream:

> Lo, Isis, the great goddess of Egypt and the land of Syria, was walking on the water of the sea of Syria, with Thoth behind her, holding her hand. She arrived at the port of Rhakotis and said: "Rhakotis is saved from destruction."[29]

Hor insinuates that the same dream also predicted Antiochus' retreat on July 30 of that year, and he continues:

> I reported this dream to the *strategos* Eirenaios on July 11, 168, when Kleon, Antiochus' commissioner, had not yet left Memphis.[30]

This last remark was evidently intended to prove that the prediction was made prior to the event. In fact, contrary to Hor's allegations, Eirenaios must have been skeptical, for he awaited the fulfillment of the prediction before he sent Hor to Alexandria with a letter to the sovereigns:

> I gave it to the pharaohs in the great Serapeum of Rhakotis on August 29, 168, and I revealed the salvation of Rhakotis and all its people, which occurred thanks to the good fortune of the pharaohs. No one can contest that [my dream] concerned the retreat of Antiochus and his army.[31]

Hor thus hoped to benefit from the attention and confidence of the monarchs as a result of the a postiori verification of the authenticity of his divine inspiration. In the years that followed, he in fact sent an ongoing account of those of his dreams that might interest the court at Alexandria, interspersed with various requests concerning the cults that were his bread and butter, in particular those having to do with the feeding and the funerals of the sacred ibises of Thoth in the Memphite necropolis, which constituted his own livelihood. Like Rasputin, two millennia later, Hor must have played on the anxieties regarding the heir apparent, Eupator, who we know died at the beginning of his adolescence, for he touches on this theme at least twice in the drafts of his reports to the monarchs.[32] We cannot but admire the ability of this simple servant of obscure sanctuaries to manipulate the anguish and credulity of the royal family, which represented a singular revenge exacted by a dominated people on their foreign masters!

THE IDEOLOGY OF RESISTANCE

We know almost nothing about the propaganda of the native insurgents who on many occasions threatened the Lagide domination of Egypt.[33] We have no program, no text denouncing the oppression and justifying their actions. All we know of their ideology is what is contained in the meager titularies of the three kings who in turn devoted themselves to these "nationalist" revolutions. Since these mysterious pharaohs left no hieroglyphic texts, we know their epithets only from Demotic documents. The first two, Harwennofre and Ankhwennofre, were both "beloved of Isis and beloved of Amun-Re king of the gods," which allows us to assume that the priesthoods of Philae (?) and Thebes were implicated in their seizure of power. Proudly proclaiming himself the "son of Osiris," Harsiese, the last of these rebel pharaohs, laid claim to a theological legitimacy in the face of Greek kings they considered to be impious usurpers.

Aside from the evidence supplied by these epithets and a few scattered allusions, the possible participation of the clergy in these revolts must remain a matter of speculation. "Collaborating" priests would always have carefully erased any trace of temple support for anti-Greek rebellions, once these were put down, in the hope of limiting possible reprisals against the entirety of a priestly class that was in fact divided. On the rare occasions when the insurgents are mentioned, their propaganda is usually turned against them; thus, in a text written shortly after his defeat, Harsiese is called "the enemy of the gods,"[34] a designation that might well have been part of his own ideological arsenal against Ptolemy VIII!

There is, however, a unique witness to the hostile sentiments of the native population, which constituted the fertilizer for these revolutions. This text, handed down on three papyri from the Roman period, is known to us under the title "The Potter's Oracle."[35] Written in Greek, curiously enough, but translated from Demotic according to one of the copies, it claims to be the story of a prophecy concerning the future of Egypt made by a potter in the time of an ancient king named Amenophis. This literary genre goes back at least to the Middle Kingdom of the pharaonic era. The principle was simple: under divine inspiration, a person, and sometimes an animal, would begin to prophesy before Pharaoh's court, foretelling both apocalyptic woes for the land and the coming of a savior who would put an end to them. Since the authors of such texts always referred to contemporary events that served as the main themes for prophecies assigned to a past that was decades or centuries old, it suffices in principle to take note of these allusions to date the texts. In "The Potter's Oracle," the main theme is the destruction or abandonment of a city "on the sea shore," inhabited by foreigners and thus called "the city of those who wear belts" (= soldiers?) or "the city under construction." It is easy to identify this city as Alexandria, all the more so as the second description (*ktizomene polis*) is a good translation of the Egyptian name for the Lagide capital, *Rhakotis* (Construction Site).[36] The inhabitants of this accursed city are called "Typhonians," that is to say, worshipers of the god Seth (whom the Greeks identified with their god Typhon), who was the very incarnation of evil in

Egypt at this time. These foreigners—it is once specified that these are indeed Greeks—would destroy themselves, for hatred and murder would tear apart families, a probable allusion to the dynastic wars of the second century. Egyptian peasants would be oppressed: "taxes would be levied (even) on grain that had not yet been sowed," and "they would flee to the districts of Upper Egypt," referring to one of the principal reasons for the desertion of the countryside under the later Lagide kings. But it was especially because of their impiety that the masters of the doomed city would perish. By "remodeling the images of the gods," that is, by Hellenizing the traditional deities—a clear allusion to the cult introduced by Ptolemy I—they would end by offending them. "Then Agathos Daimon (the beneficent tutelary god) will abandon the city under construction (Rhakotis-Alexandria) and go to Memphis, the mother of the gods." We can see how one and the same antipathy rejects Alexandria, the Greeks, and the Lagide regime. The hope that the Egyptian elites might regain power was linked to signs of divine intervention predicting a providential savior who would restore Memphis as the capital and thus reestablish the traditional order.

3 CITIES AND COUNTRYSIDE

A UNIQUE LAND

As the transition point between Africa and the lands of the Mediterranean, Egypt belonged to both and thus occupied a unique position in the ancient world. Such a strategic crossroad for any empire aspiring to universal dominion could only have been an object of conquest once such an ambition became possible. It is thus no accident that Egypt's people lost control of their destiny beginning with the sixth century B.C.E. and remained unable to regain it except for rare, brief periods until the middle of the twentieth century of our own era, which saw the demise of the British and French empires, the last in a position to view the Nile valley as the key to hegemony. To neighboring peoples grappling with harsh environments that were sometimes scorched by aridity and sometimes swept by storms, Egypt was the very image of abundance and indifferent to the caprices of climate, for it was regularly watered by a mysterious, recurrent inundation that brought it life and prosperity in the midst of a hostile desert. Its fauna, with its ibises, monkeys, and lions, as well as its flora, such as palm trees and thickets of papyrus, were themselves distinctively African and added to the fascination exerted by Egypt on its neighbors in the northern Mediterranean, inspiring works of art filled with exotic reveries, such as the famed mosaic of Praeneste (Figures 12 and 13).[1]

In Cleopatra's day, Egypt was already an ancient land, nearly three thousand years old. Its borders, which were imposed by unique geographical factors, had scarcely changed since the pyramids were built. These factors are still present in contemporary Egypt, though

FIGURE 12. Detail of the Nile mosaic in the Palestrina Museum. Photo courtesy of Paul Rehak and John G. Younger.

the ancients would have been astonished at the linearity of the frontiers established toward the end of the nineteenth century by carving borders in the desert according to meridians and parallels. It is, of course, the Nile valley and delta that constitute the heart of the inhabitable area. To these can be added the oases of the western desert, large depressions where the groundwater of the Sahara rises to the surface, sometimes in the form of permanent lakes at the bottoms of the basins, as in the case of the Faiyum, which is watered by a branch of the Nile. The rugged terrain of the eastern desert has only its mineral resources to offer. The Mediterranean coast at the north of the delta, as well as the Red Sea coast to the east, are inhospitable and barely suited to maritime activity. To the south, the traditional border was located in the environs of Aswan, where boats sailing upstream are brought to a halt by the rapids of the cataract that forms the first obstacle to passage along the Nile from the sea. South of this cataract lies a portion of Lower Nubia, a natural extension of Egypt called the Dodekaschoinos, after its length (12 *schoinoi* = about 75 miles), located south of Elephantine. Lower Nubia was won back from the Nubian kingdom of Meroe in the reign of Ptolemy II,[2] who thus became master of the gold mines of the Wadi Allaqi; the manner in which they were exploited by convict labor under horrifying conditions would forever sully the memory of the Lagides.[3]

FIGURE 13. Detail of the Nile mosaic in the Palestrina Museum. Photo courtesy of Paul Rehak and John G. Younger.

In the third century B.C.E., Ptolemy I and his three successors ruled a vast empire beyond Egypt itself. This empire included Palestine and part of Syria, which had been traditional areas of expansion for pharaonic power, but it also comprised regions that the pharaohs of old had never conquered: Cyrenaica to the west, and to the north, Cyprus, Crete, the Cyclades, Ionian islands, and numerous cities in Asia Minor and even distant Thrace. Strictly speaking, this was not a matter of an "Egyptian" empire but rather of personal possessions of the sovereign of Egypt, who treated each of them according to the traditions of its people, respecting the autonomy of the Greek cities and the customs of indigenous communities such as the Jews in Palestine. All these territories slipped from the grasp of the Lagide dynasty during the two centuries that followed, between the reign of Ptolemy IV and that of Cleopatra's father, who was obliged to stand by powerless when Rome annexed Cyprus, the last of the Ptolemaic dominions. For a very short time, Cleopatra recovered a part of her ancestors' empire,[4] but this was only through the good will of the Roman *imperator* Mark Antony, who was disposing as he pleased of territories conquered by Rome. Although these possessions served to reinforce the power of the Lagides, the unique basis of that power always remained their undisputed possession of the land of the Nile.

A MULTITUDINOUS POPULATION

Cleopatra's Egypt had a large population and was undoubtedly the most densely populated land in the ancient world. The exceptional productivity of its soil, which was watered and fertilized by a flood whose regularity and abundance aroused the astonishment and the admiration of all the classical writers, made it possible to feed an excessive (at least by ancient standards) population in a very narrow territory confined to only those lands that could be irrigated by the Nile. Another of the most widespread themes regarding Egypt was the fecundity of its women, who gave birth to twins with surprising frequency. As to the actual size of the population, we scarcely have the means to arrive at a reliable estimate. Censuses were certainly made under the Lagides for tax purposes, but we have only a single, recently published papyrus in Demotic and Greek to furnish us with an insight regarding one of the three subdivisions of the Faiyum in the reign of Ptolemy III.[5] Taking account of the risks entailed in extrapolating from a single regional figure, we can nevertheless use this source to arrive at something of an estimate.

In establishing the number of persons subject to the tax on salt (in fact, a sort of head tax) in the western subdivision of the Faiyum, the author of the papyrus in question arrived at a figure of approximately 11,000 adults, both male and female, for the year 229 B.C.E. If we add a proportional number of children and military men not included in this census, and if we assume comparable figures for the northern and southern subdivisions and add an approximation of the urban population of Arsinoe, its capital, the Faiyum would have had a population of between 50,000 and at most 100,000 persons. Moreover, the Faiyum seems to have been one of the most densely populated regions and covered a surface area equal to twenty to twenty-five percent of that of all the rest of Egypt. If we opt for the highest numbers, we would arrive at a population figure of more than 2.5 million persons, outside of Alexandria.

Another ancient source, Diodorus Siculus, supplied an estimate of the population of the Ptolemaic kingdom, drawn from a priestly source, around the year 60 B.C.E. According to him, the population of Egypt in his day, undoubtedly including Alexandria, was about three million,[6] which accords well with the maximum figure based on the local census of 229. If we admit such a total, which many historians nevertheless consider too low, we arrive at an average density of just over three hundred persons per square mile in the valley and the delta together. Such a population density, which is greater than that of France today, is no illusion: it should rather be compared to that of the non-desert portion of Egypt today, which is twelve to fourteen times greater. In terms of population density, the relationship of Cleopatra's Egypt to the various lands of Mediterranean Europe under Roman domination would have been comparable to that of present-day Egypt and western Europe, that is to say, about ten to one. To a foreign visitor, the Egyptian countryside must have seemed like a nearly uninterrupted sequence of teeming villages situated at a distance of no more than 2–2.5 miles from one another and housing sometimes more than a thousand people, though we know of a village in the Faiyum with only three inhabitants. In the reign of Ptolemy II, Theokritos[7] estimated that there were 33,333 such villages, which is approximately the number of communities in present-day France! Such a number, with its fanciful appearance, surely is not based on an official count (though Diodorus[8] and Pliny the Elder[9] reported similar figures) but rather testifies to the impression of filled space that the Egyptian countryside must have given. In comparison, the cities must have seemed like oversized small towns distinguished only by their administrative functions and the size of their religious edifices.

THE LAGIDE CAPITAL[10]

The major upheaval that affected the human and economic geography of Egypt between the pharaonic era and the time of Cleopatra was due to the creation of Alexandria. The city founded by Alexander in January or April of 331 B.C.E. on the offshore strip of land separating the Mediterranean from Lake Mariut, west of the mouth of the Canopic branch of the Nile, became the center of power while Ptolemy was still satrap. The transfer of the royal residence to a new city was in itself nothing revolutionary for Egypt. In the past, a number of pharaohs had decided to choose a new capital and had sometimes built at a site practically devoid of any prior occupation, as did Akhenaten at Amarna and Ramesses II at Pi-Riamsese, to cite two of the most familiar examples. But never had anyone dreamed of making a port the capital of Egypt. For nearly three thousand years, no pharaoh had built even a single real port on the Mediterranean, whose low and shifting coastline offered practically no shelter against dangerous currents and winds. While the establishment of a great maritime city suddenly opened Egypt to the Mediterranean world, its promotion to center of royal power reduced the rest of the country to the status of an agricultural hinterland burdened with supporting its commerce. From this strictly economic point of view, the Ptolemies turned Egypt into the rural territory of a Greek city. Laid out on the Hippodamian plan within a vast area delineated by Alexander himself, the city experienced a considerable development that soon made it the largest city in the ancient world, to be eclipsed only by Rome in the course of the first century B.C.E.

The Ptolemies made their capital a monumental city and a cultural center of the first rank by founding the Museum and its annex, the famed Library. Alexandria was indeed above all a city in the Greek sense of the word, a *polis* endowed with its necessary institutions, though lacking the political organs that would have guaranteed it an autonomy intolerable to the royal power. Like every Greek city, it was made up of a citizenry divided into *demes* and tribes, access to which was forbidden in principle to Egyptians. The latter were only tolerated in the city, and on a number of occasions, measures were taken to limit their access and thus avoid the Egyptianization of a city intended to be the showcase of Hellenism. It is only natural that the Egyptians, in their turn, viewed this foreign city on their soil with distrust and even a degree of scorn. Despite a number of official efforts, the earliest of which dates to 311 B.C.E., the kings never succeeded in having Alexandria styled "city of Alexander" in the native language. The Egyptians thus had no name for their new capital other than *Ra-qed* (Hellenized as Rhakotis), which was handed down to the Copts and the Byzantine era. The original meaning of this name was "Construction" or, better, "Construction Site," which was certainly an allusion to the actual condition of Alexandria in the first decades after its founding in 331. Such a designation surely had significant sociological implications: though excluded in principle from citizenship in Alexandria, native Egyptians were nevertheless called on to erect its public and private buildings under the supervision of Greek contractors. It was thus these workers who baptized this city so foreign to the traditions and the deities of their land and which, for this reason, would never be integrated into the cultural and religious geography of Egypt, remaining a mere "construction site" in the eyes of the natives. Later, in the reign of Ptolemy VIII, this Egyptian name for Alexandria was translated into Greek by the Hellenophobic author of the "Potter's Oracle" to predict the city's destruction without naming it explicitly.[11] Curiously, beginning with Strabo, Greek and Roman authors misunderstood this designation Rhakotis, taking it to be the Egyptian name of an age-old site on which Alexander founded his city and of which moderns have wrongly believed they have discovered the traces. No doubt, such an interpretation was derived from a desire to allot this prestigious city a legitimacy on Egyptian soil in the capacity of heir to an ancient pharaonic foundation, just as there was an attempt to legitimate Alexander's kingship over Egypt, along with that of his Ptolemaic successors, by means of an apocryphal filiation with the last king of the last native dynasty.[12]

It should be obvious that such considerations were foreign to the city's founder. Nevertheless, the opposite notion of an Alexandria "adjoining Egypt" and not really in Egypt is in conflict with the economic and political evidence. Though open to the Mediterranean, the city was nonetheless a part of the land whose produce supplied it and from which the land in turn received certain imported goods, along with those charged with administering, watching over, and exploiting it.

THE CENTER OF THE HELLENISTIC WORLD

Cleopatra's Alexandria is less well known to us than classical Athens or imperial Rome. With the exception of some cemeteries that are not very evocative, there are no surviving constructions from this famed era for the contemporary tourist to admire. Until quite recently,[13] modern archaeology had revealed only much later vestiges, such as the elegant white marble Odeon at Kom el-Dik (Figure 14). The spectacular catacombs of Kom el-

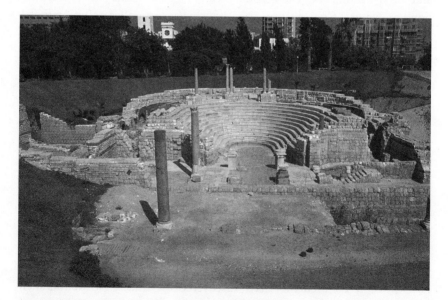

FIGURE 14. The Odeon at Alexandria. Photo by Glenn Meyer.

Shuqafa are also of the Roman era, and the imposing column known as "Pompey's pillar" (Figure 15) was in fact erected in honor of the emperor Diocletian more than three centuries after Cleopatra's suicide! To arrive at an assessment of the capital of the last queens of Egypt, we must draw on the descriptions of ancient writers, of which the most complete is that of Strabo, who visited the city around 25 B.C.E., just five years after the fall of the Ptolemaic dynasty.[14] But it is no thanks to him that we have a precise idea of the famous lighthouse constructed around 280 by the architect Sostratos of Knidos and that remained, down to the medieval era, the city's most remarkable monument.[15] The tallest construction in all of classical antiquity, at least 390 feet high, it was surpassed only by the pyramids of Khufu and Khephren, which are also more massive and were of course built more than two millennia earlier. The detailed testimony of an Arab writer, as well as representations on coins (Figure 16), vases, and other objects, have enabled attempts at reconstruction that archaeology is at present hard put to confirm. In any event, this three-staged tower surmounted by a colossal statue of Zeus Soter (Zeus the Savior) signaled ships that they were approaching the port, which lay on a coastline otherwise devoid of landmarks. A flame that was kept going on the top stage made it possible to guide ships even at night. For the city's inhabitants and for visitors, the Pharos was respectively an object of pride and curiosity, a popular symbol like the Eiffel Tower in Paris or the Statue of Liberty in the port of New York.

The city itself was built according to a monumental plan, with its principal streets being nearly a hundred feet wide. The most important one, the Canopus Street, crossed the city from east to west in a straight line. These avenues carved out five sectors labeled alphabetically, from Alpha to Epsilon. The palaces occupied a large area, for in each reign, new constructions were added to the old ones. In Strabo's day, the quarter containing the palaces constituted nearly a third of the city. Their plan and their general layout are unknown to us, but we should undoubtedly imagine them as a succession of colonnaded halls, porticos, gardens, audience halls, and offices, as well as apartments for the royal family and its servants and relations. There was even a harbor reserved for the use of royalty. A part of all this, at least, could be opened to the public on certain occasions, such as the festival of Adonis evoked by Theokritos in the most picturesque of his Idyls.[16] Near the palace was the Museum, the famous institution that made the intellectual reputation of Alexandria and to which was attached the Library. The Museum experienced a certain decline as an intellectual and literary center from the second century on, especially after 145 B.C.E., when for political reasons, Ptolemy VIII expelled from Alexandria all scholars

FIGURE 15. "Pompey's pillar" at Alexandria. Photo by Glenn Meyer.

a　　　　　　　b

FIGURE 16. Bronze hemidrachm of the Roman emperor Domitian, depicting the emperor on the obverse (a) and the lighthouse of Pharos on the reverse (b). American Numismatic Society 1944.100.53950. Photo courtesy of The American Numismatic Society, New York.

and artists suspected of opposition. Thus deprived of its reserve of talented people, the Museum found itself reduced to being directed for some years by a military man! In the first century, however, the Mithridatic wars that ravaged Asia Minor and Attica caused a return to Alexandria of a certain number of intellectuals who promised a veritable renaissance in the reigns of Auletes and Cleopatra. But it was under Cleopatra that the great Library was destroyed by fire. This disaster, an accidental outcome of the Alexandrian war, might not have been as total as has been supposed, for it is possible that it only affected warehouses containing books destined for export.[17] Whatever the case, the plunder of the library at Pergamon ordered by Antony made it possible to reconstitute it prior to the fall of the dynasty.

The final monument worth visiting would have been the *Sema*, the tomb of Alexander, which was built by the first Ptolemy and reconstructed by Ptolemy IV Philopator to shelter the deceased Lagides. Unfortunately, we have no idea of its appearance or its architecture, and even its exact location remains uncertain. Finally, Alexandria was certainly provided with all the adornments indispensable to life in any Greek city: the theater near the royal quarter; the agora, a central square traversed by Canopus Street; a stadium in the south of the city and a hippodrome in the east. Among the numerous temples dedicated to Greek deities, we should mention the great Serapeum on a hill dominating the city, the shapeless vestiges of which are still to be seen near "Pompey's pillar." The port complex, which was the very justification for Alexandria's existence, was especially grandiose, with the mole linking the island of Pharos to the coast separating its two main basins: the Great Port on the east and the Eunostos (Good Return) on the west. In the latter, an inner harbor called the "Kibotos" (literally, "Box"), was linked by a canal to Lake Mariut and the Canopic branch of the Nile. The omnipresence of water all around Alexandria cannot fail to remind us of the main public works problem on which the survival of the city depended, namely its provisioning with potable water, for that of the lake and the canals could not be consumed. There was no solution possible other than to construct, wherever possible, underground cisterns by the hundreds, with vaults that were often supported by several stories of columns. These cisterns were maintained down to the Arab period, and some still exist today.[18]

Alexandria would have had three hundred thousand free inhabitants, according to Diodorus,[19] but we do not know whether this figure includes children or only adults. We also cannot estimate how many slaves are to be added to their number. There was once a tendency to exaggerate the size of the populations of ancient cities, sometimes to the extent of advancing figures comparable to those of large European cities at the beginning of the twentieth century. In fact, it is probable that in all classical antiquity, the problems of urban management became insurmountable if the population surpassed half a million and that only the population of Rome under the Antonines reached a higher figure, thanks to the resources of an empire unprecedented in its scope, its organization, and its riches. Thus, however we manipulate the approximate information furnished by Diodorus, it would scarcely be reasonable to assign a figure of more than five hundred thousand inhabitants to Alexandria in the Ptolemaic era. Such a number would already make Alexandria a megalopolis in which about a sixth of the total population was concentrated, a demographic burden comparable to that placed by modern Paris on the French countryside. Under such conditions, it is probable that Memphis, the second-largest city, could scarcely have had more than a tenth of the population of the capital.[20]

Most of Alexandria's population had its origins in the various horizons of the Greek world or in regions of Asia Minor and the Balkans that had been Hellenized at one time or another. The great families prided themselves on being Macedonian, like the royal family, and the court long retained the use of the Dorian dialect, which distinguished the aristocracy from the commoners of Alexandria. Though the sovereigns always wanted to keep the Egyptians in the minority, they favored the settlement of Jews, at least down to Ptolemy VI. Jews completely dominated one of the five sectors of the city (Delta), not far from the royal palaces, and they had synagogues scattered throughout the city and its suburbs, where they would gather to read the Torah. The persecution they suffered under Seleucid rule in Judaea had provoked an exodus on the part of Jewish persons hostile to Antiochus IV's policy of enforced Hellenization. Ptolemy VI and Cleopatra II, sovereigns who were especially benevolent toward the Jewish population, extended their beneficence to the point of authorizing their high priest Onias IV to build a temple at Leontopolis (Tell el-Yahudiya) in the

FIGURE 17. Obverse of a gold octodrachm depicting Berenike II. From the Ottilia Buerger Collection of Ancient and Byzantine Coins, photograph © 1995 courtesy of Lawrence University, Appleton, Wisconsin.

eastern delta, in compensation for the loss of the temple at Jerusalem, which had been sullied by Hellenistic practices.[21]

The coastline around Alexandria was progressively urbanized. Thirty miles to the west, Taposiris Magna was adorned with a temple in the Egyptian style, whose totally white enclosure wall still faces the sea in our own day. The vines cultivated on the offshore strip of land between this city and the capital yielded a reputable vintage suitable for aging. To the east, Canopus, at the mouth of the branch of the Nile which bears its name, was a vacation spot favored by Alexandrians, who went there via canal in boats, surrounded by flowers and to the accompaniment of flutes and tambourines.[22] The city was also noted for its many sanctuaries, of which the temple of Sarapis was famous for its oracles. North of the city, at the tip of Cape Zephyrion, which sheltered its port, rose the temple dedicated to Arsinoe Philadelphos assimilated to Aphrodite, on whose altar Queen Berenike II (Figure 17) had consecrated a lock of her hair. It was this humble offering that inspired the poet Kallimachos' loveliest elegy, later rendered into Latin by Catullus, for it was claimed that the lock disappeared, only to reappear in the heavens as a constellation of stars.[23]

THE DELTA

Alexandria and its coastal annexes were separated from Egypt proper by a fringe of lagoons and swamps, running along the north of the delta, which has been traversed since time immemorial by a sparse and imperfectly assimilated population living on animal husbandry and fishing.[24] It was a marginal and indeterminate zone where Egyptian tradition located a number of myths, such as those concerning the childhood of Horus, who, with his mother Isis, found shelter from the murderous rage of Seth in the papyrus thickets there. On the eastern end, opposite Alexandria, was the fortified city of Pelusium, Egypt's line of defense against invasions from Asia via the route through northern Sinai, and whose fall was often the prelude to occupation of the land by foreign troops. Conversely, Pelusium also played the role of a place for concentrating troops and a base of departure for offensive expeditions into Syria.[25]

Beyond Alexandria and the coastline with its inhospitable surroundings, the traveler encounters immemorial Egypt, the Egypt of pharaohs and deities whose fabulous antiquity impressed foreigners then as much as it does tourists now. We would love to be able to describe the land through the eyes of a Scipio Aemilianus in 139 B.C.E.,[26] or those of Caesar, who sailed up the river in the spring of 47 in the company of the last Lagide queen. Unfortunately, no travel diary has come down to us recording the impressions of such knowledgeable and illustrious visitors. We must therefore trust in our imagination, with the assistance of the description left by Strabo, a Greek from Asia Minor and a contemporary of Cleopatra VII, but who visited Egypt only after her death, when it was under Roman administration.

For the most part, Strabo's brief notes are scarcely evocative unless they are supplemented by archaeological evidence or by epigraphic or papyrological documentation. A number of places he cites are difficult to identify, and the documentation is unevenly distributed; thus it is with the vast triangle formed by the Nile delta. This important region, which served as the hinterland of Alexandria, was traditional Lower Egypt, whose importance was roughly equal to that of the Nile valley proper south of Memphis, from the economic and demographic point of view as well as the administrative and religious. But most of the nomes and cities of the delta are scarcely more than names to us—famous to be sure, though we can no longer associate them with monuments, for in the great majority of cases, they have completely disappeared.

Yet this was a rich territory whose cultivable land, which was flooded during the inundation season, stretched far beyond the line of sight under its vast horizons. Numerous cities and towns were located along the branches of the river as they spread northward, flowing toward the seven canonical mouths by means of which the Nile donated its waters to the sea. These habitation sites occupied the summits of mounds that were spared by the floods and were formed by the accumulation of rubbish during the centuries of occupation. During the inundation, these towns would have seemed like so many islands studding the surface of a motionless sea. The major cities offered visitors and pilgrims a view of their grandiose temples, certain of them quite prosperous because they were consecrated to popular deities, such as the Isieion of Behbeit el-Hagar, and others already deserted and perhaps already in ruins, like the venerable sanctuary of the sun god at Heliopolis. All these ancient capitals—Sais, Mendes, Bubastis, Sebennytos, Tanis—must have witnessed a greater or lesser degree of decline as the economic activity of this entire region was diverted to Alexandria. In the west, the Ptolemies respected the autonomy of the old trading post of Naukratis, Egypt's first Greek city, founded around 650 B.C.E. on the Canopic branch of the Nile, though the founding of Alexandria robbed it of all its significance to commerce. The Bubastite branch of the Nile was connected to the Red Sea by an artificial canal begun by the pharaoh Necho of Dynasty 26 and completed by the great Persian king Darius. Put back into service by the Lagides, this canal followed the valley of the Wadi Tumilat as far as the Bitter Lakes and then forked off to the south toward the port of Arsinoe, opportunely renamed Cleopatris, corresponding to the modern site of Suez. Its economic importance was nevertheless relative, undoubtedly because of its narrow width and the constant threat of its sanding up. Traffic between the Red Sea and the Nile had always made use of the ancient trails that crossed the eastern desert, such as that which, from earliest times, linked Myos Hormos to Koptos by way of the Wadi Hammamat.[27] Other ports were founded on the Red Sea coast by the first Ptolemies in order to receive African merchandise or to serve as intermediaries for elephant hunting, such as Berenike of the Troglodytes or Ptolemais of the Hunt, but the cessation of the latter activity at the end of the third century dealt them a nearly fatal blow.[28] These ports did not regain their prosperity until the very end of the second century, when the discovery of the monsoon permitted navigation on the Indian Ocean and resulted in increased maritime activity in this region.[29]

MEMPHIS AND THE FAIYUM

Someone journeying from the north, whether from Alexandria via the Canopic branch of the Nile or from the northeast frontier by way of the Pelusiac and Bubastite branches, would in either case arrive at Memphis at the apex of the delta.[30] The city's geographical location 25 miles upstream from where the Nile splits into its branches and near the beginnings of important routes to the Faiyum and the western oases, as well as the antiquity and prestige of its monuments and cults, were assets that prevented any other city from disputing its preeminence. It was also the largest city in the land prior to the founding of Alexandria. We can make only a rough estimate of the size of its population: fifty thousand at least, but not likely much more than that if we bear in mind the figures of three million for all of Egypt and five hundred thousand for Alexandria.[31] Satrap Ptolemy had made it his residence before his final move to the new capital a little before 311 B.C.E. Bordered on the east by the river, Memphis was protected from its floodwaters by a series of dikes averaging 12 cubits (about 20 feet) in height, which completely surrounded the city. Fitting comfortably within this enclosure wall nearly five miles in length, the city was divided into a number of quarters, certain of which were reserved for foreign communities long before the conquest of Alexander: Greeks in particular, but also Carians, Syrians, and Jews. The temple of Ptah, whom the Greeks identified with Hephaistos, served as Egypt's premier sanctuary, since the pharaohs celebrated their coronation there, a tradition the Lagides themselves respected, at least from Ptolemy V on. Memphis was also the abode of a living deity, the Apis bull, which played an essential role in the creation of Sarapis, the tutelary god of Alexandria. But the city was not just a religious center, for its location made it the obligatory transit point for all merchandise coming from the valley. Linked directly to the Faiyum by a heavily traveled desert road, Memphis was the natural outlet for all its rich agricultural production. It was also an industrial center, famous for its output of weapons, textiles, and faience.

South of Memphis begins Upper Egypt, a long ribbon of verdure between two deserts. To its west stretches the depression of the Faiyum, in the north of which is a lake fed by a natural canal that branches out from the Nile. This long-neglected region experienced a boom under the first Ptolemies, who successfully completed a vast development project on an unprecedented scale. Remarkably well-planned irrigation and drainage efforts permitted the cultivation of both the Faiyum's desert borders and the marshy areas near the lake, whose level was also lowered in order to free new land. The talent of the Greek engineers appointed by the king and the mobilization of an Egyptian work force enabled the rapid success of this enterprise, which considerably enriched the crown and permitted it to distribute land to the soldiers recruited as cleruchs. Although a part of the Faiyum was developed directly by the state, huge domains were conceded to important personages to assure their systematic exploitation. The best known of these was the domain given to Apollonios the *dioiketes* (minister of finance) in the reign of Ptolemy II. This domain of 10,000 *arouras* (6,810 acres) was

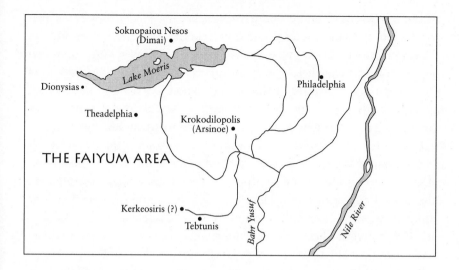

The Faiyum Area

administered by a certain Zenon of Kaunos, his agent; his archive, which was discovered by chance in his office at Philadelphia, constitutes the most important collection of papyri from all antiquity.[32]

The capital of the region, which the Greeks had called "Krokodilopolis" because the city was dedicated to the crocodile god Sobek, was renamed Arsinoe in honor of the king's deceased wife, and it became an important city. A number of other towns were founded, some of them built in Greek style on the Hippodamian plan, such as Philadelphia, the "capital" of Apollonios' fief. Remarkably, most of these, which were once magnificent rural towns adorned with temples and public buildings, now lie buried under the sands, sometimes at considerable distance from the fields under cultivation today. During the past hundred years, excavations have made it possible to bring them back to life, and they have also yielded quantities of papyri written in Greek and Demotic. From Soknopaiou Nesos (present-day Dimai) in the north to Tebtunis in the south, these towns formed an almost uninterrupted circle of ancient habitation sites all around the basin of the "Land of the Lake," which was also called "The Sea" (ancient Egyptian *P-iom* = Faiyum).

UPPER EGYPT

All along the valley, the capitals of the ancient nomes received new Greek names relating to the deity or sacred animal that dominated each of them. Thus, ancient *Hu-nen-nesu,* dedicated to Herishef (Harsaphes), a ram god whom the Greeks identified with Herakles, became Herakleopolis. Further to the south, *Wenu,* the city sacred to Thoth, was named Hermopolis, "City of Hermes." Between Panopolis, the "City of Pan (= Min)" and Abydos, the ruined city where one could still see the Memnonion or tomb of Osiris described by Strabo, lay Ptolemais, the only Greek city in the valley, which was founded by the first Ptolemy. Strabo indicates that it was the largest city in the Thebaid, comparable only to Memphis, but hardly a trace of it remains today, except for an impressive stone quay that signals its importance as a riverine port. Destined in the mind of its founder to replace Thebes as the capital of Upper Egypt, it must have presented the unexpected appearance of a Hellenistic city in the midst of an Egyptian countryside, with the political institutions and cultic and cultural edifices of a Greek *polis:* a theater, a *boule* (city council), a *prytaneion* (city hall), and a temple of Dionysos, where artists came to make sacrifices.[33]

But it was difficult for Ptolemais to supplant the old capital of the New Kingdom, which the Egyptians called *Wase* or even just *No* (the city), and which naturally became Diospolis (City of Zeus), because Amun was at that time identified with the lord of Olympus. But it was its other name of "hundred-gated" Thebes, far more venerable because it went back to Homer, that was handed down to posterity. A veritable museum of pharaonic architecture and sculpture, Thebes extended over a vast area, with urban concentrations around and even within the vast enclosures of Karnak and Luxor on the right bank and Medinet Habu on the left bank. The great temples, which had grown so huge that they were impossible to maintain, were in certain cases partly or entirely abandoned, to the extent that the city already presented the appearance of a huge ruin field. Religious life had retreated into sanctuaries on a more human scale, sometimes entirely new buildings like the temple of Hathor at Deir el-Medina, and sometimes old buildings that had been scrupulously restored, down to the details of their decoration, such as the small temple at Medinet Habu. The population of Thebes, which was still quite large, was very much attached to its traditions and proud of its heritage; it was one of the most prone to rebellion in the Ptolemaic kingdom, along with that of its near neighbor Hermonthis, city of the war god Montu, which prided itself on being home to the sacred Buchis bull, the Upper Egyptian counterpart of the Memphite Apis.

It is in part to this impetuosity that Thebes owed the accelerated decline in importance that it experienced under the last Lagides. Already deprived of its function of southern capital by the foundation of Ptolemais, which became the administrative center, Thebes suffered the consequences of its multiple rebellions against the central power. The most severe of these repressions seems to have descended upon the city at the time of the unrest that accompanied the fall of Ptolemy X Alexander and his replacement by his older brother Ptolemy IX Soter, recalled from exile in 88 B.C.E. Thebes was stormed three years later and sustained considerable damage; but it was not entirely ruined, as the Greek historian Pausanias seems to imply, for a number of inscriptions attest to a degree of activity in the temples of Karnak and Medinet Habu during the reigns of Auletes and Cleopatra.[34]

During the second century, Thebes and Hermonthis had been kept under strict surveillance by garrisons at Pathyris and Krokodilopolis to its south; these were manned by soldiers of mixed origin and with a lifestyle more Egyptian than Greek, but who remained loyal to the Ptolemaic monarchy. These cities went into a decline and even disappeared after the events of 88 B.C.E. The great cities of the southern nomes—Latopolis (Esna), Apollinopolis (Edfu), Ombos, and Aswan (this last with its neighboring islands of Elephantine and Philae)—were able to escape these vicissitudes, as witnessed by the splendid temples erected there at that time.

Most of these cities experienced increasing prosperity under Lagide rule. Unable to conceive of a civilization other than an urban one, Greeks tended to converge on centers whose size was already increasing because of the royal policy of centralization of administration and economic management. These centers did not, however, obtain the attributes of autonomy that attached to the status of a Greek *polis,* which were granted only to Ptolemais. Nevertheless, the presence of an increasing Greek or partially Hellenized population led to the addition of institutions foreign to Egyptian tradition, notably the *gymnasia,* where the rudiments of a Hellenic education were taught. A city's Egyptian temple was thus not its only center; other, more profane buildings were introduced, such as public baths, which made their appearance in even the smallest villages from the third century on.

ARCHITECTURE AND URBANISM

Aside from the temples, which were built of sandstone or limestone, the dominant material for the construction of houses and most public buildings was brick. The raw material was abundant and easily obtained, for it consisted of the Nile silt itself. Since rain was rare, the bricks were molded and dried in the sun, but left unfired, a technique that had scarcely changed since predynastic times. For practical reasons, fired bricks were used only in the construction of wells, cisterns, and baths. Stone, preferably pink granite from Aswan, was used for foundations, thresholds, and sometimes the frames of doors and windows, though these last were generally of wood. Marble, the building material par excellence for the Greeks, does not occur in Egypt, and only certain prestigious buildings—the palaces and the richest private homes of Alexandria—knew the benefit of marble imported at great expense, and that more as an element in their decoration than in their construction. Timber is also scarce and of mediocre quality in Egypt, and so it was rarely employed. Even at Alexandria, most of the houses were evidently topped by masonry vaults, for at the time of the Alexandrian war, the lack of wooden roofs saved the city from being burned down.

In the towns and cities, houses[35] usually had one story, with living and service quarters often arranged around one or more courts. Basements or vaulted cellars were quite frequent, leading to an elevation of the ground floor that made it necessary to gain access by means of front steps or even a ladder. The entrance most often faced north, so as to profit from the fresh breeze that blows from that direction. Exterior windows were few in number, small, and located high on the walls. They were often adorned with trellised screens of wood or stone and closed by means of wooden shutters to keep out the sun and the heat. Certain buildings had more than one story, sometimes assuming the form of two-, three-, or even four-storied highrises as much as 100 feet tall, which characterized the urban and sometimes even the rural landscape. In the cities, such buildings could be rented out in the form of apartments, and their ground floors often had shops opening on the street. In living and reception areas, the walls and ceilings were often painted with figurative motifs or in imitation of precious materials such as marble, alabaster, or onyx. This decoration was arranged in registers according to contemporary fashion in the Hellenistic world. In the most luxurious homes, the floors could be paved with mosaics. Thus, with greater or lesser success, Egyptian architectural tradition was combined with Hellenistic decorative style.

The former entailed not only the materials employed but also a certain taste for pharaonic forms that grew ever stronger toward the end of the Ptolemaic period, when the country homes of the rich were adorned with a massive entrance pylon imitating those of the native temples. The two towers of the pylon, shaped like truncated pyramids, contained several rooms, including the doorkeeper's lodging. Their decoration also borrowed more and more from the traditional Egyptian repertoire, often reinterpreting it, and one might thus see sphinxes, grooved cornices, and other such features side by side with columns and entablatures in the Greek style.

As everywhere in the Near East, pharaonic cities and towns had developed in a haphazard manner. The temples and the long processional routes associated with them constituted the only stable elements in the organization of urban space. All the rest—houses, shops, granaries, and such public buildings as existed—were arranged willy-nilly around the sacred enclosures and the *dromoi*—that is, the processional routes, often lined with sphinxes, which linked the temples to their landing stages or to other sanctuaries. The houses of the priests were located within the temple enclosures, where they were packed as tightly as those of the artisans and shopkeepers outside them. The available surface area was doled out frugally, and public spaces were rare, being limited practically to the temple forecourts and the streets. The latter, which were simple access routes, were inconvenient and narrow; they did not form a coherent network, and they often came to dead ends.

Both in Greece itself and in Asia Minor, the Greeks had long since developed principles of urban planning and monumentality. These found their expression in the construction of Alexandria and, at least we might suppose, of Ptolemais in Upper Egypt. The effects of these new concepts, which were of course linked to the way of life that accompanied them, made themselves felt progressively in the remainder of Egypt. Not only did towns newly founded in the area of the Faiyum developed by the first two Ptolemies, such as the Philadelphia of Zenon's archives, follow such a plan in its entirety, but even ancient cities benefited from real improvements thanks to the introduction of the Greek juridical notion of the public street (King Street or Street of Pharaoh). The intensification of commercial exchanges and the use of coinage, both occasioned by the Greek takeover of the economy of the land, also led to the construction of market places that replaced the old, informal *souks,* at least in the most important cities. These constructions, which sheltered numerous shops under porticos and arcades, constituted a new element in the organization of the urban landscape.

Despite all the changes in architecture and urbanism that Ptolemaic domination was able to effect, the general appearance of cities and towns in the reign of the last Cleopatra must have remained quite eastern, with their mud-walled, flat-roofed buildings, and their streets littered with heaps of garbage and livened by vendors surrounded by sounds and smells that scarcely differed from those to be experienced in the villages of Upper Egypt today.

4 ECONOMY AND SOCIETY

THE WEIGHT OF BUREAUCRACY

The Ptolemies encountered an ancient administrative tradition in Egypt, one whose origin lay more than twenty-five centuries in the past. The very conditions of agricultural production in the Nile valley necessitated a system of decision making to organize the efforts needed to apportion the waters of the annual flood. Administrations had thus developed at the local level, prior to their being brought together under the authority of a central government: it is no exaggeration to say that in Egypt, bureaucracy preceded the state. The scribal class from which the bureaucracy emerged had always formed the elite of Egyptian society, and without any major changes, it survived any and all upheavals in the land from the Old Kingdom on. Once they had become masters of Egypt, the Lagides did well to refrain from dismantling the structures of this bureaucracy. They made use of the preexisting framework, adapting it progressively to the new priorities they assigned to it. The three principal themes underlying the administrative reforms of the early Ptolemies were the exercise of strict control over the various parts of the land by consigning the upper levels of the administration to Greeks, the facilitation of the settlement of foreign colonists in the countryside, and the reorientation of agricultural and craft production so as to maximize tax revenues.

The territory of Egypt was traditionally divided into about forty more or less stable districts, which were at one and the same time geographic, economic, administrative, and religious entities. In predynastic times, these had been political entities, chieftainships of a sort, each with its own emblem; alliances among them created the primitive kingdoms that were the origin of the first unified Egyptian state. At a relatively late date, a canonical list of these districts was established: twenty for Lower Egypt and twenty-two for Upper Egypt. The Greeks called these entities *nomoi,* a term that correctly evokes the division of space into autonomously organized agricultural territories, for that was the primary function of these districts. On the whole, the Ptolemies maintained these divisions, though when local conditions necessitated it, they eliminated certain nomes and created others. These nomes, whose Egyptian names were those of their age-old emblems, were rebaptized by the Greeks according to the names of their administrative centers. Thus, for example, the Hare district became the Hermopolite nome and the Dolphin district became the Mendesian nome—a sign of the importance the Greeks attached to the provincial centers in their urban conception of the organization of space, and in consequence of which the administrative centers of the nomes experienced constant expansion down through the period of Roman occupation, when as a supreme gift, they were endowed with political institutions and became genuine cities.

THE STRATEGOS[1]

Under the Lagides, the capital of a nome remained no more than the seat of the local administration, a status inherited from pharaonic Egypt. According to custom, the chief official of a nome was a civil servant, appointed by the king, who was first and foremost in charge of all the annual agricultural activity, from the management of the waters of the inundation to the levying of the harvest taxes that were due. This *nomarch,* as he was called in Greek, stemmed from one of the great local families and drew his personal revenues from the many benefices he held in the temples of his district. A veritable hereditary lord when the central power was weak, the nomarch was evidently kept under strict control during the prosperous periods of the Egyptian monarchy. Under the first Ptolemies, the nomarch continued to be a civil administrator charged with purely agricultural matters,[2] but a newcomer quickly deprived him of most of his powers, relegating him to a subaltern position. This official who eclipsed the nomarch was called the *strategos,* a purely Greek title that originally designated a military commander. The *strategos* of a nome was thus at first the commandant of the Greek troops stationed there, but his jurisdiction soon extended into the civilian realm, and he became the official responsible for his territorial district, while his military powers devolved upon specialized officers: *hipparchoi* for the cavalry units and *phrourarchoi* for the garrisons of fortified towns.

For the sake of efficiency and to limit the number of these high functionaries, it was often the case that several nomes were united under the authority of a single *strategos;* this was the rule in the Thebaid down to about the end of the second century B.C.E.[3] At the beginning of that century, an *epistrategos* of the *Chora* was appointed to be the superior of the *strategoi;* he was a sort of minister of the interior whose power extended to all Egypt outside of Alexandria. A second *epistrategos* was appointed in the Thebaid[4] so as better to assure the security of that troubled region, which had been the source of the nationalist rebellion of 205–186 B.C.E. Nomes grouped under a single command each had an *epistates,* a representative of the *strategos,* at its head. All these officials were at first exclusively Greek, but toward the end of the second century, Egyptians began to appear in these positions. At just that time, the number of *strategoi* grew larger, because of a tendency to limit their jurisdictions to a single nome. In the reigns of Ptolemy XII Auletes and Cleopatra VII, most of the nomes of Upper Egypt had Egyptian *strategoi,* who often succeeded to office from father to son, thus reviving an old pharaonic practice. This was the case with a certain Haremephis in the Panopolite nome under the last Cleopatra,[5] Pachomios surnamed Hierax (Figure 18) at Dendara and Edfu,[6] and Monkores in the Peritheban nome.[7] But their superior in the hierarchy, who was at that time Kallimachos,[8] the *epistrategos* of the Thebaid, was still a Greek.

As the local representative of the king, the *strategos* exercised executive power in his domain, and his jurisdiction also extended into the judicial realm. He was supposed to have knowledge of all the affairs of his district, and he thus received complaints addressed to the king by private persons regarding legal matters.[9] To assure that his decisions would be respected, the local police forces were placed under his direct authority.

The *strategos* was assisted by a large staff. Among his subordinates, those occupied with economic and tax matters were the most numerous. It was necessary to demarcate, measure, and register the agricultural lands according to their status, which could vary, and orders needed to be issued for irrigation works (canals, dikes) and for the obligatory requisitions for corvée labor. Once the size of the fields to be sown was determined, the next step was to estimate the harvest on which the rents and taxes due to

FIGURE 18. Statue of Pachomios, *strategos* of Dendara under Cleopatra VII. Detroit Institute of Arts 51.83. Founders Society Purchase, William H. Murphy Fund. © The Detroit Institute of Arts 1988.

the state would be drawn. In addition, it was necessary to organize the shipment of the wheat belonging to the king to Alexandria or to the various garrisons that had to be supplied in this manner. Finally, it was necessary to organize the bidding for the tax farms and the royal monopolies. These numerous, enormous tasks were supervised by various officials who were represented by subordinates at the level of the territorial subdivisions of the nome: the cantons (*topoi*) and the towns. From the first, the *oikonomos* played a prominent role; local agent of the *dioiketes*, the all-powerful minister of finance, he was in charge of everything in the nome that concerned the royal revenues, assisted, inter alios, by an accountant (*eklogistes*) and a checking clerk (*antigrapheus*).

THE OFFICIAL SCRIBES

Yet another personage came to assume more and more importance: the royal scribe.[10] Unlike the *oikonomos* and his subordinates, the scribe stemmed from the ancient Egyptian tradition; his Greek title of *basilikogrammateus* is a literal translation from the native language (*sesh-nesu* in the classical language, or *sekh-en-peraa* in Demotic), and the office was the prerogative of Egyptians. In the administration of the nomes, royal scribes eventually supplanted the *oikonomos* in the course of the second century B.C.E., to the point where they became the second-ranking official after the *strategos*. The reasons are undoubtedly the bilingualism of all the Egyptians working in the royal administration, for the Greeks learned the Egyptian vernacular only rarely and with difficulty, as well as their better knowledge of the rural milieu and the Egyptian mentality—a precious asset in carrying out tasks related to agricultural production. At a lower level, the royal scribe was represented by the scribes of the cantons (*topogrammateis*) and the scribes of the towns (*komogrammateis*),[11] all of them evidently Egyptian. Their role in the management of rural land was an essential one, as shown by the preserved archive of the *komogrammateus* of Kerkeosiris in the Faiyum, a certain Menches.[12]

As the guarantor of the public interest at the level of his village, the *komogrammateus* kept an eye on all the activities of the people he administered, which lent him a prestige that would have made him the envy of the other village notables: the local *epistates*, the police chief, and the *komarchos*. We do not know how Menches first obtained this coveted post, but we do know the conditions under which he was able to renew his position in 119 B.C.E.[13] In part, to obtain his reappointment by the *dioiketes,* who named all the officials dealing with finances, he was obliged to agree to undertake the cultivation of 10 *arouras* (a little less than 7 acres) of unproductive royal land at his own expense and to pay the tax office an annual rent of 50 *artabai* of wheat. This was certainly a convenient way for the administration to develop uncultivated land, but it also meant that candidates for office already had the means to meet the expenses of cultivation, expenses that peasants on royal lands would generally not have been able to undertake. Moreover, Menches had to give the village a "bonus" consisting of 50 *artabai* of wheat and 50 *artabai* of lentils and other edible vegetables, which indicates that the other village worthies—undoubtedly the *komarchos* and the elders—had been consulted regarding his appointment to the position of local scribe and that they exacted a price for their favorable recommendation.

This was an influential position, to be sure, but one that exposed its occupant to all sorts of local intrigues, as shown by the following curious misadventure reported by this same *komogrammateus* in December, 118 B.C.E.:

> On 17 Hathyr of year 53, I learned of the arrival in the village of Asklepiades, the assistant of Aminias, the police chief of the nome. As is customary, I went to meet him, accompanied by the *komarchos;* some elders of the tenant farmers; Demetrios, the constable and acting police chief of the village; and others. When we greeted him, he arrested us: myself, Demetrios, and one of the peasants, Marres son of Petos, on the pretext that a complaint had been lodged against us, as well as against (several other individuals), by Haryotes son of Harsiese, an inhabitant of Krokodilopolis, according to which they had tried to poison him while they were dining together in a tavern in the village. On the 19th of the same month, Asklepiades had us appear before Aminias, who had us released for lack of the appearance of the opposing party. . . .[14]

In this petition, which was addressed to the sovereigns while they were touring the provinces, Menches requested that since there existed no real charge against him, the *strategos* be ordered to see to it that "no one be able to repeat such a procedure with a view to slander or blackmail." The tactic, which was undoubtedly intended to discredit Menches and the members of his circle, came to naught, but Menches must have had good reasons to fear fresh attempts to dispossess him of his office.

THE BURDEN OF TAXATION

Taxation was the keystone of the Lagide administrative system. As managers of the land, the Ptolemies above all behaved like proprietors of a productive domain from which they desired to draw maximum profits. Though certain aspects of the economic control they imposed on the land—borrowing in large part from the pharaonic system that preceded them—once inspired admiring historians to speak of a "planned" or "state-controlled" economy, the purpose of this control was not so much the rationalization and centralization of a traditional economy for the sake of productivity as it was the guarantee of the return of abundant and regular revenues into the coffers of the treasury.

Like the entire structure of exchange, the system of taxation was based on two complementary units of value: coins and wheat. Though it had been introduced into Egypt in the fifth century B.C.E. under the Persians, coinage was only adopted as a standard means of exchange under the Lagides, whereas wheat had constituted the basis of the traditional system of commerce. Salaries, rents, and taxes could thus be paid with either. In consequence of this, the revenues of the state were organized according to two parallel systems based on different principles. Levies on fields of wheat were made in kind, right on the threshing floor, by royal functionaries known as *sitologoi*. The wheat was then stored in royal granaries before being divided up according to its various destinations: payment of personnel fed by the king (functionaries, soldiers), the provisioning of Alexandria, and exportation to other lands. The taxes on most other products and on all other activities were collected according to a different system, whose goal was to bring coins rather than payments in kind into the royal coffers. To attain this objective, the Lagides introduced the farming out of taxes, a system developed in Greece to collect imposts on risky production on which it was impossible to organize direct collection. Such a system presupposed the existence of banks and capital ready for investment. The latter, for the most part, came from outside Egypt, and potential investors saw a means of enriching themselves through this tax farming.

In fact, the intervention of private profit in the tax system in no way "liberalized" the economy. Quite the contrary, the state was obliged to exercise close and careful control in order to prevent embezzlement of its revenues. Production taxed by the state was subjected to a preliminary estimate by specialized functionaries, and the harvest, thus estimated, was the object of a public auction of the total of the tax that the bidders committed themselves to pay to the treasury. The bidders were capitalists organized into firms that had the means to guarantee the collection of the tax. The growers were obliged to sell the entirety of their harvest at a fixed price to the tax-farming firm that had won the marketplace. The harvest was then processed in approved factories belonging to private persons and to temples; the factories were themselves taxed according to a similar system. Finally, the tax farmers sold the consumer product to wholesalers or retailers who obtained their licenses from the state by bidding.

It should be evident that the laws of a free marketplace did not come into play at any point in the process. At every step, from the grower to the retailer, the prices were fixed by the state. Only the amount of the tax was subject to variation, because it depended on the bids. It was thus in the interest of the state to optimize its guarantee of the estimated quantity and the quality of the harvest, so that the tax farmers would make the highest possible bids for the tax they estimated they could pay to the state while hoping for a reasonable profit for themselves. To limit risks, controls had to be as strict as possible, and the state itself furnished the cultivators with seed grain. The officials who estimated the actual harvest were responsible for shortfalls, and they did not fail to pass these on to the peasants if need be. The workers and other employees of the factories were obliged to turn up for work and to furnish guarantees by taking an oath. The tools of their trade, such as oil presses, were kept under lock and key outside of official work hours so as to prevent clandestine production and contraband. As for the tax farmers and the resellers who made bids, they were obliged to guarantee their debts by offering their property as security. All sums paid were in the firm's account at the royal bank, where they were kept until the taxation process was completed. A monthly meeting brought together the *oikonomos* of each nome, his *antigrapheus,* and representatives of the firm and the bankers to examine the profits and arrive at intermediate balances. These were transferred under lock and key to Alexandria, where they were kept in the care of the *dioiketes* and his *eklogistes,* the chief accountant of the kingdom.

We could discuss the theoretical organization of the system of taxes on agricultural products other than wheat, in particular oils, with the help of the royal regulations on farm duties transmitted to us in a lengthy papyrus from the reign of Ptolemy II,[15] but it is difficult to tell whether they conformed to reality in every detail. In any event, it is evident that the system had its risks. If its merit was to guarantee revenue for the state from the labor of the peasants, its defect was that it put a straitjacket on production and exchange, thus preventing any economic growth. In the absence of private initiative, production could only stagnate, and retail prices were kept at an artificially high level: ordinary cooking oil was, on average, twice as expensive in Egypt as on the foreign market. This situation could not lead to competition because of high customs tariffs that often reached 50 percent, while the small number of points of entry into Egypt made it possible to control or considerably limit the possibility of bringing in contraband merchandise. The system also necessitated internal customs barriers. Taxes were in fact farmed out in the individual nomes, so that free circulation of merchandise subject to taxation had to be limited to protect the interests of the tax farmers and to prevent competition among the nomes, which could have lowered the bids on the value of the taxes.

RESISTANCE AND CONTRABAND

The social consequences of such a heavily taxed economy were anything but small. While the system offered certain guarantees to producers, whether cultivators or artisans, assuring them in advance that they could sell the fruits of their labor, it left them with low incomes and a poor standard of living. Further, the artisans were protected only for the short term, in consequence of the annual or biennial renewal of the licenses they acquired through bids. And since they were entirely at the mercy of the bureaucrats who oversaw the economy, as well as the agents of the tax farmers and the banks, while they had no means of control over the requisitions to which they were subject, whether justified or not, one can understand how their situation could quickly become insupportable. The sovereigns and their counselors were aware of the danger that abuses committed by their own subordinates could represent for producers, and they often tried to alleviate the situation with decrees of amnesty, as well as admonitions directed at those responsible for these abuses. But it was the system itself that invited its own abuse, making crises inevitable.

One possible cause of bankruptcy was internal contraband, which was inevitable because of the many levels of taxation of agricultural and craft production. Notwithstanding severe repression, a whole segment of production and commerce escaped royal control, thanks to a vast network of collusion in which it was not rare to find servants of the state. Unfortunately, it is impossible to evaluate the size of this parallel economy or to estimate the loss of revenue it entailed for the treasury. The prime victims were evidently those who held the concessions on the royal monopolies, who were quite disarmed in the face of such unfair competition, as shown by the following complaint addressed in 113 B.C.E. to Menches, our *komogrammateus* of Kerkeosiris:

From Apollodoros the concessionaire of the sale and tax on oil for the village in year 4 (of Cleopatra III and Ptolemy IX).

My business has been ruined by people bringing olive oil and castor oil into the village on the black market. On Mechir 11 (February 28, 113 B.C.E.), it was reported to me that a certain Thracian (from the village) of Kerkesephis, whose name is unknown to me, had stored oil in the house of the cobbler Petesuchos and was selling it illegally to Thaese, a woman living in the same house, and to a goose farmer and his daughter, of the same village. Since you were absent at that time, I immediately advised the chief of police and someone from the police guard to go to the house of the said cobbler. We found the Thracian there, but the merchandise had been hidden. Performing a search, we discovered some [jars] hidden under a piece of leather and under some lamb skins belonging to the cobbler. [While the search was being carried out, the Thracian managed to] flee, and the contraband oil [that was recovered represented only a small part of the bootleg merchandise], causing me a dead loss of fifteen copper talents (= about 180 silver drachmas). I therefore submit this report to you so that you might countersign it and transmit it to the competent authority.[16]

In this case, the authority in question was the royal scribe (*basilikogrammateus*) residing in Krokodilopolis/Arsinoe, the capital of the nome, to whom the local scribe Menches was supposed to forward this sort of complaint. His role was to defend the interests of the king and his tax farmers, but we might well wonder whether the measures at his disposal would have been effective. Such contraband would have entailed highly organized networks, from its clandestine manufacture down to its retail sale. The principal malefactor, a Thracian and thus a privileged foreigner, had succeeded in escaping the police. Only the poor small fry, all of them Egyptians—the recipient of the contraband and its eventual purchasers—could therefore be punished. Under the circumstances, it is likely that the plaintiff could ask for nothing more than some relief from his contractual obligations to the state, given that the latter had proved itself incapable of enforcing respect for his monopoly.

On other occasions, the tax farmer could simply come up against the ill will of taxpayers who had organized to seek protection from his demands, as we observe in the following letter dating from 117 B.C.E.:

To Amenneus the *basilikogrammateus* (of the Arsinoite nome), from Pnepheros son of Paous, the concessionaire of the tax on beer and natron at Kerkeosiris for the year 53 (of Ptolemy VIII). Having been informed that the inhabitants have agreed to ask for your protection, and being myself desirous of good accord with you, because it is up to you more than any other to watch out for the interests of the Crown, I am asking you to write to Demetrios, the *epistates* of the village, to Nikanor, the chief of police, to Menches, the *komogrammateus*, and to the elders of the peasants, that they might urge the inhabitants to follow the ancient customs, so that I can pay my due (to the state). Greetings.[17]

A note from the addressee shows that the message had been well received and that there was no question of the royal functionary's siding with the villagers against the tax farmer, because the interest of the state lay first and foremost in the efficient collection of taxes.

A CASH ECONOMY

Money had not been entirely unknown in Egypt in pharaonic times. Traditionally, transactions were based on a system of references to weights of metals. Actual coins, however, appeared only toward the end of the first Persian occupation, with the massive introduction of Athenian tetradrachms bearing a depiction of an owl (Figure 19), which were at that time the dominant means of exchange in international commerce.[18] In the fourth century B.C.E., the last native pharaohs struck some coins of sorts (Figure 20), but it was Ptolemy son of Lagos who, after some trial and error, defined a coherent system of coinage.[19] It was trimetallic, though only silver and bronze played an important role in exchange. The system was closed, that is to say, only coins struck by the king were legal tender within the country. Since the Ptolemaic standard was of less weight than that employed in the rest of the Mediterranean world (about 14 grams instead of 17 for a four-drachma coin), the state recovered the difference in metal by means of money changing, which was obligatory for all merchants who came to purchase Egyptian merchandise with foreign currency. Such a means of holding on to this precious metal was all the more necessary in that the Lagides had no silver mines at their disposal, either in Egypt or in the neighboring lands they were able to dominate, so that there was scarcely any means of obtaining it other than the foreign coins acquired in exchange for merchandise. Bronze was used essentially for exchanges within Egypt. Under Ptolemy II, these multiplied to the point where it became necessary to strike an unprecedented gamut of denominations, with

FIGURE 19. Athenian silver tetradrachm depicting the goddess Athena on the obverse (a) and an owl on the reverse (b). American Numismatic Society 1944.100.24201. Photo courtesy of The American Numismatic Society, New York.

FIGURE 20. Gold daric struck under one of the last native pharaohs, depicting a horse on the obverse (a) and the hieroglyphs for "good gold" on the reverse (b). American Numismatic Society 1963.268.72. Photo courtesy of The American Numismatic Society, New York.

weights ranging from 3 to 96 grams. Contributing to this phenomenon was the obligation to pay certain taxes exclusively with coins.

With coinage becoming an indispensable element of the economy, the Lagides had to create instruments of credit, that is, a banking system. The banks, both royal and private, were entrusted to franchisers who paid for the privilege of exchanging money and receiving deposits.[20] There were banks in all the nome capitals and many of the towns. The royal banks also collected all payments to the king's account in the form of taxes and fines, for which they provided receipts written on *ostraca* (fragments of pottery); they also kept the guarantees and securities furnished by the bidders of the tax farms. All the banks could manage accounts on behalf of private citizens and make payments in their name. They also made loans at a rate of interest that was administratively fixed and whose high level (24 percent) scarcely encouraged the development of credit. Since they handled both public and private funds, the banks were closely supervised, though this did not prevent instances of embezzlement, such as that to which the royal bank at Thebes fell victim in 131 B.C.E. under the following circumstances.[21]

At a particularly grim point in the civil war between the partisans of Ptolemy VIII and those of his sister Cleopatra II (Figure 21), a high local official, the vice-thebarch Dionysios, had ordered the banker Diogenes to transfer ninety talents, coming from sums that had been deposited or paid, to the profit of a certain Harsiese, the leader of a party of rebels. Dionysios was undoubtedly acting under pressure from the latter, who was for the moment master of Thebes, but as soon as he learned of the imminent arrival of royal troops in the city, he feared being accused of high treason and misappropriation of funds. Not having the sum in question at his disposal, he pressed the priests of Amun to give him the disposition of two accounts they had at the bank and into which the state deposited money for the maintenance of their cult. He knew how to be convincing, for the priests ended by agreeing to loan him the sums deposited in their accounts, which exactly covered the amount misappropriated. Dionysios then ordered the banker to remove all traces of the orders regarding the transfer. The latter, conscious of being guilty of the serious offense of falsifying the public accounts, took the precaution of keeping a copy of the letter from the vice-thebarch concerning the affair—this sole piece of evidence serves to inform us of it. The denouement eludes us somewhat: the priests were never able to obtain reimbursement of the money they had loaned to Dionysos without security, and they were undoubtedly obliged to complain directly to king Ptolemy VIII when he passed through Thebes in July, 130 B.C.E. The affair was quickly found out, for all the local financial administration was almost immediately replaced, including not only the banker and the vice-thebarch but also the latter's immediate superior, the thebarch Demetrios, though he seems to have been entirely unaware of his subordinate's exactions.

THE RAVAGES OF INFLATION [22]

The Ptolemaic system of coinage, which was relatively stable during the first three reigns of the dynasty, experienced a serious crisis under Ptolemy IV, due in part to the arming and mobilization efforts necessitated by the fourth Syrian war. The reduced agricultural production caused by the conscription of Egyptian peasants and the requisitions that were made to feed the army provoked a crisis that threatened the provisioning of Alexandria. To protect the capital city's marketplace from an excessive rise in prices, the *dioiketes* Theogenes decided around 210 B.C.E. on a drastic change in the relative value of silver and bronze, which had hitherto remained unchanged, to the detriment of the bronze coins. With the aim of radically uncoupling the

FIGURE 21. Statue of Cleopatra II holding a cornucopia. MMA 89.2.660 (Gift of Joseph W. Drexel, 1889). Photo courtesy of the Metropolitan Museum of Art.

two types of metal, a new unit of currency was created for everyday transactions: the copper drachma, sixty of which equaled one silver drachma, which was legal tender only in Alexandria. The new system had a practical, though secondary, advantage: it enabled the simplification of accounts by doing away with the obol, a subdivision of the drachma. The only other denomination that continued under the new standard was the copper talent, the equivalent of six thousand copper drachmas but only one hundred silver drachmas.

The economic, social, and political consequences were tremendous. The authorities had undoubtedly hoped to recover the silver in circulation by way of tax payments, because taxes were calculated according to the old standard, making it advantageous to pay one's taxes in silver. But in fact, the silver vanished entirely, while the bronze coins were caught up in a spiral of inflation that caused the price of goods and services to shoot up. A whole class of small rural savers was ruined, which was doubtless one of the causes of the huge revolt that broke out in the Thebaid five years later. In the forty years that followed, inflation forced the government to double the ratio of silver to bronze on two occasions, in 183 and 173 B.C.E. Ptolemy VI seems to have succeeded in stabilizing prices by reestablishing the circulation of silver coins in the land. But the civil war that broke out under his successor caused a repeat of the phenomenon, leading once again to a devaluation of the copper standard in 130–128. At this time, an ordinary silver coin of four drachmas, bearing the effigy of the first Ptolemy, was worth more than two thousand copper drachmas! No further devaluations were imposed, even though prices experienced some further speculative skyrocketing, as at the time of the civil war of 89–88. While the situation in the country did not really improve, the overall lack of cash set a material limit on the inflationary pressure. Toward the end of the reign of Ptolemy XII, however, the Lagide state experienced a grave financial crisis because of the large sums expended by the king to obtain Rome's recognition, and because of the astronomical amounts he borrowed to reestablish himself on the throne while he was in exile between 58 and 55. On this occasion, the silver coins were devalued to prevent bankruptcy.[23] In 53–52, the purity of the silver coins fell from 90 percent to 33 percent. It is not known whether this step, which was the ancient equivalent of printing money, was sufficient to pay back the king's debts. In any event, it undermined the credibility of the Ptolemaic coinage and rekindled inflation, this time of the silver standard. To put an end to the disorder, the last Cleopatra tried to reform the bronze coinage by introducing two new coins of eighty and forty drachmas, but it fell to Octavian to resolve the situation by doing away with the copper standard created in 210, thus ending 180 years of financial instability.

THE MISERY OF THE PEASANTS

The scintillating, bustling life of Alexandria and some of the Greek and native cities should not lead us to forget that the vast majority of Egyptians lived by working the land. The various foreign dominations scarcely affected the difficult living conditions of ordinary peasants, conditions that were cast in the immemorial mold of agricultural traditions, themselves ruled by the annual cycle of the Nile inundation. In the oases of the western desert, the Persians had introduced new techniques of irrigation through drainage of the water table, but only highly marginal areas of Egyptian territory were affected. The Greeks in particular tried to acclimate or increase cultivation of items that were familiar to them and that furnished the products they most consumed and exchanged: wheat, wine, and olive oil.

Wheat was the staple food of the civilizations of the Mediterranean. The arrival of the Greeks coincided with a small revolution in this domain: the cereal constituting the staple of Egyptian nourishment had traditionally been a type of emmer wheat the Greeks called *olyra* (*Triticum dicoccum*, called *boti* in the Egyptian language), and this was progressively replaced by hard wheat, which was the only variety consumed by the Greeks and thus exportable. As for viticulture, they had few improvements to offer to a science the Egyptians had mastered in remotest antiquity. The peculiarities of the country, however, considerably limited their success in expanding the cultivation of olive trees. Hardly any of the land in Egypt was favorable to them, and at best they yielded an oil of mediocre quality. To these contingencies imposed by nature was added the ill will of the native cultivators. This last was due not only to the inertia of a society fixed in a routine for millennia but was also linked to a care to preserve equilibria acquired through a long experience that the newcomers, overestimating their own cultural superiority, remained ignorant of or quite wrongly disdained. When an item from an archive[24] incidentally reports the opinion of some poor laborers, these frankly claim the status of experts in Egyptian agriculture, to the great displeasure of the agronomists who came running at the bidding of the king or of great personages to whom domains had been granted. Further, the eating habits of the native population could not easily be upset: *olyra* was always preferred to wheat, beer made from fermented barley to wine, and sesame oil to olive oil.

Certain technical innovations gained ground rather quickly, however, especially in the area of irrigation. In the course of the second and first centuries, the water wheel (*saqiya*) and the Archimedean screw progressively competed, at least in the delta, with the old balancing-pole device invented in the New Kingdom and still in use today under the name *shaduf.* The more sophisticated inventions of the Alexandrian savants, such as the force pump devised by Ktesibios in the reign of Ptolemy II,[25] must have made only anecdotal appearances in the Egyptian countryside. Even iron plows, which were made of imported metal lacking in Egypt, are likely to have been furnished to peasants only in the few domains that were especially productive.

It was rather through the introduction of new economic demands that the life of the native peasants changed. The land had never belonged to them, for the pharaoh had always been its sole legal owner, though he could concede its exploitation to his favorites and to the temples. However, rents and taxes could previously have had no aim other than to sustain all the social classes not directly engaged in production: scribes, priests, soldiers, and so forth. The agricultural economy thus remained fundamentally redistributive. Bringing with them the notion of profit, the Greeks would profoundly modify the structures of rural Egyptian society.

Native peasants had no single status. The simplest case was that of the "royal peasant" (*basilikos georgos*). The village scribe (*komogrammateus*) entrusted a parcel of land to him and imposed on him a program of sowing it.[26] The latter was determined in advance by the local authorities in consideration of directives from the capital and according to the height attained by the Nile inundation. The needed seed grain and agricultural tools were loaned, and the division by type of land sown was duly controlled.[27] It should be evident that the cultivator was given no initiative and hardly any responsibility. He seems to have had only one alternative: to submit to the program or to refuse to work the parcel of land offered to him, at the risk of not being able to feed his family. If there was a shortage of labor or conditions were pressing, even the latter possibility was disallowed, and he was constrained to make a tenancy agreement. In any case, he was obliged to deliver his harvest to the threshing floor, where it was divided up. The king took his rent, which amounted on average to 40 percent, though it could be as high as 50 percent on the best fields, and he also collected various taxes and received a reimbursement for the loan of the seed grain, which on average corresponded to a tenth of the harvest. In sum, the royal peasant was left with scarcely more than a third—and in any case less than half—of what he had produced, at best enough for his family to subsist until the next harvest. This bleak picture, however, is only theoretical. Such centralization in the organization of agricultural production presupposed means that the central power did not always have at its disposal. Coercion had its limits, too, for if the duress exerted on the peasants became insupportable, there was a risk the fields would be abandoned. In 118 B.C.E., at Kerkeosiris in the Faiyum, a group of peasants collectively refused to farm, under the conditions imposed, an area of land left uncultivated during the preceding civil war. After having tried in vain, under orders from Alexandria, to rent the land in question to others, the royal scribe was obliged to ask the *dioiketes* to order its downgrading, entailing a lowering of the rent, to induce the peasants to end their strike and sow; less rent for the king was better than no rent at all![28]

Moreover, the peasants were compelled to endure new and ever more burdensome constraints, even as those of a purely administrative order tended to weaken. First of all, for crops other than wheat, they were subject to the control of the representative of the company to whom the state had entrusted the tax farm on the crops in question. The profit of the farm depended on the amount of the harvest, and we can imagine the pressures brought to bear on cultivators to optimize their yield. Next, a significant portion of the land did not belong directly to the king. There were the sacred lands reserved for the maintenance of the temples, though their exploitation was controlled by royal officials. And in particular, there were lands granted by the king, either to great personages in the form of vast domains, or to soldiers (cleruchs). The latter could exploit their plots personally, perhaps with the aid of some hired help, but they could also entrust the cultivation to third parties. Often enough, these were not professional farmers but entrepreneurs who served as intermediaries between the cleruchs and the peasants who worked the fields. The latter were thus the source of a whole pyramid of profit: profit for the enterprise that managed the exploitation of cleruchic lands, profit for the cleruch to whom the land had been granted, profit for the tax farmer, and profit for the king, who in the end received revenue from the various taxes on the land itself and its crops.

Peasants working cleruchic land were not, however, unhappier than those farming royal land. To a certain extent, they escaped the arbitrariness of officials anxious to fulfill the objectives of the production plan. More-over, cleruchic land was not submitted to as strict a control, for there was a free choice of what to grow on it.

AUTOPSY OF A VILLAGE: KERKEOSIRIS[29]

We have the unique good fortune to be able to acquaint ourselves with the life of a whole Egyptian village at the end of the second century B.C.E. In January 1900, at Tebtunis in the south of the Faiyum, one of the workers on the staff of an Anglo-American archaeological expedition, disappointed that he was finding only crocodile mummies where he had hoped for sar-cophagi, gave one of them a swift kick, splitting it open. The desiccated reptile turned out to be completely wrapped in rolls of papyrus reused as cartonnage by the embalmers. Thus was discovered the official archive of Menches the *komogrammateus,* that is, village scribe. Curiously, he did not hold office at Tebtunis itself but at Kerkeosiris, a place whose location is uncertain, thus making for the paradox that it is at one and the same time an archaeological nonentity and the village whose organization at a specific time in the Ptolemaic era is the most thoroughly described for us.

The principal task of the *komogrammateus* was to assemble annually a complete register of the village lands according to the various tax cate-gories of the fields, as well as a list of the concessionaires of the plots, the sowings organized according to the species cultivated, and predictions re-garding the yields. At regular intervals, the *komogrammateus* was sup-posed to send a report to his superior, the royal scribe (*basilikogramma-teus*) of the nome, on the progress of the sowing and the harvesting under way. Work commenced at the beginning of September, when the flood sub-sided, and was not over until the harvest. These documents, some of them written on huge rolls thirteen to twenty feet long, constitute a goodly part of Menches's archive. Aside from this engrossing activity, the *komogram-mateus* had a whole gamut of responsibilities that made him the most visible local official, though perhaps also the most vulnerable, as shown by the anecdote noted earlier. He did not just do paperwork but also had to go out into the fields and personally supervise people and work, such as when the canals and dikes were inspected to assure that the irrigation nour-ished by the inundation occurred under optimum conditions.

Since it was a village in the Faiyum, Kerkeosiris was not directly affected by the inundation. The waters of the Nile arrived there by way of a canal that irrigated a large part of the oasis and began at the Bahr Yusuf, a branch of the Nile that emptied into Lake Moeris. The village was a recent creation, founded under the first Ptolemies in connection with the vast works they undertook in order to make the region into a rich agricultural province where numerous colonists could be settled. The territory of the village amounted to an area of about 4,700 *arouras*, or 3,200 acres. The village itself occupied 50 acres. Taking into account 116 acres of land incapable of exploitation, 119 acres of pastures, and 15 acres of orchards, these last belonging to private persons, there remained 2,900 acres that could theoretically be cultivated. More than half of this area—about 1,650 acres—comprised royal lands, while the rest was made up of 1,055 acres allotted to cleruchs and only 195 acres of fields consecrated to deities. It is far from certain that all village territories, even those in the Faiyum itself, were similarly configured. In particular, the proportion of cleruchic lands (36.4 percent) seems to have been higher at Kerkeosiris than elsewhere, which can easily be explained: it was a new village founded for the particular purpose of assigning land to Greek soldiers. The fields conceded to them constituted, in their turn, two distinct categories, if not in their status then at least in the way they were exploited. About 740 acres were registered in the names of about thirty *katoikoi*, cavalrymen, all with impeccable Greek pedigrees, who had domains of between 20 (14 acres) and 80 *arouras* (54 acres); the remaining 315 acres were divided among Egyptians, fifty-five infantry (*machimoi*) and eight cavalrymen, who had respective holdings of 7 and 15 *arouras* (4–9 acres).

These lands were not all exploited at the same time. For one reason or another—a ruptured dike or faulty drainage turning a field into a swamp, salinization, desertification—some parcels of land would become uncultivable from one season to the next. From another point of view, the years covered by our archive (121–110 B.C.E.) correspond to a phase of agricultural crisis provoked by dynastic war. The period preceding the decrees of amnesty in 118 B.C.E. was especially difficult. Of the 1,650 acres of royal lands, the area actually cultivated was only 890 acres in 121 B.C.E. and declined to 783 acres in 118–117, or only 47 percent of the cultivable surface area. Such a situation can only be explained by a shortage of labor due to the flight of peasants. The amnesty measures had only a modest and limited effect, for in 112–111, the cultivated surface area (867 acres) had not yet returned to the level of 121. The loss to the crown was all the greater in that rents had to be lowered several times to induce the peasants to return to work. The figures furnished for the lands given to the cleruchs are more puzzling: from 119–118 to 116–115, the proportion of land left uncultivated rose from seventeen to 48 percent! There is no evident reason for such a phenomenon. Is it to be blamed on general causes or purely local circumstances? This evident process of abandonment is much the same in the case of the Greek cavalry (from 24 to 58 percent) as in that of the Egyptian *machimoi* (from 6 to 24 percent). The proportion of *cleruchs* personally exploiting their fields also presents an interesting development: in 119, only a third of the *katoikoi* and 42 percent of the *machimoi* were cultivating their own fields; three years later, the situation remained practically the same with regard to the former, whereas 98 percent of the infantrymen were present in their own fields! The reason for this is surely the demobilization that followed the official end of the dynastic war. The Egyptian infantrymen, freed from active service in the royal army, had no means of subsistence other than to return to their fields, while the Greek cavalrymen were content to receive income by renting their lands and otherwise devote themselves to more lucrative activities.

What species were cultivated at Kerkeosiris? Wheat always accounted for more than half the sown area, on the order of 50–55 percent of the royal lands, and more still on the cleruchic lands—as much as 62 percent in 119–118 B.C.E. Next were lentils (13–15.5 percent of the royal lands); with their high nutritional value, they must have figured prominently in the local diet along with fava beans, though the latter were grown in smaller quantities. Vetch, a leguminous plant used to feed beasts of labor, and barley, the principal ingredient in Egyptian beer, were constantly cultivated, the former alternating with the cereals according to a triennial rhythm. Various other fodders and certain species of condiments—garlic, black cumin, and fenugreek, the latter used in preparing broths—complete the list. Notable by their near absence are *olyra,* the native grain, oleaginous plants (olives, and sesame and castor-oil plants), and flax. Since the Faiyum was otherwise an important producer of oil and linen, these absences can only be explained as indicating a certain territorial specialization. Kerkeosiris was thus essentially a wheat-producing community, though it is impossible to establish what considerations, at the nome level, determined the choice of what would be grown in the various villages.

Domestic animals played an important role in the village economy. Generally the property of private individuals, cows and oxen were raised almost exclusively for work in the fields, and their owners sometimes rented them out to farmers who had none of their own. Herds of sheep and goats belonged to private people and more often to temples, which entrusted them to seminomadic herdsmen, usually Bedouins, as is still the case in our time. The poultry yards were invariably filled with geese, whose flesh was offered to deities and furnished an occasional protein supplement for the peasants. The chicken, which had been unknown under the ancient pharaohs, became more and more common, as did consumption of its eggs. The most striking element of the countryside, though, was the immense dovecotes to be found on the outskirts of the villages. At Kerkeosiris, one of these constructions sheltered a thousand nests, a third of which were consecrated to the god Sobek of Tebtunis. Fed lentils and wheat, these pigeons were a source of manure with their droppings, and also of meat, of which Egyptians, both ancient and modern, have always been quite fond.

Finally, honey production was expanded, largely at the instigation of the Greeks, who were great consumers of it. The art of apiculture, already well known in pharaonic times, was practiced according to an itinerant method in which the hives were moved after the flowering of the various crops to obtain a gamut of different varieties. This practice often provoked conflicts between the beekeepers, who were more concerned with the yield of their hives than with administrative boundaries, and local functionaries unable to grasp the subtleties of the natural cycle of bees.[30]

ARTISANS AND SHOPKEEPERS

Craft industries and commerce were the other side of Egypt's riches. Agricultural products had, for the most part, to be transformed into consumable goods. Oleaginous seeds had to be pressed into oils, whether these were for food (sesame, olive) or for lighting (castor oil). We have seen that the production and sale of these oils, as a royal monopoly, were assured by licensed artisans and merchants under the strict control of agents of the state and the tax farms. The same was true of the manufacture of papyrus, which was an almost exclusively Egyptian specialty. Conscious of the economic and political interest of this resource, the Ptolemies expanded the export of papyrus throughout the Mediterranean world, where it had already long been the privileged medium for all prestigious uses of writing, in particular for the publication of literary, philosophical, and scientific texts.

Though they were in large part heirs to pharaonic traditions, local artisans charged with supplying the markets of Egyptian cities and towns were certainly stimulated in the Ptolemaic period by the changeover to a cash economy. Because it facilitated the circulation of goods, the new economy enabled the formation of larger industrial enterprises that could sell their products at a distance. Certain localities or urban quarters specialized in a given activity, according to a widespread usage in the Greek world. Artisans engaged in the same trade were organized into corporations that were collectively responsible to the treasury. Among these numerous activities, we may mention those connected with textiles: spinning, weaving, fulling, dyeing.[31] The two principal raw materials were flax and wool, cotton being still only an exotic commodity not cultivated in Egypt. Linen continued to be manufactured according to old native traditions. To obtain thread for weaving, it was necessary to use castor and natron when boiling the fibers, and these two products were subject to monopolies, which enabled the king to maintain control over every stage in the manufacture of the cloth. The best quality was the "royal linen" (byssos), woven exclusively in workshops attached to temples, which consumed a great deal of it for the clothing of their deities. The price paid for this privilege by the temples was that they were obliged to deliver a stipulated quantity to the tax office or to pay its value in silver. Linen of other qualities was manufactured by independent artisans organized into corporations and charged with production quotas imposed by the administration. When not in use, looms had to be kept under lock and key to prevent clandestine production that could escape taxation. Woolen fabrics had not been highly prized in pharaonic Egypt, for a taboo prohibited its use for anything having to do with priests, deities, and the dead. This did not prevent the Greeks from greatly expanding its production, thanks to the introduction of Milesian sheep (from Miletos, a city in Asia Minor), which supplied large amounts of high-quality wool. The scouring of the raw material required the use of a saponiferous plant called *stroutheion,* whose supply was strictly controlled and taxed, as in the case of natron. The organization of production did not differ from that of linen, except that the state was more involved because of its need to supply the army with woolen clothing. Wool was also used in making rugs and tapestries, which became ever more popular as time went on.

Pottery making was one of the most widespread craft industries. All who visit the ancient sites in Egypt find themselves treading with amazement on quantities of potsherds so huge as to be the despair of archaeologists. Though it was generally of poor quality, clay was abundant everywhere in Egypt, thus accounting for the essentially local aspect of production. We must also note the passion for "Egyptian" faience, a sort of green or pale-blue enameled frit used for all sorts of small containers, figurines, and inexpensive trinkets. Alexandria was the center of production of more luxurious vases, as well as painted figurines of more exclusively Hellenic style, both for local sale and for export.

Without doubt, Memphis was the principal center of metalworking.[32] This was, in fact, an industrial tradition reaching far back into the city's pharaonic past, for its local god Ptah was the patron of blacksmiths and goldsmiths, which led the Greeks to identify him with Hephaistos. This activity was directed especially at the manufacture of weapons. We know that in the winter of 218–217 B.C.E., the workshops at Memphis armed the troops of Ptolemy IV, who carried off the victory at Raphia on June 22, 217. The proximity of deposits of copper near Dionysias in the southwest of the Faiyum made Memphis an advantageous location for bronze work. Iron, on the other hand, had to be imported. Aside from weapons, artisans working with metal produced agricultural implements and luxury items such as containers, lamps, ornamental wall lamps, figurines, and sacred objects. Gold and silver were also worked, and the reputation of the Memphite goldsmiths was an ancient one. Silver vessels were especially prized, for they constituted capital that could on occasion be pawned.

The commercial distribution of all these goods beyond the local markets, as well as the transport of agricultural products destined for Alexandria or for export, largely depended on navigation on the river.[33] Transposing their traditional occupation into the Egyptian framework, a large number of Greeks invested in the chartering of barges on the Nile. There was no royal monopoly in this domain, so there could be private flotillas devoted to traffic in merchandise both private and public, the latter mostly wheat and oil. The owners were regularly rich Alexandrians holding high office at court or sometimes even members of the royal family, for these alone had the means to invest in shipbuilding. They rented their ships to charterers, who were often organized into companies to limit their risk. These were generally Greeks but sometimes also Phoenicians, such as the partners in a company at Memphis under Ptolemy XII, where we encounter a Zabdion and a Malichos.[34] Certain charterers personally piloted their cargo boats, but they could also entrust them to captains, who were often Egyptians well accustomed to the hazards threatening such heavy loads on the Nile.

GREEKS AND EGYPTIANS BEFORE THE LAW[35]

Until the conquest of Alexander, Egypt had a largely homogeneous population. Despite the various foreign occupations, immigrants constituted only a limited portion of the total population, mainly Greeks at Naukratis; Greeks, Carians, and Syro-Phoenicians at Memphis; and Syrians and Jews who were settled by the Persians in certain garrison towns such as Elephantine. Alexander and his successors opened Egypt to colonization, which resulted in complex socioethnic cleavages affecting the entire land.

Among the divisions separating the two communities, that having to do with law is one of the most easily discernible. The Lagides respected the totality of the native Egyptian law, which was the fruit of a long juridical tradition shaped by the Saite pharaohs, principally Amasis (570–526 B.C.E.), and compiled into a coherent corpus of laws under the Persians.[36] There could be no question of applying these laws to the Greeks, whose usages derived from an entirely different cultural tradition. Quite unlike the Egyptians, however, the Greeks did not have a single set of laws. Each city had developed distinct juridical usages and had in principle its own body of laws. All Greeks residing in Egypt could therefore lay claim to the law of their respective cities of origin. In the area of private law, it was therefore necessary to develop a common norm, a synthesis of the laws in use in the various city-states of the Greeks who had settled in Egypt; this was called the "law of the cities." It goes without saying that because they were theoretically autonomous entities, Alexandria, Naukratis, and Ptolemais had laws of their own applicable to their respective citizens. To these levels of law was added the abundant legislation of the Ptolemies, which principally concerned the public law. This legislation took the form of ordinances (*prostagmata*) and regulations (*diagrammata*) that chiefly concerned, as one might expect, matters relating to taxation. While there were sometimes ad hoc measures that rather quickly fell into oblivion, these ordinances could also have a long life, such as that of Ptolemy II forbidding attorneys to defend private persons in conflict with the tax office before tribunals, which was still being cited under Ptolemy VI more than a century later.

Such a plurality of laws was bound to entail a multiplication of jurisdictions for treating litigation between private persons. Aside from certain special tribunals and others that were discontinued over the course of time, two types of jurisdiction are well attested: that of the *laokritai*, made up of priests who applied Egyptian law, and that of the *chrematistai*, judging according to the law of the cities. The latter were originally circuit judges, but they soon became permanent, sitting in each of the nome capitals. The respective competence of these jurisdictions was in fact not so clearly defined, for personal status did not in itself define the nature of the applicable law, except in the special case of the three Greek cities of Egypt. In other words, there was nothing to prevent a Greek from asking that Egyptian law be applied, or vice versa. Eventually, there were so many resulting confusions, especially in cases where the opposing parties were respectively Greek and Egyptian, that one of the ordinances promulgated by Ptolemy VIII and his two wives along with the decrees of amnesty in 118 B.C.E. concerned this very problem.[37] From that time on, the language of the contracts in question would determine the competent tribunal: Greek for the *chrematistai*, and Demotic for the *laokritai*. The only notable exception was the case of a Greek contract drawn up between two Egyptians, which had to be submitted to the *laokritai*, notwithstanding its language. This can be explained by a desire on the part of the sovereigns to protect this native jurisdiction from possible encroachments by the Greek tribunals.

Among the differences between Egyptian law and Greek law, we should at least point to that concerning the juridical capacity of women. It is rather more a matter of a fundamental opposition of two concepts of women's role in the family and in society than of a simple difference in laws. For the Egyptians, women enjoyed complete legal autonomy, which among other things permitted them to dispose freely of their own goods. For the Greeks, a woman was dependent on a guardian, literally a "master" (*kurios*), generally her father or her husband, or otherwise a relative or a third party outside the family. It can easily be seen how this difference in treatment weighed heavily in the choice of Greek or Demotic when drawing up a marriage contract, for example, or dividing goods among heirs, according to whether one wanted to favor the wife in the one case or the daughters in the other.

Whether native or Greek, the tribunals did not always find favor with plaintiffs, who more and more often preferred to address themselves directly to the special jurisdiction of high officials. In fact, nearly twenty centuries before Montesquieu, Ptolemaic Egypt was ignorant of the principle of the separation of powers. By royal delegation, all representatives of public authority in the nomes had a power of administrative coercion permitting them to judge any case brought to their attention and to cause their decision to be executed. Originally, this competence could only be exercised in matters where royal interest was at stake, that is to say, essentially cases concerning taxation. But more and more plaintiffs, recognizing the greater effectiveness of a jurisdiction with effective control over the police force, addressed themselves directly to it. Thus, for example, we see a Hermias who, tired of the impotence of the *chrematistai*, took his case before the tribunal of the *epistates* of the Peritheban nome;[38] he did not win his case, though, despite his status as a Greek. Since it increased the authority of the local functionaries by concentrating all the administrative, judicial, and police powers in their hands, such a development could only lead to abuses, which the kings attempted to combat. The amnesty laws of 118 B.C.E. included several measures aimed at limiting the powers of the *strategoi* and other public officials in matters of jurisdiction and coercion. The effort was in vain, for their constituents were in search of protection that could only be provided by the local holders of any authority whatsoever, in exchange for docile loyalty and some possible profit. Inevitably, corruption and clientelism grew rife in the Egyptian countryside, transcending differences in status and law between Greeks and Egyptians and thus sweeping aside, in an unexpected manner, any and all ethnic antagonism.

SLAVERY[39]

Slavery, the scourge of all ancient societies, had certainly existed in pharaonic Egypt, though it never played a very important economic or social role. It does not seem that the Macedonian conquest was followed by a considerable influx of slaves, even though at home, the Greeks considered slave labor indispensable to the proper functioning of the economy. The organization of agricultural and craft production under the Lagides rendered it in no way necessary. From the point of view of those who held the land— the king, the temples, and the cleruchs—the use of slaves to work the land would have been much less advantageous than its exploitation by the peasants, who theoretically were free. In the cities and countryside of Egypt, there were scarcely any slaves other than household slaves, whose origins were quite diverse: the victorious wars of the third century B.C.E. brought a large number of prisoners into Egypt, but this source dried up in the centuries that followed. Piracy on the Mediterranean was always a potential source of slaves, but it was effectively combated by the Ptolemaic navy until about 250 B.C.E., and then by the Rhodians until the middle of the second century. It was only between 150 and 67, the date of their overwhelming defeat by Pompey, that pirates were able to supply the great market of the free port of Delos with human cargo; at that time, however, the slaves were generally shipped along to Italy, the biggest buyer, and not to Egypt. The exposing or sale of children by parents driven into poverty, on the other hand, made it possible to renew the stock of slaves, as did, in certain cases, servitude imposed on debtors, though the sovereigns seem finally to have denied this ability to private creditors, reserving for themselves the right to exercise it only at the expense of those indebted to the tax office. Children were the most desirable, for they could be taught all sorts of occupations useful for the household or the business of their owner. They could even be entrusted to specialized instructors to learn the craft of weaving, writing or bookkeeping, or certain medical specialties.

Though slaves were only a negligible part of the population in provincial Egypt, the same was not true at Alexandria and the other Greek cities.

Besides the innumerable domestic slaves of the royal court and the rich, the staffs of many workshops are supposed to have been composed of slaves, as everywhere else in the Greek world, though we have only a little information regarding them.

Slaves did not always tolerate the conditions imposed by their status, even in the households of highly placed personages, as is shown by a missing persons report dated to August 13, 156 B.C.E. regarding the flight of two of them:[40] one, a Syrian by birth, belonged to an ambassador of the Carian city of Alabanda, and the other to a high functionary of the royal palace. In addition, the first had stolen three gold coins and some jewelry from his master, while the other had only been able to carry off some clothing. Though the escape took place at Alexandria, the file stems from the police station at the Anoubieion of Memphis, where it was borrowed by Apollonius, the brother of Ptolemaios the recluse, of whom we shall speak again.[41] Without doubt, it was feared that the fugitives would mingle with the crowd of pilgrims at the Serapeum in order to take advantage of the asylum of temples. The notice, accompanied by the offer of a reward, had been issued by the office of the *strategos* of Memphis, an unusual procedure for a private matter that can only be explained by the high rank of the owners. Such assumption of responsibility by the authorities did not insure greater effectiveness, for a second hand was obliged to emend the text, raising the amount of the reward.

5 PRIESTS AND TEMPLES

THE MOST RELIGIOUS OF PEOPLES

Herodotus'[1] sentiment regarding the religiosity of the Egyptians, which he expressed in the fifth century B.C.E., would also have been voiced by any visitor four centuries later, whether Greek or Roman. There is in fact scarcely any land where religion has been so linked to cultural identity. In the last analysis, traditional religious concepts constituted the backbone of pharaonic culture and guaranteed its continuity through historical vicissitudes. The political regime, the social structures, and even the economy could experience profound upheavals, but so long as the foundations of the ancient cults remained unshaken and could adapt to new conditions, the permanence of pharaonic civilization was assured. Thus, the conquest of Alexander in 332 B.C.E. did not affect the vitality of this religious culture any more than the Persian invasion under Cambyses in 525 had done, and it would also not be threatened by the Roman occupation. It was not without reason that the astonishing vigor of this religion aroused the fascination of foreign peoples who came into contact with the Nile valley. Bringing it to an end took the cultural revolution prompted by the expansion and triumph of Christianity in the third and fourth centuries of our own era.

Like every belief system, Egyptian religion was traditionally founded on a certain implicit representation of the world and society. Within its framework, the relationships among the constitutive elements of nature and society were conceived in terms of a struggle between order and chaos, with the divine being the creator and the guarantor of the former against the latter. Without doubt, this cultural representation was closely tied to the special conditions of life in the Nile valley and the principles of economic, social, and political organization to which they led. Communal at first, this religion left little room for the individual, who emerged only slowly as a subject of religious devotion. From the king, the unique interlocutor of the gods, through the priests' monopoly of the religious domain, to ordinary Egyptians establishing relationships of their own with the divine, the evolution was long and complex, but with no major break. The genius of Egyptian religion lay not only in facilitating the coexistence of these successive modes of the relationship of the human to the divine—the royal, the sacerdotal, and the personal—but also in combining them according to a unique and interchangeable scheme beyond the apparent multiplicity and diversity of divine figures and the myths associated with them. This process enabled religion to play a central role in pharaonic society, furnishing a normative model for the structures of power by means of its founding myths, as well as a practice extending to all areas of social life and appropriate responses to the inevitable tensions, whether fundamental or transitory.

We must not think, however, that Egyptian religious beliefs constituted a closed system fixed forever in its own coherence, incapable of change and impervious to outside influences. The latter, especially those from western Asia, were rather common during and after the New Kingdom, bringing new deities and even new forms of religiosity, though these innovations had first to be adapted to native modes of expression and the basic concepts they articulated. These conditions met, Syro-Canaanite deities such as Astarte or Baal were able to find a place in the Egyptian pantheon, at least in certain locales. In other cases, adaptation proved impossible, as when the Persian kings settled Jewish military colonists in the delta and in the far south of the land, at Elephantine. The fundamental principles of the Jewish religion were irreconcilable with Egyptian religious sensibilities, and mere cohabitation proved difficult and even conflictual, culminating in the destruction of the Jewish temple at Elephantine in 410 B.C.E.[2] The religious attitude of the Greeks could not occasion such mental blocks. Since they viewed Egypt as a possible source of their own culture, the Greeks evinced a curiosity regarding Egyptian mythology. Well before Alexander, they elaborated a system of identifying the deities of the two pantheons: Amun–Zeus, Mut–Hera, Osiris–Dionysos, and so forth. Certain pharaonic sanctuaries, such as that of Amun in Siwa Oasis, were visited by Greek pilgrims two centuries before Alexander's conquest. Under such conditions, it is scarcely surprising that exchange between the two religious systems was almost entirely one-sided.

NEW SANCTUARIES

The Ptolemaic period witnessed the repair and construction of numerous religious edifices in the Nile valley. This architectural activity, which continued under Roman domination during the two centuries following the death of Cleopatra, was so considerable that the majority of the temples one can visit in Upper Egypt today are contemporary with the Lagide kings or with Rome of the Caesars.

The temple of Edfu[3] (Figure 22) is without doubt the best preserved, with its pylon, its walls, its courtyard, and its interior layout all intact. It also has the distinction of having been entirely constructed and decorated during the Ptolemaic era. Begun under Ptolemy III, it was completed about 170 years later, in the reign of Ptolemy XII, though there were interruptions due to economic or political conditions, such as the period of the great revolt in the Thebaid, which closed the construction site for nearly twenty years. The temple of Dendara[4] was begun around the time that Edfu was completed. This is surely no coincidence; the same gangs of workmen were probably transferred from the site of Edfu to that of Dendara.[5] The latter was thus begun under Ptolemy XII, in whose name the crypts were decorated. The construction work was well advanced in the reign of Cleopatra, making it possible for the sculptors to cover the southern exterior wall with the famous scene depicting Ptolemy Caesar and Cleopatra before the local gods and goddesses. Most of the decoration, however, was executed under the Roman emperors, from Augustus to Nero. Along with the greater part of the temple of Kom Ombo (Figure 23), which has the peculiarity of having been laid out along two parallel axes, and the main temple at Philae, dedicated to Isis, these edifices represent the bulk of the architecture surviving today from Ptolemaic Egypt. Contrasting with the disappearance of all contemporary monuments in the Hellenistic style, the preservation of these buildings, with their purely pharaonic style and intent, has often led historians to adopt too Egyptophilic a view of the religious policy of the Lagides. In fact, they were almost exclusively interested in their capital city, whose architectural heritage turned out to be more vulnerable to eventual destruction than the sanctuaries of Upper Egypt.

Thanks to the exceptional preservation of these temples—in particular, those of Edfu, Dendara, and Philae—visitors today can form a precise picture of a functioning pharaonic temple. It can seem strange that these late constructions furnish the best illustrations of what a traditional Egyptian

FIGURE 22. Statue of the falcon god Horus in the temple of Edfu. Photo © Michael S. Schreiber.

FIGURE 23. Temple of Kom Ombo. Photo © Dr. Howard Schreiber and Mrs. Arlene J. Schreiber.

temple was like, ones far more evocative than the confused ruins of the great New Kingdom edifices at Karnak or Luxor. These vast spaces where dead silence reigns when crowds of tourists are absent, and where the half light becomes ever fainter and the spaces smaller as one advances toward the sanctuary, arouse a feeling of the sacred in even the most skeptical of individuals. An Egyptian temple was not a church; it was a domain from which humans were normally excluded, except for the servants of the gods and goddesses. Its external appearance was that of a fortress, intended more to bar intruders than to welcome pilgrims. Its exits, few and narrow, were closed by heavy doors. Its layout, with many interior corridors, courts, hypostyle halls, and vestibules separating the outside world from the holy of holies, was intended to screen access according to the status of the persons allowed to penetrate inside. The temple served to protect the divine image, and it was designed to enable the performance of the tasks needed to maintain the image's supposed effectiveness, tasks that constituted the essence of the daily cult ritual. The role of the decoration of the temple was at one and the same time normative, commemorative, and substitutive, indicating the ideal form of the divine cult, recalling its mythical origin, and in the event that reality fell short of the ideal, taking over by means of the pregnant quality of its images.

Necessary but routine, the celebration of the daily cult ritual (Figure 24)

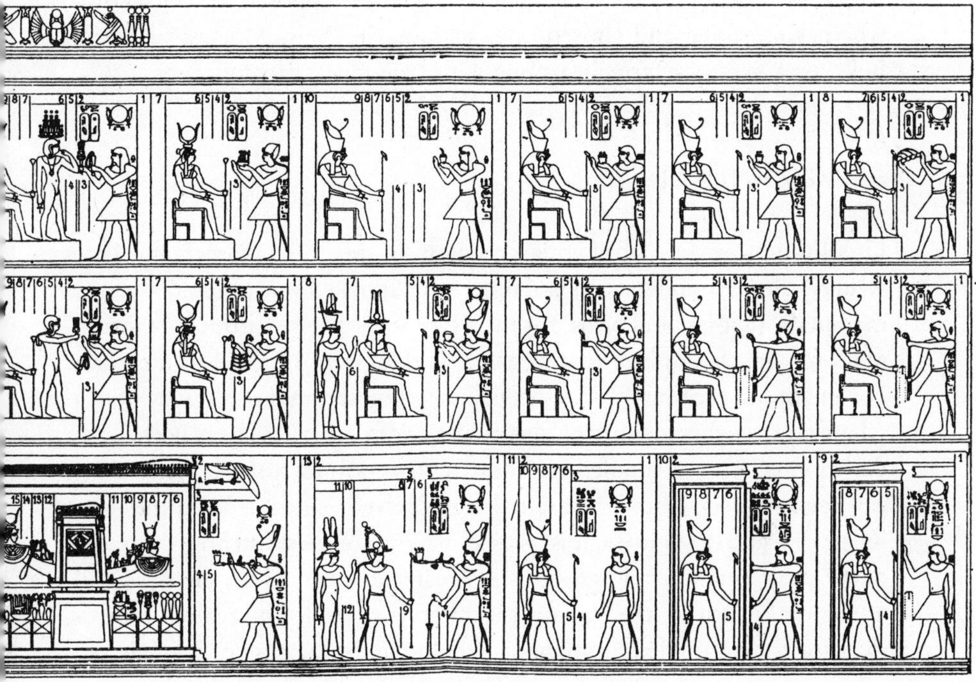

FIGURE 24. Scenes from the daily cult ritual depicted on the interior of the sanctuary of the temple of Horus at Edfu. After M. de Rochemonteix and E. Chassinat, *Le Temple d'Edfou,* Vol. I, Mémoires publiés par les membres de la Mission Archéologique Française au Caire 10 (Cairo, 1892–97), Pl. XII.

was far from the only human activity in the temple. There were festivals, of course, and the calendar was filled with them. Their frequency in fact varied from temple to temple: thus, there were 91 festival days each year at Esna in Upper Egypt[6] but as many as 153 at Dimai in the north of the Faiyum.[7] There was a general participation of the local clergy, from the high priest down to the humblest *pastophoroi,* but above all, these festivals occasioned the gathering of laypeople who thronged to catch sight of the deities who were carried out in gilded wooden chapels perched on emblem-covered barques that pitched on the shoulders of the priests in the course of interminable processions. While these manifestations followed general prescriptions fixed by age-old traditions, new theological developments tended to redouble the popular fervor that accompanied them. Thus, the epiphanies of sacred animals assumed a privileged place among the other solemnities because of the attraction exerted on the faithful by these living divine hypostases, which were more susceptible of emotional investment than inert wooden images. Each temple was thus supposed to keep its own, whether a unique and chosen one, such as the Apis, Mnevis, or Buchis bulls, or a livestock farm swarming with crocodiles, cats, or ibises.

SACRED ANIMALS

Of all the bizarreries of Egyptian religion, in the eyes of Greek and Latin writers, the least understood and most often mocked was the cult of certain mammals, reptiles, and birds, for the animals themselves attracted more attention from the faithful than the deities they were believed to incarnate. For the pious, the animal was the visible, tangible vessel of a divine power, whatever the exact identity of that power might otherwise have been. Their devotion otherwise entailed two apparently contradictory aspects. If one can easily conceive how the animal could have been considered the living image of a god or goddess, it is more difficult to understand how the corpse of the dead animal could arouse still greater interest. Thus, the Apis bulls are better known for their grandiose funerals, attended by zealous crowds, than for their daily lives in their sacred stable. In the case of animals venerated en masse, like the ibises of Thoth, the cats of Bastet (Figure 25), or the crocodiles of Sobek, examination of the hundreds of thousands of mummies found in the cemeteries has shown that a great number of these unfortunate animals were deliberately killed, most often well before reaching maturity. Such findings seem to contradict the famous passage in Diodorus relating the sad fate of a Roman citizen, a contemporary of Ptolemy Auletes, who was lynched by a mob enraged by the fact that he had accidentally killed a cat just when the king was seeking the recognition of Rome![8] In fact, these instances of euthanasia discovered by autopsy were intended to enable each pilgrim to bury an animal, that is, to pay the expenses and carry out the rites. Participation in the burial of a sacred animal was an especially popular act of devotion, in return for which the faithful hoped for divine grace. The dead animal, duly mummified and buried, was thus more auspicious and useful to its adherent than its mewing or growling counterparts in the livestock yards of the temples. In this respect, better cared for in death than in life, the sacred animals of Egypt shared the fate of their human devotés!

In certain cases, there was more curiosity than authentic piety in the interest that drew pilgrims to the divine livestock farms. This was undoubtedly the case with the crocodiles venerated in many temples in the Faiyum, where Sobek was lord. According to Strabo, Roman tourists flocked there

FIGURE 25. Bronze statuette of a cat goddess, probably Bastet. Brooklyn Museum 78.243. Gift of Alice Heeramaneck. Photo courtesy of the Brooklyn Museum of Art.

to watch the feeding of the repugnant reptiles, which the obliging priests organized into spectacles.[9] But when one of these crocodiles died, the personnel of the temple were overcome with sincere emotion as they hastened to prepare for the funeral, as witnessed by the following response to an urgent request from the priests of Dimai, who were anxious to organize the transport of one of the divine carcasses to its final resting place at the beginning of 132 B.C.E.:

> In receiving your letter, we were aware of the preoccupations the god arouses in the hearts of us, the notables, regarding the resting place of the great god Osiris (= the dead crocodile). You wrote [us] to say that you have [already] asked for a barque to be taken to the pier. We have passed this request along to the priests [of the necropolis]. They have ordered that the barque of the [sacred] crocodile which is on the lake be taken to the place in question until an embalming tent is set up. Let us know what you need down there.[10]

Behind the epistolary formulas, we can easily see the scrupulousness with which the priests applied themselves to the performance of their duty toward the defunct incarnation of their god.

THE PRESTIGE OF THE PRIESTS

If one defines a priest as the privileged intermediary between the human and the divine, there was only one priest in Egypt, the one depicted performing the offering rituals in all the temple reliefs: the King of Upper and Lower Egypt, the Son of Re, Ptolemy, perhaps accompanied by his queen, Cleopatra. This was a fiction, of course, all the more so as the Greek kings must have been almost entirely ignorant of the complicated rituals of the native religion. It was thus the Egyptian priests, heirs to a millennia-old tradition, who were charged with maintaining the fragile equilibrium of the universe by meticulously observing all the prescriptions aimed at assuring the good will of the divine.

Priests did not constitute a homogeneous social class. There were various categories of priests, and the size of their ranks was proportional to the number of active cult places, from simple chapels with a lone servant to huge temples with hierarchically organized staffs. Many priests accumulated several appointments to office in one or more temples, each position furnishing an income, which was often modest enough in the case of the many lower-ranking priestly offices. These offices were theoretically in the hands of the king, who alone delegated ecclesiastical responsibilities to those who were supposed to represent him before the gods and goddesses, but in fact they were venal. They could be passed along from father to son or sold to third parties. In cases of transfer, the new incumbent paid a special tax to the state. To enter into the priestly class, he also had to meet cer-

tain conditions: he had to attain a certain level of instruction, to be cir-
cumcised, to observe a certain number of physical and moral precepts, and
undoubtedly also to belong to a priestly family, if we are indeed to speak
of an actual sacerdotal "caste" in Egypt.

The organization of Egyptian temples was such that purely religious duties occupied only a limited amount of the priests' time. In fact, the servants
of each temple were divided into five groups (called *sa* in Egyptian and
phyle in Greek), each of which performed the divine service for one lunar
month on a rotating basis. Traditionally, there had been four such groups,
but the Canopus decree of 238 B.C.E. added a fifth in honor of the reigning
sovereigns, Ptolemy III and Berenike II, the gods Euergetes, which had the
effect of commensurately shortening each group's period of service and left
them free for other activities. In principle, the "pure ones" (*wabu*) were
supposed to refrain from certain activities that could defile them. They
were thus not allowed, at least in principle, to engage in commerce, agriculture, or crafts. But the priests did play an important role in native society in the areas of law, education, and culture.

The Ptolemies left the application of Egyptian law to the priests, a body
of law that applied to the relations between natives and originated with the
pharaohs Bocchoris and Amasis, the Saite lawgivers. It was priests who
wrote, in Demotic, the many contracts regarding sales, loans, divisions,
and marriages, by means of which the native population disposed of their
movable and immovable property. It was also priests, sitting as tribunals of
laokritai, who decided litigations stemming from the application of these
contracts.

In the domains of education and culture, the temples had traditionally
exercised a veritable monopoly on the teaching of the hieroglyphic and Demotic writing systems and on all branches of pharaonic learning and science, from secular and sacred literature to medicine and the interpretation
of dreams. For the native culture, the Egyptian temple thus played the role
enjoyed by the Greek *gymnasion* in the dominant culture, the two institutions constituting opposite poles that defined the Januslike civilization of
Lagide Egypt.

PIETY OUTSIDE THE TEMPLES

The temples did not, however, have a monopoly on the spiritual life of
Cleopatra's contemporaries, indeed, far from it. There is considerable
archaeological evidence that the gods and goddesses were not forgotten in

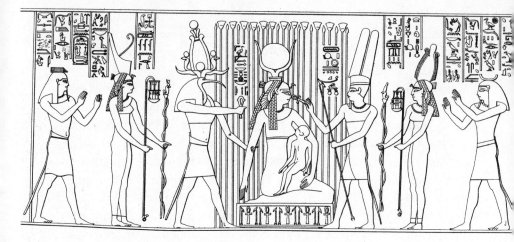

FIGURE 26. Isis, attended by other gods and goddesses, nursing her son Horus. Mammisi (birth house) of the temple of Isis at Philae. After H. Rosellini, *Monumenti dell'Egitto e della Nubia,* Vol. III (Pisa, 1844), Pl. XIX.

the privacy of homes. The large numbers of bronze or terra cotta statuettes found in houses attest to everyday piety. Niches in walls were often the location of personal cults. Sometimes a painting on a panel of wood, the veritable ancestor of the Christian icon, served as the object of this devotion in the home. Along with tutelary deities such as the dwarf Bes, who chased away evil spirits, divinities of quite a different stature have been found: Sarapis, of course, in his Hellenized form, but more often Isis, whose prestige was to grow even greater when Egypt became a Roman province. In the Ptolemaic period, she competed with Cybele, whose zealous devotés spread her ecstatic cult wherever Greeks were most numerous. But she quickly assumed her less exotic and more universal traits. Isis was the omnipotent goddess of salvation, whose ten thousand names revealed the extent of her powers. In her guise of mother nursing her child Horus (Figure 26), she was the mother of all gods and goddesses and the protectress of suffering humanity. Though major temples were dedicated to her, such as that of Philae (Figures 27 and 28) in the far south and that at Behbeit el-Hagar (Figure 29) in the far north, her greatest temple was that which grew ever larger in the hearts of all the inhabitants of Egypt and eventually won those of the subjects of Rome; under another name, but with the same consoling mission, she was able to escape the shipwreck of ancient paganism and survive to our own time.

Beyond the home, religiosity also found expression in professional or private associations. These had been known in both classical Greece and

FIGURE 27. Temple of Isis at Philae. Photo © Dr. Howard Schreiber and Mrs. Arlene J. Schreiber.

pharaonic Egypt, and as the two traditions blended together in Ptolemaic Egypt, they became a dominant feature of social life in the towns and villages. They often brought together people of the same profession, such as that founded in 110 B.C.E. for the Theban *choachytai,* but sometimes also local notables and petty bourgeois who had in common only their devotion to one and the same deity. Some of these associations enjoyed official encouragement, such as those dedicated to Dionysos (Figure 30)—the *thiasoi* —which became numerous at the end of the third century under the influence of Ptolemy IV Philopator, whose enthusiasm for the god of Bacchic ecstasy is well known. We even have the text of an edict enjoining those initiated into the Dionysiac mysteries, who were supposed to play a major role in these associations, to come to Alexandria and register so that the orthodoxy of their initiation could be verified.[11] It is clear that membership in these *thiasoi* was tantamount to a display of loyalty to the regime. Otherwise, in certain cases, the sole religious obligation of the association's members was to make sacrifices and libations in honor of the king and the queen, like the synod of Zeus Hypsistos (the Highest) at Philadelphia in the Faiyum, whose meeting place in the temple of Zeus constituted the only evidence of the group's devotion to the divine patron of the sanctuary.[12]

FIGURE 28. Falcon-headed god Horus (detail of figure 27). Photo © Dr. Howard Schreiber and Mrs. Arlene J. Schreiber.

FIGURE 29. Temple of Isis at Behbeit el-Hagar, viewed from the north. In the foreground, the ruins of the hypostyle hall and of the sanctuary, with its façade dominated by a huge block. In the background, the south brick wall, on which there is a modern cemetery. Photo © Christine Favard-Meeks.

Regular meetings, usually monthly, could take place in a temple forecourt, in a specially outfitted place, or in a private home. The pretext was always a banquet, washed down with plenty of drink. Less secular obligations were generally also incumbent on members, such as participation in various festivals and processions in honor of their deity and the organization of the funerals of sacred animals. Finally, they had obligations to assist one another. Not only was there a code of good conduct to be observed, on pain of being assessed a fine, but members were also obliged to assist their fellows who were ill, needy, or imprisoned, and especially to provide for their funerals when they died. As we know, this last burden could be heavy indeed in Egypt, and it is not surprising that many tried to avoid it, hence the importance of the sanctions provided for in case of failure to perform this ultimate duty.[13]

GREEK PRIESTS

In the three Greek cities of Egypt, there were official cults for Hellenic or Hellenized deities according to the traditional forms of the Greek world.

FIGURE 30. Marble statuette of a satyr carrying the infant Dionysos. The features of the satyr suggest the piece was made in Alexandria. Walters Art Gallery 23.69. Photo courtesy of The Walters Art Gallery, Baltimore.

The same was true in the *Chora,* where any number of cult places, usually modest in size, were established in honor of the deities of Olympus or the deified royal ancestors. Thus, we find mention of temples dedicated to Zeus, Demeter, or the Dioskouroi in the villages of the Faiyum.[14] For their priests, the rites performed in these temples did not impose requirements as strict as those of the Egyptian cults. In the cities, a priesthood was a public office like any other, and it could be held by any citizen for a limited period of time. At Alexandria and Ptolemais, the most prestigious of these priesthoods were those dedicated to the dynastic cults, in particular that of Alexander and the Lagide sovereigns. In the course of the third and second centuries B.C.E., these priestly offices grew in number until they reached a total of eight at Alexandria and thirteen at Ptolemais.[15] The holders of the most important of these were replaced each year, while the others could retain their positions for several years in a row or even for life. These were purely honorific positions awarded to members of the important families of these two cities, and their duty was essentially to participate in processions organized periodically in honor of the deified kings and queens. The official titles of several priestesses evoked the object they carried in these processions: *kanephoros* (she who carries the basket of gold), *athlophoros* (she who carries the trophy), *stephanephoros* (she who carries the crown), and *phosphoros* (she who carries the torch). The greatest privilege enjoyed by these priestesses was that of eponymy, that is, of being mentioned along with the king and queen in the dates of all documents, both official and private. This custom fell into neglect in the course of time, however, and from the end of the second century on, eponymous priests and priestesses were no longer mentioned in the dates of documents. We thus do not know the names of the holders of these offices, though they continued to succeed one another until the end of the dynasty, as proved by scattered allusions to them, the last one dated only six months before the death of the last Cleopatra.[16]

TEMPLE ECONOMY

Egyptian temples were not just sacred places where hordes of priests carried out arcane rituals. They were also centers of economic activity. An Egyptian cult was an activity consuming many items that had to be replaced on a regular basis: food items ranging from bread to burnt meat offerings, feed for the sacred animals, textiles for the clothing of the statues and the priests, oil to light the sanctuaries, unguents and perfumes, combustible material for the sacrifices, wood and metal for ornamentation and the paraphernalia used in processions, not to mention the salaries of the servants, priests, and minor personnel who maintained the temple. In the pharaonic era, the kings had provided the temples with estates to furnish them with all they needed in order to function. These royal donations, made over the course of the years and confirmed at each change of reign, in the end constituted impressive domains like those of the temples of Thebes, Memphis, and Heliopolis, which were inventoried at the end of the New Kingdom in the lengthy Papyrus Harris I.

In the framework of their policy of control over the economy, the Ptolemies decided to limit the autonomy of the native temples. Without their being confiscated on the theoretical level, the sacred lands, or at least the great majority of them, were removed from the administration of the temples and entrusted to royal peasants. In theory, the state turned the income over to the temples in the form of a rent called *syntaxis,* but in practice this was a much smaller amount than what would have been derived by direct management. For their most immediate needs, however, certain lands could be ceded back to the temples, which had them cultivated by peasant slaves of the deity, who were in fact farmers who paid a fixed annual rent to the divine proprietor. The temples also received income from a tax levied on all the orchards and vineyards belonging to private persons. This tax, called the *apomoïra,* had been intended by Ptolemy II for the special maintenance of the cult of his deified wife, Arsinoe Philadelphos, a cult that had to be celebrated in all the temples of Egypt. The income from this tax, which was collected by the state and redistributed to the temples, thus depended on their carrying out an act of allegiance to the dynasty, assuring the loyalty of the native priests.

Aside from this, certain craft and industrial activities were controlled by the temples, such as the manufacture of *byssos,* for the use of any other textile was forbidden to the deities and their priests. With regard to production otherwise subject to royal monopoly—for example, the pressing of oil—the temples were authorized to produce only what was absolutely necessary to supply their cults. The temples also often had flocks of sheep and goats, which were under the care of herdsman-slaves of the god.

Finally, a significant part of the revenues of the temples came from the offerings of pilgrims and of the faithful who came to ask for divine intercession. Wealthy private individuals even went so far as to dedicate land to the gods, generally orchards, gardens, or vineyards.

ORACLES AND OATHS

Beyond their economic role, the temples of the Ptolemaic period played a vital social role in the native towns and villages. People came to the temple to request oracles. Every important decision in individual or family life was often made after consulting the deity through the mediation of his or her priests. Minor cases at law between private persons could also be resolved in this manner, if both parties were agreeable to this recourse. The exact details of the procedure varied from one temple to another. The consultation could take place at the main entrance or at a less important doorway specially set aside for this purpose. Each of the two alternatives submitted for divine decision was written down on a separate piece of papyrus. These were given to a priest, who presented them to the statue or to a sacred animal, and the single papyrus corresponding to the divine entity's choice was given back to the person making the consultation.[17]

In a similar manner, a god or goddess could be requested to serve as guarantor of an oath. Any number of conflicts between private persons could be resolved in this manner. In a case of petty larceny, for example, and of course excluding flagrant delicts, the accused could get out of the affair by making a public denial, in front of the temple gateway, of participation in the theft in question. Before being solemnly pronounced, the text of the oath was carefully set down by a priest on a piece of papyrus or a potsherd. Perjury, if proven, could have had serious consequences for the guilty party. The number of oaths that have been found attests to the popularity of this practice, which avoided longer and more hazardous procedures.[18]

STRANGE SLAVES

A more enigmatic form of temple intervention in the life of the society is to be found in an unusual group of papyri written in Demotic and found in great number at Tebtunis and in other temples in the Faiyum, though we might suppose that the practices to which they attest existed elsewhere as well. In these documents, individuals, both male and female, declare themselves slaves of the local deity, along with their descendants, generally for a period fixed at ninety-nine years. Such "slavery" seems to have been more theoretical than real, however, for the only obligation stipulated for the person who made the declaration was the payment of a monthly sum to the deity, one that in truth was quite modest. For their part, these deities were supposed to protect their servants from evil acts committed by various supernatural entities—phantoms, wandering ghosts, demons, evil genies—all of them duly listed.

At first glance, this slavery would seem to be nothing but a way of obtaining protection against the evil eye. But those who entered into such peculiar servitude would seem to have belonged to certain very precise categories: their fathers were frequently unknown, and they were often "born in the domain (of the temple)." There must thus have been special ties between the temples and the individuals in question from the time of their birth, and these contracts could have been intended to confirm these ties and make them official. These could have been, for example, infants who had been exposed or born of the prostitution that was tolerated in the sacred domain. In such a case, this curious voluntary slavery might have been motivated by nothing other than an award of long-term public assistance on the part of the temple. Not all the examples are susceptible to such an interpretation, however, and we must admit that many were seeking, by this means, a real spiritual protection against dark forces and the human anguish they caused.[19]

THE DEITIES OF MEMPHIS[20]

Though it is relatively easy to define and describe social forms of devotion in ancient religion, personal attitudes most often escape us and, with them, the religious conscience and innermost convictions of individuals. At best, we are confronted with conventional and ostentatious elaborations that distort rather than reveal the actual underlying religious sentiment. It is thus exceptional to have a group of documents affording a glimpse of the link between real life and spirituality, even if the latter can only be read between the lines, as a possible driving force behind individual choices. Discovered by accident in the Memphite necropolis at the beginning of the nineteenth century, the archive of Ptolemaios son of Glaukias constitutes one of the rare opportunities granted us to penetrate the troubled conscience of ordinary folk, simple and unpretentious, but whose deeper motives perhaps exceeded the simple need for material survival and social recognition.

Memphis, the second city of Egypt after Alexandria and the veritable capital of the native land, was also its premier religious center, where pilgrims converged from both the valley and the delta in search of mystical experiences or in hope of a cure for their physical or spiritual ills. The object

FIGURE 31. Head of a statue of the goddess Sakhmet. New Kingdom. Detroit Institute of Arts 31.69. Gift of Mrs. Lillian Henkel Haass and Miss Constance Haass. © 1988 The Detroit Institute of Arts.

of this feverish anticipation was not the traditional lord of the ancient city, the venerable Ptah, the creator god who watched from his shrine over royal coronations and his own local craft industries and whom the Greeks identified, for the latter reason, with their divine blacksmith Hephaistos. Nor were these devout souls attracted by his closest associates, his consort, the lion-goddess Sakhmet (Figure 31), despite the dominion over illnesses that was attributed to her, or his son, Nefertem of the lotus crown (Figure 32). Too closely tied to long-gone political and social conditions, the theology of all these ancient deities could scarcely serve to inspire a piety that was ever more based on a personal relationship with a savior god.

FIGURE 32. Bronze statuette of Nefertem. MMA 10.175.131 (Rogers Fund, 1910). Photo courtesy of the Metropolitan Museum of Art.

FIGURE 33. Bronze statuette of Apis. Late Period. Detroit Institute of Arts 1994.46. Founders Society Purchase, Hill Memorial Fund and William H. Murphy Fund. © 1998 The Detroit Institute of Arts.

These new needs were satisfied by other manifestations of divine power, ones nearer and more tangible.

First and foremost among these was the Apis bull (Figure 33). Far from being a latecomer, he was one of the most ancient religious institutions of pharaonic Egypt. His cult had grown separate from that of Ptah, to which it was originally closely linked, and from the New Kingdom on, it was split up into two distinct aspects, that of the living Apis and that of the dead one.

FIGURE 34. Head of Sarapis. Walters Art Gallery 23.120. Photo courtesy of The Walters Art Gallery, Baltimore.

The living Apis, symbol of fecundity and guarantor of Egypt's prosperity, led a quiet life in his stable-sanctuary at Memphis, along with his mother (who was identified with Isis), his harem, and his numerous progeny. Assimilated to Osiris, the dead Apis became a chthonic deity, all-powerful in this world and the next, and he was buried with great pomp, surrounded by mourning crowds who had come from throughout the land. Above their subterranean necropolis in the desert northeast of the great Step Pyramid of the ancient pharaoh Djoser stood the vast buildings of the great Serapeum, where the dead bulls had a cult of their own. It was this mummified Apis, Osorapis, who had been adopted by the Greeks of Memphis under the name Sarapis long before the arrival of Alexander the Great. They had made him into a composite and syncretistic deity, identifying him with Hades, their own god of the netherworld, and attributing oracular powers to him. By decision of Ptolemy I, this Sarapis (Figure 34) became the tutelary god of Alexandria, whence his cult would later spread throughout the Mediterranean world.

Curiously, a whole sacred menagerie came to be associated with Apis, venerated in a collection of nearby temples and buried in their own catacombs: cats of Bastet, dogs of Anubis, ibises and baboons of Thoth-Hermes, falcons, and so forth. The Serapeum was thus but the center of an immense sacred city built among the pyramids and the ruined cemeteries of the kings and nobles of the Old Kingdom. Colonnades and statues in purest Hellenistic style were nestled amid the massive Egyptian monuments, a setting perfectly suited to the bicultural nature of the devotions that took place there.

THE LIFE AND DREAMS OF PTOLEMAIOS THE RECLUSE[21]

The eldest of four sons of an ordinary Macedonian soldier, Ptolemaios was born around 200 B.C.E. in a little village in the Herakleopolitan nome, where the oasis of the Faiyum opens onto the Nile valley and where his father worked a plot of land granted by the king. We know nothing of his childhood and upbringing except that he received enough instruction to enable him to write in Greek, though not enough for him to do it easily or correctly. Around the age of thirty, he decided to retreat from the world and to live confined in an annex of the great Serapeum of Memphis (Figure 35), more specifically, in the sacristy (*pastophorion*) of a small temple dedicated to the Canaanite goddess Astarte, the Astartieion.

Ptolemaios remained there for at least twenty years; he was apparently strictly cloistered, though we are uncertain whether this extended to the entire Serapeum or whether it was limited to his own small lodging. There is no doubt that he was a voluntary recluse, but nowhere does Ptolemaios explain why this was so; perhaps there were material considerations or perhaps a compulsion of a mystical sort. The former can be justified by details furnished by Ptolemaios concerning his means of subsistence. We know that the temple gave him a monthly grain ration for his nourishment, and that his situation enabled him to perform some minor services for

FIGURE 35. Entrance to the Serapeum at Saqqara. Photo © Al Berens, Suredesign Graphics.

remuneration and even to engage in a little peddling, but the total he could earn by these means remained quite insufficient, and he could scarcely have scraped together a living without outside help. Even with a guarantee of (very) relative security, such a low standard of living would not have been attractive enough to compensate for his total lack of freedom, even if it was consensual in origin, and this without interruption for at least twenty years. We must thus allow that it was divine inspiration that had guided Ptolemaios to his voluntary retreat.

The many complaints and requests written by our recluse to various high officials, and even to King Ptolemy and Queen Cleopatra themselves, enable us to put together an account of the lifestyle of Ptolemaios and those around him. And there is more: the very privacy of souls is bared to us by his carefully transcribed accounts of the dreams that agitated his nights and those of his companions in retreat. Two thousand years before the birth of Freud, dreams were not considered to be disguised expressions of unconscious drives but rather manifestations of divine power bearing tidings of hope or forebodings of menace. The belief that dreams could reveal the will of the divine had long been common among the Greeks, for the expression "a dream comes from Zeus" is already to be found in Homer. The Egyptians also paid great attention to their nocturnal fantasies, ever since the famous dream of King Tuthmosis IV at the feet of the Great Sphinx, in which he was commanded to free the august statue from the sand that had covered it. The form taken by the messages was usually not all that clear, so each temple library had to have books on the interpretation of dreams, veritable keys to dreams whose study enabled certain specialists to come to the aid of dreamers by deciphering strange visions sent to them from the divine realm.[22]

Not every dream was equally inspired, and the environment of the sleeper played an essential role. Deities usually manifested themselves to the faithful only in sacred places. This was certainly the case with Imhotep (Figure 36), whom the Greeks called Imouthes. This great man had been a minister of Djoser and the architect of the Step Pyramid, which loomed in the vicinity of the Serapeum; he was progressively deified, becoming the patron of scribes and of the arts and sciences, among which medicine became more and more prominent, to the point where the Greeks could easily identify him with their own healing god Asklepios. Those who were ill or members of their family thus requested admission into the Asklepieion, to sleep there and perchance to obtain, by means of a dream, an indication of the remedy prescribed by the god himself. This practice of therapeutic incubation, known from other sanctuaries in the Greek world, made a fortune for the temples of the Memphite necropolis.

The dreams recorded in Greek or Demotic in Ptolemaios's archive were mostly not therapeutic in nature. They express other preoccupations, ranging from existential angst and identity crises to other, more sordid concerns. Evidently Ptolemaios did not view them as a manifestation of his own fears but rather as forecasts of their ultimate resolution by divine intervention, with that confusion of cause and effect that is the compost heap of all superstition.

On at least one occasion, however, Ptolemaios had a premonitory dream of general interest. Just as the temple of Ptah at Memphis was the home of Apis, the temple of Atum-Re in the neighboring city of Heliopolis (whose name means "city of the sun") sheltered another sacred bull, Mnevis. The latter had died on December 17, 159 B.C.E., and the priests thus had to search for a young calf to take its place. Such a quest could turn out to be long and difficult, for the required signs were many and precise. Six months later, the search was undoubtedly not yet over, prolonging the pious anxiety, and on June 2, 158, Ptolemaios experienced this nocturnal apparition:

In my dream, I had the impression of continually calling on the very great god Amun to come to me from the north in his trinity. He finally appeared, and there seemed to be a cow in this place, and she was pregnant. He seized the cow and laid her on the floor. He plunged his hand into her belly and removed a bull.[23]

The identity of the divine obstetrician (an Amun of the delta?) might have served as an indication of the place where the new Mnevis was to be found. Such revelations, if verified, would undoubtedly have conferred con-

FIGURE 36. Bronze statuette depicting Imhotep. Late Period. Detroit Institute of Arts 64.574. Gift of Mr. and Mrs. Bernard F. Walker. © The Detroit Institute of Arts 1998.

siderable prestige on the dreamer. At just that time, a certain priest from Sebennytos named Hor was being haunted by political visions. For his part, Ptolemaios was habitually seized by torments much closer to home.

COVETED VIRGINS

What was the situation troubling Ptolemaios at this point? He was not alone, for other recluses lived in the enclosure of the Serapeum. In particular, there was Harmais (in Egyptian, Haremhab), a native who shared Ptolemaios' lodging and adversity. But the persons who counted most in the latter's eyes, at least in the critical period of 164–158 B.C.E., were twin girls named Taus and Thaues. The story of these highly unusual girls begins with a sordid affair of criminal adultery. Their mother Nephoris was infatuated with a Greek soldier, Philippos son of Sogenes; desirous of marrying him, she persuaded him to use his swashbuckling talents on her husband, the father of the two young girls. Philippos, however, was able to escape by jumping into the river from the roof of his house. He succeeded in swimming to an island, and he was picked up by friends who took him to Herakleopolis, where he soon died of a broken heart. Meanwhile, Nephoris took possession of her husband's goods, and she did not hesitate to expel their three daughters from their home, depriving them of their inheritance. These girls, the twins and their older sister Tathemis, were left without means of support and took refuge in the Serapeum.

Now, it happened that the Apis bull died in the month of April, 164 B.C.E., at the ripe old age of twenty-two. The complex rites and ceremonies that had to take place during the seventy days of the embalming period required young people to play the roles of the various deities who had participated in the funeral of Osiris, with whom the deceased Apis was identified. Prominent among these were Isis, the widow of the god, and her sister Nephthys. Because they were both virgins and twins, this prestigious responsibility was entrusted to the younger daughters of Nephoris. They acquitted themselves well indeed, for the temple continued to employ them to perform the daily libations of the cult of Osiris-Apis, and six years later, they were called on to perform the same task at the burial of Mnevis, the sacred bull of Heliopolis.

Though their position was highly regarded and remunerative, the twins were nevertheless vulnerable. In particular, their half brother Pachrates, child of their mother's first marriage, succeeded in swindling them of the oil provision that constituted an important part of their wages. Unable to defend themselves, inasmuch as they did not know Greek, they placed themselves under the protection of Ptolemaios, who wrote a number of petitions on their behalf. Our recluse's devotion to their cause was undoubtedly sincere but in part self-interested. The emoluments of the two sisters, which were proportional to the importance of the ritual task they were called on to perform, were incommensurate with the meager income Ptolemaios received from the temple. He could thus legitimately hope for some small profit in exchange for his good offices. Nevertheless, the degree to which the girls preoccupied Ptolemaios, and especially his dreams, shows that such an explanation is insufficient. Ptolemaios was genuinely convinced that he had been invested with some sort of divine mission with regard to them, as had been revealed to him in a dream inspired by the god Sarapis himself. Such a conception of his role otherwise conflicted with his own sexual urges, which led him to desire at least one of the two sisters and which were exacerbated by his enforced celibacy. The torments of his conscience are revealed in the dreams he regularly recorded:

I seemed to see Thaues singing gaily, . . . and I saw Taus laughing, and her foot was large and clean.

Two men were working in the vestibule. Taus was sitting on the steps, joking with them, but hearing the voice of Chemtosneu, she suddenly became quite gloomy. They said they would instruct her [. . .].[24]

Two men came toward me and said, "Ptolemaios, take the money for the blood." They paid out one hundred bronze drachmas to me, and a purse full of bronze *staters* to Thaues, the twin. They said to her, "Here is the money for the blood!" I said to them, "She has more coins than I do!"[25]

During the night of February 10–11, 158 B.C.E., Ptolemaios had a more explicit dream:

I seemed to be walking in Memphis, from west to east, and I climbed up a pile of straw, and a man coming toward me from the west also climbed up. My eyes were as though closed, and when I suddenly opened them, I saw the twins in Tothes' classroom. They were calling (me). I answered, "Don't be discouraged, Tothes is tired of finding the way to me, because I've overturned my bed!" I then heard Tothes answer, "Go away! Why are you saying that? I'll bring you the twins." [. . .] I walked toward them until I reached them, and I walked in the street with them. I said to them: "I have very little time left outdoors, and what I was [will disappear] tomorrow morning." Immediately I saw one of them go into a dark corner of a house, and she sat down and urinated. I then saw that the other one had gone and sat on the other side [. . .]. I saw many other things as well, and I begged Sarapis and Isis with these words: "Come to me, goddess of goddesses, have pity and hear me. Pity the twins whom you have made twins. Save me! I am old, and I know the end will soon come. But they will be women, and if they are sullied, they will never again be pure." [26]

Besides these dreams and the petitions Ptolemaios wrote on behalf of the two sisters, accounting documents in particular shed some light on their day-to-day existence. We thus know that in their spare time, they were supposed to devote themselves to some small-scale trade in linen cloth and clothing in which Ptolemaios played the role of a middleman, bringing into play his connections in the Herakleopolitan and Arsinoite nomes. Their surplus rations, sold at a fair price, could thus yield a profit. But it was necessary for these rations to be supplied regularly, which was far from being the case, considering the number of complaints in this regard. For not only had their half brother Pachrates got hold of the official document giving them the right to a certain quantity of oil provided by the offices of the royal monopoly, but their bread rations, normally furnished by the temple, were frequently misappropriated by temple administrators, who engaged in traffic in the grain intended to feed the personnel. Despite all, the twins were not badly off, inasmuch as their diligence in performing their religious duties was so much appreciated that they were entrusted with other tasks, such as the daily libation to Imhotep/Asklepios, the great healing god, with of course a corresponding salary. Moreover, their food purchases show that they did not live on bread alone and that all sorts of cakes, fruits, and vegetables figured in their diet, along with honey and beer.

THE WOES OF AN EGYPTIAN MENDICANT FRIAR

The situation of their sister Tathemis was much more precarious. She was also despoiled by her mother Nephoris, and she had followed the twins to the Serapeum. But unlike them, she did not have the good fortune of being entrusted by the priests with a ritual task. Fairly enough, she was tolerated in the sacred enclosure as a refugee, but she had to resort to various expedients to survive. She thus mingled with the beggars who clustered around the crowd of pilgrims, and almost surely, she sold her charms, following a practice then common in and around the very enclosures of certain temples and found in this an additional and not negligible source of income.

Like her sisters, Tathemis found a protector in the person of the Egyptian Harmais, none other than the roommate of Ptolemaios. Though Harmais took on the task of watching over the nest egg that Tathemis was slowly accumulating, it would be an exaggeration to cast him in the role of a pimp. In fact, like Tathemis, he lived by begging in the temple of Astarte, an allowable activity for the followers of the Syrian goddess, though it was usually condemned by Egyptian deities. Curiously enough, Tathemis intended her savings, which were at least partly the product of prostitution, to form a dowry that would have enabled her to find a husband! But the treachery of her mother put an end to her dream. Nephoris found Harmais and persuaded him to give her the money, pretending that she needed it to pay for the clitoridectomy Tathemis would require before marriage according to Egyptian custom (in fact not attested elsewhere),[27] as well as for the dowry, which she herself would pay to the future husband. The naive Harmais fell for the lies of this awful mother, and Nephoris once again robbed one of her daughters. Poor Tathemis turned on Harmais, who was in no way able to compensate her and who could do nothing more than submit yet another petition to the *strategos* Dionysios.

Harmais himself specialized in being a dupe and a punching-bag. The Serapeum and its temple of Astarte were anything but safe havens from the vicissitudes of the surrounding world. Times were hard, the country was in a situation of latent civil war, and the tensions without had their effect on the close circle of priests, minor lay personnel, recluses, and refugees. Rumors circulated and suspicion reigned, exacerbating secret jealousies and old grudges. The slightest incident could lead to the settling of scores. When Ptolemy VI and his wife Cleopatra II visited Memphis after returning from an exile of several months in Rome, turmoil spread to the Serapeum, for a rumor went around that weapons were being hidden in the temples and that the lives of the sovereigns were in danger. The representative of the local police conducted a search in the temple of Astarte to no avail, but some minor priests who had been present decided to come back that night; by torchlight, they roughed up Ptolemaios, Harmais, and their companions, and they seized their effects. In the days that followed, they returned and committed more acts of violence, going so far as to enter the goddess' holy of holies and make off with her cult objects! At his own, more modest scale, Harmais thus found himself relieved of the jar containing his savings. Less than a month later, bakers who made bread for the offerings and members of the cleaning staff broke into the sanctuary to beat up the recluses. On this occasion, Ptolemaios managed to lock himself in, but Harmais was left outside and was severely beaten with blows from bronze scrapers. Harmais once again wrote a complaint in Demotic,[28] and to have some chance of being heard, he had it translated into Greek.

TO BE GREEK IN AN EGYPTIAN TEMPLE

Given that these hostile acts kept occurring, the many reports and petitions Ptolemaios addressed to the sovereigns or to the *strategos* of Memphis seem to have been practically useless. On two occasions, he expressed indignation that people had dared to mistreat him even though he was Greek.[29] This insistence was of course intended to move the authorities, who were all Greek at the level he was addressing, and to provoke a reaction of solidarity. But this insistence also reveals a paradoxical and disquieting situation: as a Greek, or someone claiming to be one, in a strictly Egyptian milieu, Ptolemaios could only have aroused the animosity of people who were steeped in millennia-old religious traditions and jealous of the privileges of the dominant ethnic group. Since this resentment could scarcely have expressed itself otherwise, Ptolemaios was the perfect scapegoat, though such an explanation cannot account for the ill treatment inflicted on Harmais and the other Egyptian recluses. These testify rather to an endemic, generalized violence infesting interpersonal relationships among the minor clergy and the lower-ranking temple personnel, and that occurred at other times and in other Egyptian temples.[30]

In the seclusion of his retreat, Ptolemaios did not forget his family, who remained in his native village. There, his younger brothers led a difficult existence after their father was killed by rebels during the unrest of 164 B.C.E. They were the target of humiliations and encroachments at the hands of their Egyptian neighbors, and Ptolemaios was often obliged to use his talent for making petitions to come to their aid with the authorities. His youngest brother, Apollonios, was the special object of his solicitude. Born on December 14, undoubtedly in 175, Apollonios was a generation younger than his older brother, which explains the paternal attention the latter lavished on him after the death of their father. An intelligent, gifted, vivacious, and even boisterous child, he learned to read and write Greek, and perhaps Demotic, at a very early age, and he became an even better scribe than his brother who entrusted him with writing numerous memoranda. From 164 to 158, he played a vital role not only for his brother but also in the service of the twin girls, acting as a messenger and an intermediary between the outside world and the confined milieu of the recluses. Without him, there would have been no trafficking to improve their everyday fare and no contacts with high officials to submit complaints and reports. The resourceful youth even succeeded in winning the confidence and even the friendship of Dionysios, the *strategos* of Memphis, who often authorized him to make use of the services of his office. When he arrived at the threshold of adulthood, he decided to follow his brother's example and become a recluse in the Serapeum. This experience was a complete failure and undoubtedly left the young man permanently disgusted with temples and their narrow-minded, sordid personnel. Three months after his entry into religion, he managed to get into a dispute with the sons of the man who furnished wood to the Serapeum, and these youths, who were donkey drivers by profession, beat him with sticks like one of their animals.

Deprived of his jaunts into the nomes south of Memphis, Apollonios in particular felt like he was suffocating. The dreams he carefully set down in Demotic reveal the adolescent's identity crisis, caught as he was between two cultures and two worlds in underlying conflict:

> Second dream—A man is singing, that is, Apollonios in Greek and Petehorempi in Egyptian, who knows [the answer to] this riddle?[31]

If we understand that Petehorempi was his Egyptian name, we might suppose a split in his personality. Were there two people in him, a Greek and an Egyptian? To this question was added the trouble caused by the continual presence of the twins, a nagging temptation that had already tormented his brother some years earlier:

> First dream—I was going up toward the *dromos* of Sarapis with a woman named Thaues, who is a virgin. I was chatting with her and said, "Thaues, is your heart sad [at the idea] of my making love [to you]?" She answered, "If that happens, my sister Thotortaios (*sic!* = Taus?) will be angry with me" (what follows is obscure).[32]

Did Thaues actually allow herself to be seduced by this handsome and endearing young man? Nothing is certain, but there was indeed an alarm: was she going to become pregnant? The possibility of such a scandal was too much for Ptolemaios, who understood that it was not his brother's destiny to remain confined within the small circle of the temple of Astarte.

AN INFORMER IN THE TEMPLE

The king and queen announced their arrival at Memphis for the New Year celebration in the month of October, 158 B.C.E. Ptolemaios decided to address a request to them in which he begged them to order that his younger brother be enlisted in the garrison of Memphis, noting that their father Glaukias had been a cleruch and had died in the king's service, that Apollonios was his only family and his sole support, and that in return he could serenely continue offering sacrifices in their honor and that of their children. Apollonios personally handed the document to the king through the "window of appearances" that was specially set up at the Serapeum on October 3, 158. The request was immediately granted on condition of an investigation into the cost of the induction. After administrative complications that dragged on for nearly five months,[33] Apollonios indeed became a soldier on February 23, 157, with the theoretical benefit of regular pay. But punctual payment of salaries was rendered problematic by the chronic financial difficulties of the state, depriving Ptolemaios of the profit he had counted on from his brother's pay. Moreover, the latter was posted far from Memphis for long periods of time, leaving our recluse in ever more critical distress, assaulted and mocked by a pack of enemies who went so far as to throw stones through his window.

In 156 B.C.E., by dint of repeated complaints, Ptolemaios managed to have his brother assigned to the office of the police chief of the Memphite necropolis as an intelligence agent. Maintaining surveillance on both the crowd of honest pilgrims and the more dubious characters thronging in the forecourts of the temples, he reported on all suspicious characters, especially those profiting from the right of asylum to escape taxes or royal justice. Since he was in a position to intimidate his brother's enemies, the latter gained a measure of tranquillity. Especially appreciated by his superiors for his perfect knowledge of the Serapeum, Apollonios was authorized to carry on his person the police identification cards and other assorted files that could help him gather information and were found among his personal papers.[34] But his zeal did not just win him the esteem and admiration of his chief, it also gained him mortal enemies. We barely know the details, but the contents of his letters grow ever more worried, leaving us to understand that he fell into a trap: he was sentenced to a fine of fifteen talents, evidently because of a certain fugitive named Menedemos, who haunted his nightmares and even threatened his life. Eventually, he named the cause of his troubles: it was the dreams of his brother, inspired by Sarapis and the other deities, which were responsible for his situation. In a final letter filled with distress and sarcasm, he threw it all in his face:

> I swear to you by Sarapis, if I didn't still have some scruples, you would never see me again! Since you only lie, and the gods with you, for it is they who have cast us into the mire, where we are all but dead, and if you saw (in a dream) that we were going to be pulled out, it means that we will be pushed down (even deeper)! . . . I should be ashamed when we have devoted our-selves to chimeras sent by the gods and to belief in dreams in which we have made errors. Good luck! [35]

On the verso, next to the address, we can read this last ironic barb: "For those who speak the truth!" It is easy to imagine the bitter disappointment of Ptolemaios, who saw the fundamental values of his universe scorned by a brother whom he looked upon as a son. Some time later, on September 20, 152 B.C.E., the police chief wrote to Ptolemaios and complained that Apollonios had deserted, leaving him alone to confront a state of near anarchy in the temples of the necropolis.[36] Under these somber auspices, Ptolemaios' string of documents breaks off suddenly, leaving the ending of the story a matter for conjecture: the death or forced departure of Ptole-maios from the Serapeum, the restless wanderings of his brother with his shattered morale. The gods had certainly abandoned them, but could it have been otherwise in the robbers' dens their temples had become?

6 LIVING ON THE DEATH OF OTHERS

THE LAND OF THE DEAD

Since the end of the Middle Ages, the mummy has served as the incarnation of ancient Egypt in Western imagination. Once very much in use as a raw material in making fertilizer and medicaments, it later fed the morbid fantasies of a romantic vision of this civilization. If Egypt seems like a land of the dead to us, it is not that death played a more important role there than in other ancient societies but because relatively recent improvements in standards of living, hygiene, and medicine have rendered death less prominent in our own mental universe. But nowhere as in Egypt have natural conditions joined forces with human effort to preserve the remains of the dead, to a degree that the ancients themselves undoubtedly did not suspect and that never ceases to astonish us today.

The funerary beliefs and practices of pharaonic Egypt endured for more than three millennia and came to an end only with the triumph of Christianity, whose eschatological concepts required less concern with the corpse. A number of changes occurred in beliefs and practices, as attested not only in texts, of which we have a large corpus, but also through archaeology, whose spectacular finds have contributed more than anything else to modern Egyptomania. In the period under study here, we can observe the final phase of this evolution. As in every area of culture in this civilization so conscious of its past, change most often occurred through the accumulation and integration of different levels of belief and practice, with the tradition becoming ever richer as new developments occurred in basic, age-old concepts governing faith in the survival of the individual. The funerary rituals, written in hieratic on papyri and sometimes in hieroglyphs on stelae or sarcophagi, testify eloquently to ongoing revisions and reinterpretations of the tradition: we find new developments, corresponding to new concerns, mixed with various chapters of the New Kingdom Book of the Dead and extracts from ancient Osirian liturgies once reserved only for deceased kings.[1]

The most obvious tendency in this evolution was the ongoing democratization of these practices. By the Ptolemaic period, these had long since spread through all levels of Egyptian society. As early as the fifth century B.C.E., Herodotus was able to describe three methods of mummification available to the families of deceased persons, with the third, most perfunctory type affordable even to the humblest.[2] Both texts and archaeology indicate that under the Ptolemies, few Egyptians escaped this post-mortem treatment. For that to happen, it would have been necessary for a body to disappear, swallowed up in the waters or carried off by a crocodile, or for someone to die in absolute poverty with no relative or next of kin willing to spend the required minimum.

THE GREEKS AND THE EGYPTIAN AFTERLIFE

What was the attitude of the Greeks settled in Egypt toward native funerary customs? At home, Greeks and Macedonians preferred cremation and burial, though the scarcity of combustible material rendered the former more costly. Their funeral rites were relatively summary, and their graves were generally modest. It must be admitted that the few traditional beliefs of the Hellenes concerning the afterlife did not measure up to the richness and the sophistication of Egyptian eschatology. Though there had been some evolution since Homer's depressing portrayal of Hades, they were scarcely such as to induce a preoccupation with one's lot after death. This absence of hope of eternal life in Hellenic culture, which was anthropocentric and Promethean, exalting above all the accomplishments of the individual in this life, can explain the fascination that the promise of an afterlife with many possibilities exercised on the Greeks in Egypt, leading them to adopt the funerary customs of that land. In the Saite period, the son of Alexikrates and Zenodote had an immense stone sarcophagus made for himself, thus demonstrating his adherence to native values.[3] Greek and Egyptian motifs are mixed, though, on a series of pre-Ptolemaic stelae belonging to the Hellenomemphite and Caromemphite colony settled in the

Egyptian capital from the sixth century on.[4] At Alexandria itself, the cemeteries of the Ptolemaic era were Greek in style, with some Egyptian elements, though later, in the Roman period, pharaonic influence would become preponderant, culminating in the astonishing decoration of the so-called tomb of Tigranes and that of the necropolis of Kom el-Shuqafa, the work of Alexandrian artists transposing purely Egyptian religious representations into their own style. In the *Chora,* from the Ptolemaic period on, many of the Greeks who frequented the *gymnasia* did not turn up their noses at typically Egyptian burial equipment, and their names can be found side by side with those of natives in lists of mummies. There were only rare pockets of Hellenistic resistance in the matter of burial customs, as in the cemetery of Hermopolis, where an Egyptophobe proudly boasted in his epitaph that he had been cremated[5]—abomination of abominations to native sensibilities!

SPECIALISTS IN THE SERVICE OF THE DEAD

It is not merely the result of chance that we are better informed about mortuary specialists than about most other social groups. Nor is it because they represented a class that was great in number or in prestige but rather because they proved better able than others to preserve their archives from destruction. In fact, they had the habit of putting their documents—familial, patrimonial, and professional—in jars stored in disused or unoccupied tombs that they employed as storerooms. These turned out to be excellent places for preservation, and the papyri have been recovered intact by digs, both official and unofficial, during the past two centuries. A number of these archives have been preserved to us in this manner, principally from the Theban[6] and Memphite[7] areas.

The bodies of the deceased were entrusted to these persons, who were called in Greek *choachytai,* "libation pourers," a term unknown from classical sources and to which the earliest papyrologists incorrectly attributed an Egyptian etymology, the literal translation of the Egyptian title *wah-mu,* "(he) who pours water." The libations evoked by these names were supposed to be made on behalf of the deceased, though they constituted only a part of the work of the *choachytai.* They were not, however, charged with mummifying the bodies. This delicate operation fell to another group of professionals. The embalmers were known in Greek as *taricheutai,* "salters," a term that graphically evokes the process of impregnating the corpse with a saline solution (natron). The Greek texts also mention the

paraschistai, (incisers), a title relating to the cut made in the side of the ca-
daver so that the internal organs could be removed. Diodorus carefully dis-
tinguishes the two groups: the *paraschistes* was detested because he sought
to undermine the integrity of the body by mutilating it, whereas the
taricheutes, master of the art of embalming, was honored and admitted
into the sacerdotal class.[8] In fact, the documentation does not confirm his
assertions, for the same persons are sometimes designated *taricheutai* and
sometimes *paraschistai.* At Thebes, there was only one Egyptian title corresponding to both, *khery-heb,* "he who holds the roll (of papyrus),"
which refers specifically to the role of ritualist played by the priest charged
with supervising the embalming of the body. It might seem surprising that
Greek employed prosaic, even trivial terms, whereas Egyptian used ancient, pompous expressions. This contrast was in fact cultural in origin: the
Greeks had at first seen only strange and even repugnant operations in
these Egyptian funerary practices because of their inability to understand
the Egyptian religious universe into which they were integrated. Thus, the
title *khetemu-netjer,* attested at Memphis and in the cemeteries of the
Faiyum and Middle Egypt, and which means "chancellor of the god,"
seems to have been rendered into Greek as *entaphiastes,* "gravedigger."

All these activities must have been relatively lucrative, to judge from the
transfers of property attested in a number of documents and that sometimes reveal sizeable inheritances of land. It is difficult to assign a particular task to each of these specialists in the preservation of the body. The re-
sults of their work are known archaeologically, and they can be compared
to the descriptions given by Herodotus and especially by Diodorus. The
three methods of mummification they describe have yet to be discerned by
examining the many mummies preserved to us intact. Their categories
must thus have been theoretical, though the quality of mummification
seems to have been quite uneven. The essence of their concerns was especially manifest in the care taken with the linen shrouds and bandages—the
only part of the process that the relatives of the deceased could verify with
their own eyes. A large quantity of cloth was usually required for this process and, in theory at least, linen of a certain quality (*byssos*), with fibers of
animal origin formally excluded because they were considered impure. In
fact, many pieces of used clothing were employed, and various fabrics were
recycled. A cartonnage mask, modeled from old papyri glued together or
from plaster-soaked cloth, and painted with bright colors, was often placed
on the head of the deceased and extended by a breastplate over the chest.
The feet could also be protected by a cartonnage case. Beyond that, funerary equipment was scanty, being reserved for the very richest. There could

FIGURE 37. Vignette to Book of the Dead, chapter 125, depicting the judgment of the deceased (second from right) before the god Osiris (far left), lord of the afterlife. Detroit Institute of Arts 1988.10.13. Founders Society Purchase, Mr. and Mrs. Allan Shelden III Fund, Ralph Harman Booth Bequest Fund, and Hill Memorial Fund. © The Detroit Institute of Arts 1994.

be one or two wooden coffins, a box for the viscera intended to replace the canopic jars, which were no longer used, and a funerary papyrus written in hieratic containing a version of the old Book of the Dead (Figure 37). In the first century B.C.E., funerary literature was diversified by the appearance of compositions specially intended to restore the senses of deceased persons, such as the Books of Breathing;[9] to allow them free movement in the afterlife and free access to Osiris, such as the Book of Traversing Eternity;[10] or to indicate the means by which they could assume various animal and magical forms, such as the Book of Transformations written in Demotic.[11]

THE CHOACHYTAI AT WORK[12]

As for the *choachytai,* they were concerned only with the last stage, the placing of the body in its final resting place, usually after an obligatory waiting period in a provisional tomb. Sometimes, the family decided to keep the body of the deceased at home for a while after it was mummified. Cases made especially for this purpose have been found, with panels that could be removed to permit the face of the deceased to be viewed through a window.[13] Further, we know that the mummy of a relative could in certain cases serve as collateral on a loan,[14] though we are not informed as to what would have happened to the body in case of default. To transport the corpse itself, the family had to call on other professionals known in Greek as *nekrotaphoi,* "undertakers," about whom little is known except that they were a markedly inferior socioprofessional group, the employees rather than the colleagues of the *choachytai.* The latter also had the duty of paying the various taxes levied on mummies, in particular those owed to the "president of the necropolis," the official charged with the general administration of the immense Theban cemetery.[15] The work of a *choachytes* was not finished, however, when the mummy was finally placed in its resting place with the customary last rites. The deceased was supposed to receive regular libations and offerings, which only the *choachytai* could carry out. At an earlier time, in the sixth century, well-to-do families assigned the *choachytes* a field whose revenues were supposed to supply the funerary offerings. Under the Ptolemies, for lack of available fields, there was a change in the way the *choachytai* received their support: from then on, they were paid a salary by families intending to perpetuate the funerary cult of their departed relatives. The mummies in the care of the *choachytai* were thus a permanent and regular source of income, a veritable patrimony that could be handed down or sold. Mummies could thus be divided up among the heirs of a *choachytes* or sold to other *choachytai* like any other goods.

Such a situation was possible only because the *choachytai,* who were organized into corporations of sorts, which were very much closed, benefited from a monopoly. At second-century Thebes, whence stem the most important archives, we know of four great families of *choachytai,* which were often linked by marriage. Within each of them, the care of the dead and the related income were passed down directly by inheritance; the women were not excluded, and they were able to practice the profession with no special restrictions. In an urban center as large as Thebes, there were doubtless other families at work in other sectors of the necropolis, but their archives have not survived to us. The Theban *choachytai* all lived on the west bank, at Djamet, in a village built within the great enclosure of the funerary temple of Ramesses III at Medinet Habu, which is today the best-preserved monumental complex in this entire area. The great temple itself seems not to have been used at this time, but its enclosure wall sheltered the small temple of Amun of Djamet, which was almost entirely reconstructed in the Ptolemaic period and was at that time the principal cult place on the west bank.

We do not know how the *choachytai* had originally been recruited. Only native Egyptians seem to have exercised this profession, but we do not know whether this requirement was obligatory or whether a foreigner could enter into their circle, for example, by marriage. Moreover, the *choachytai* were also involved in other activities. At this time, the Egyptian texts in fact no longer accord them the title *wah-mu*, "water pourer," but rather *wenenper*, "shrine opener," which the Greeks translated as *pastophoros*, "shrine carrier." It would be tempting to translate the title as "verger" or "sacristan." These titles seem generally to have been attached to the temple of Amun of Djamet. But if the *choachytai* were thus part of the minor personnel of the temple, they did not belong to the sacerdotal class itself (the *wabu*, pure ones), though they were sufficiently linked to the divine cult to have been authorized to occupy themselves with its pale substitute, the mortuary cult of simple mortals. We also know that they were recruited on certain occasions to assist in the carrying out of processions and festivals; thus, they were supposed to spread sand on the *dromoi* of the temples of Amun and Mut at Karnak, on the east bank of Thebes. Moreover, when the same god Amun crossed the Nile once a year to visit his temples and chapels on the west bank of Thebes, it was their task to conduct the procession and to make the prescribed libations along the route.[16]

A PROFESSIONAL ASSOCIATION

So as better to organize the exercise of their profession, the Theban *choachytai* founded an association in 109 B.C.E. Such associations, which were both religious and professional, are known from other places in Egypt at around the same time and in other milieus, undoubtedly in imitation of the Greeks, who were fond of forming ethnocultural groups. The regulations of this association are preserved to us, along with its membership list.[17] To have a right to membership, one had to be a member of one of the families of *choachytai* and to be a male age sixteen years or older; boys who had reached the age of ten could be registered along with their fathers as minor members. At the time the regulations were written, there were twenty-three active members of the association and eight minors. It was run by a board made up of five persons, including a president, whose Egyptian title was *lesonis,* a vice-president, and three assistants. As a religious brotherhood, the association was dedicated to the god Amenemope, the Amun of Djamet, and all its members were his *pastophoroi.* They were supposed to celebrate a certain number of festivals on specified dates, known as "drinking days." These periodic drinking sessions, intended to reinforce the reciprocal ties of affection among the members, were strictly limited to the consumption of two jugs of wine. The members also owed one another mutual assistance, especially when one of them died. In the same spirit, they promised to observe certain rules of good conduct within their community; failure to respect those rules was punishable by a fine and by a double amount if the infraction was committed by the president. No one was to exercise the profession of *choachytes* without being a member of the "association of Amenemope," a veritable union, or lay claim to any revenue related to it, even if such revenues had theoretically been acquired by inheritance.

Each *choachytes* had rights to a certain number of families, which were supposed to entrust their deceased to him and whose living members constituted a supply of future clients. We have seen that these rights could be transmitted by inheritance or ceded away. From another point of view, the families in question had no choice but to turn to the sole *choachytes* who had acquired, by inheritance or purchase, the right to attend to the funerary cult of their departed relatives. The compensation they paid for the care of the latter must have been, of course, a small amount. The modest budget of most of the families concerned, which was almost entirely devoted to the basic needs of existence, could have supported little more than symbolic sums for such expenditures. Though the wealthiest individuals could purchase a family tomb of brick from a *choachytes,* built by the latter himself, and entrust its maintenance to him, most had to content themselves with collective tombs that were the common property of the group of *choachytai.* In fact, these were ancient tombs that had long since been plundered and, in many cases, had belonged to high officials of the New Kingdom who had died a thousand years earlier. The Theban mountain was literally riddled with such tombs, but only a small number of them had been reused. The largest and best known of these was called *Thynabounoun* in the documents written in Greek; this is actually an Egyptian expression meaning "the tomb of Nabunun," in which we can recognize, scarcely changed, the name Nebwenenef, an important personage in the Theban clergy during the reign of Ramesses II. This tomb, a tunnel more than one hundred yards long, is still visited today. We can imagine the number of mummies that must have been stored there.

"SAINTS" SOMETIMES DISTURBED

Having in his charge several hundred mummies, grouped by family, the *choachytes* compensated by quantity for the low sum paid for the maintenance of each one of them. The long lists of mummies preserved to us in the archives show that they did not all have the same status. Thus, some of the deceased had the title *p-hesy,* "the favored, the blessed," or *p-hery,* "the eminent, the saint." We do not in fact know how such privileged status was acquired. The ambivalence of the Egyptian term *hesy* has led to the hypothesis that these were persons who had drowned, for drowning in the Nile was equivalent to an apotheosis, but such an explanation cannot have applied in the majority of cases.[18] Offerings and libations constituted the essence of the duties the *choachytai* were supposed to perform on behalf of their inert boarders for as long as a surviving relative continued to pay the expenses. The equipment used by the *choachytai* in their cultic tasks, consisting of libation vases, censers for fumigations, portable altars, and so forth could have a certain value, as shown by a complaint addressed in 127–126 B.C.E. to the police chief of the Peritheban nome, Diophantos, by the *choachytes* Osoeris son of Horos. The latter reported that when all the police had been called to the east bank on the occasion of a visit to Thebes by the *strategos*-general Lochos, three persons had taken advantage of the situation to force the door of a provisional tomb belonging to him and make off with all the tools of his trade. Moreover, the bodies that were being temporarily stored there had been devoured by jackals that got in later through the open doorway. The plaintiff estimated the value of the stolen goods at ten talents, or sixty thousand bronze drachmas, a sum that could feed a family of five for an entire year![19]

DIVISION OF LABOR IN THE OTHER CORPORATIONS

Like the *choachytai,* the *taricheutai* had a monopoly, with the activity of each of them strictly limited to a specific place. But unlike the *choachytai,* whose exclusive rights were limited to the tombs they tended, the *taricheutai* had rights to a certain village, a certain quarter, or a certain socioprofessional group that served as the source of the dead persons with whom they were occupied. Thus, on July 1, 119 B.C.E., an agreement was made by two *paraschistai*, Petenephotes and Amenothes son of Horos, carefully delimiting their areas of activity. The villages cited in this agreement belonged to three different nomes around Thebes: the Peritheban nome, the Pathyrite nome to the south, and the Koptite nome to the north. The area of Thebes itself was divided thus: the west bank (*Memnoneia*) went to Petenephoris and the east bank (Diospolis and Madamud) to Amenothes, except for the priests of Amun and their slaves, who were to be mummified by Petenephotes. The terms of the division must not have been self-evident, for on at least three occasions in the four years that followed, one or the other of the contracting parties submitted a complaint in Greek to the tribunal of the *epistates* regarding repeated infringements on the part of his colleague.[20]

At Memphis, the *entaphiastai* also shared the various quarters of the urban area and its surrounding villages, as shown by a number of Demotic papyri containing long lists of these potential sources of cadavers, which were drawn up by *entaphiastai* dividing up their goods on behalf of their heirs. Unlike those of their Theban colleagues, their daughters were unable to exercise the profession themselves, though as heirs, the women had a right to its income. Thus, in 75 B.C.E., Taynchis, a member of an important family of Memphite embalmers, ceded to her daughter Senamunis the rights to the funerals of

> . . . a third of the village called "Crocodile Tail" in the district of Unchem, with all its inhabitants; a third of two villages in the "New Lands of Ptah," with all their inhabitants; a third of the Greek quarter of Memphis; [. . .]; a third of the *pastophoroi* (minor priests) serving Osiris-Apis and Osiris-Mnevis; a third of the winegrowers (in the Memphite nome) . . .

to which were added the use of and income from a third of each of three funerary chapels in the necropolis.[21] We may suppose that like her mother Taynchis, Senamunis would have been highly desirable to the other *entaphiastai* and that such transfers of goods favored endogamy within this closed professional group. We do not know how, in practice, this monopoly over the villagers and socioprofessional classes mentioned in this document was shared with those who held the rights to the other two thirds. We can only hope there was a *modus vivendi,* whether tacit or established in writing, so as to avoid disputes over encroachments, as in the sad case of the Theban *taricheutai.*

The archives of the *choachytai* have brought us some very curious documents. There are two verdicts and a detailed report on a lawsuit that saw the community of *choachytai* in conflict with a certain Hermias in year 53 of Ptolemy VIII Euergetes II and his two wives, Cleopatra II (Figure 38) and Cleopatra III, that is, in 117 B.C.E. Hermias belonged to a family of Greek soldiers who had been settled in Egypt for at least a century. In the reign of Ptolemy IV Philopator, his father Ptolemaios had been garrisoned at Thebes, where he had a large piece of property. At the death of the king in 205, there had been a major revolt against the Alexandrian authorities in Upper Egypt, and the Thebaid seceded under a new native pharaoh, Harwennofre. Along with all those attached to the Lagide regime, Ptolemaios fled, abandoning his home. We may suppose that it was seized by the rebels and perhaps sold to the highest bidder. Twenty-three years later, in 183, and at least five years after the rebellion had been successfully put down and Ptolemy V Epiphanes reigned over a reunified land, this property was divided among three families, one of which, represented by two sisters,

FIGURE 38. Ptolemy VIII (far right) and Cleopatra II (?) making offerings, accompanied by a male fecundity figure and a goddess personifying fields. Temple of el-Dakka in Nubia. After J.-F. Champollion, *Monuments de l'Égypte et de la Nubie*, Vol. I (Paris, 1835), Pl. LII.

sold its share to a forager named Herieus. Apparently none of the owners lived there, because the building is described as being in ruins. The different shares passed from hand to hand, and then, beginning in 153, the property began to interest the *choachytai,* who bought it up bit by bit, share by share. Meanwhile, what was left of Ptolemaios' former house must have completely collapsed, for from then on, the site is described as a bare lot with traces of foundations. In 127, the *choachytai,* who owned nearly three quarters of the original surface area, undertook to construct a new building there. The following year, the owner of the remainder of the lot, a member of the cavalry named Apollonios, filed a complaint with the Greek tribunal of *chrematistai* against the *choachytai,* who had, according to him, encroached on his portion. The latter agreed to negotiate, and Apollonios agreed to withdraw his complaint and to cede all his rights to the *choachytai* in exchange for a financial consideration.

It was at this point that Hermias son of Ptolemaios, the former owner of the ruined home, intervened. At that time between sixty and seventy years of age, Hermias had settled at Ombos, an important military center about 110 miles south of Thebes, with the impressive rank of infantry captain. Since his age and position undoubtedly allowed him some free time, Hermias devoted himself to recovering the property his family had left behind at Thebes. Thus, he easily enough succeeded in having himself recognized as the owner of 20 *arouras* (more than 13.5 acres) of wheat fields that a priest of Amun, a certain Harmais, had bought from another Apollonios, who must have appropriated it at the time of the great revolt of Harwennofre, for Hermias was able to prove that the land had been registered in the name of his mother's grandfather. At the same time, he persuaded himself that the house of the *choachytai* was built on the site of his own family's house. He had no document to support his claim, however, and he would spend the next eight years using all possible legal means in an attempt to recover what he considered to be his heritage. Since the *choachytai* had kept all the documents of sale, which attested to the legitimacy of their acquisition of the disputed property, Hermias turned on one of the sellers, a woman named Lobais, who for her part could not prove that she had had legal possession of the share she sold to the *choachytai,* which she acknowledged by means of a certificate of relinquishment signed before the Greek tribunal of *chrematistai* to whom Hermias had submitted a complaint. Armed with this document, Hermias tried to secure the appearance of the *choachytai,* but they withdrew to the west bank, where they otherwise usually lived. On six occasions between 125 and 117, Hermias turned to various high officials to have the *choachytai* expelled from his home, but until 119, they consistently employed the tactic of ignoring every summons. From that year on, however, the pressure exerted by Hermias became stronger, for he left Ombos permanently to retire at Thebes. They thus appeared before the tribunal of the *epistates* of the Peritheban nome assisted by a competent attorney and armed with all the necessary documents. Hermias, who failed to obtain assistance on this occasion, was defaulted from his complaint. But he did not despair, and he addressed himself to the highest authority in Upper Egypt, the *epistrategos* of the Thebaid, to no real avail. Finally, in 117, he made a second petition to the *strategos,* who referred the affair—for the second time—to the tribunal of the *epistates* of the Peritheban nome, evidently with the same result, though this time Hermias was accompanied by an attorney who had prepared a speech against the *choachytai.*

CADAVERS IN THE CITY

Among the arguments elaborated by Hermias' attorney before the tribunal of the *epistates,* the most interesting concerned the use the *choachytai* were making of the house they built at Thebes. In fact, it was serving as a storage place for as-yet unmummified bodies awaiting transfer to the west bank of the Nile. Now, the house of the *choachytai* stood near the *dromoi,* that is, the processional ways, which led from the Nile to the sanctuaries of Hera—the Greek name for Mut, the consort of Amun—and of Demeter, who corresponded to Opet, the hippopotamus-goddess of fertility, whose temple had at that time just been rebuilt. For these goddesses and their priests, the proximity of "cadavers and those who deal with them is an abomination." [23] Already, according to Hermias' attorney, the royal physician Tatas had transmitted an order from the royal court to the local *strategos* concerning the relocation of all mortuary activity to the west bank. Later, acting on a complaint of the priests of Amun and supported by a report from the *topogrammateus* (district secretary), the successor of this *strategos* wrote to the *epistates* in order to effect this transfer. If this had been done, Hermias might have been able to take possession of the disputed house, but the *choachytai* did not move. The main reason cited by their attorney was that the various injunctions concerned only the *taricheutai,* not the *choachytai,* whose presence on the east bank was justified by their participation in the major processional festivals. Such a justification, which was admitted by the tribunal with no further comment, seems somewhat stamped with bad faith: it did not matter whether or not the *choachytai* were occupied with mummification, the fact is that they were storing bodies in their house. Such an "abomination" was inevitable, however, for it was certainly not possible to transport all the Theban dead to the opposite bank immediately, so they had to be accepted somewhere. Nevertheless, the background of the argument is perplexing, and one might wonder about the convergence of viewpoints between the Greek and Egyptian personalities regarding the elimination of activities related to cadavers around these great temples. A dead body as a taint was in fact a Hellenic notion, not an Egyptian one. In Egypt, sanctuaries and cemeteries were often located near one another with no major inconvenience. We must thus suppose that the motives of the priests of Amun were not the same as that of the Greek physician, and that far from their having any concern for public hygiene or religious taboo, they were hoping only to settle a score with a rival corporation, using any ammunition at hand.

This affair, with whose details chance alone has acquainted us, was thus not as insignificant as one might think after only a quick glance. Aside from its purely juridical aspects, which are scarcely surprising except for their modernity in form and content, it sheds light on many revealing cultural and social facts. It was in fact a proceeding initiated by a Greek against Egyptians practicing a profession that was contemptible from the point of view of the dominant ethnic group. The various legal actions were conducted in Greek before jurisdictions composed solely of Greeks (*chrematistai,* the tribunal of the *epistates*), but which nevertheless took into account arguments and interests foreign to their culture. The motives of the chief protagonist seem clear: Hermias clearly intended to spend his retirement at Thebes—despite its decline at this time, the city must still have had some attraction for a Greek junior officer who had spent his entire career in a provincial garrison center like Ombos—and, so as to lead a comfortable enough life there, he tried to recover property his forebears had abandoned. He must have assumed that his rank and his status as a Greek would have enabled him to prevail easily over Egyptians of a lower class. But contrary to his expectations, those in authority considered only the purely legal aspects of the affair. Though he had succeeded in regaining cultivated land from the hands of a priest of Amun, this was because he could cite an official document to establish his claim. But he had nothing of that sort to claim ownership of the house of the *choachytai,* though that did not stop him from initiating several proceedings before authorities he hoped would be partial to his cause, first the *chrematistai* and then the *epistates;* at one point, the latter even ordered the expulsion of the *choachytai.* But the latter, aware of their lower social status and the fact that they were in the right, and after first having employed flight as a tactic to discourage their opponent, confronted him successfully on two occasions, taking care each time to secure the assistance of a Greek attorney, and a good one at that. Whatever sympathies reinforced by a feeling of solidarity among people of the same sociocultural group that the authorities might have felt toward Hermias, they could not ignore the position, which was not a negligible one, of the *choachytai* in native Egyptian society. In charge of funerals and of the cult of the dead, they counted, along with other categories of priests, as guarantors of the ancient pharaonic culture. To treat them unjustly would be to run the risk of exacerbating the resentment harbored by the non-Hellenic part of the population toward the Greeks and thus to fan the flames of a revolt that was always ready to be rekindled. In the absence of an indisputable title to the property, the authorities could not have ruled in favor of Hermias against the *choachytai,* for the same reasons they were unable to enforce the royal regulations banning the presence of cadavers within city walls, regulations that were inspired by basically Hellenic principles but ran counter to the ancestral customs of the Egyptians.

AN EMBALMER COMPLAINS TO THE KING[24]

The attention paid by the Greek authorities to these eminent representatives of Egyptian culture was manifested even more dramatically in another affair, whose setting this time was the Memphite necropolis. On October 15, 99 B.C.E., King Ptolemy X and his niece-wife, Queen Cleopatra-Berenike III, visited the Serapeum of Memphis. An embalmer named Peteese submitted a petition written in Greek directly to them to complain of having been assaulted by certain individuals in the necropolis. He asked the sovereigns for their protection in the form of a royal command written on a wooden tablet that could be posted, forbidding anyone from laying a hand on him or his goods from that time on. Less than a week later, a copy of the petition bearing the royal seal was sent to Apollodoros, the *strategos* of the Memphite nome. Timonikos, the latter's subordinate, forwarded it to the *epistates* of the Anoubieion, the area of the temple of Anubis where the embalmers of the Memphite necropolis exercised their profession, along with an order for immediate execution. The wooden plaque requested by Peteese, bearing the king's instructions in Greek and Demotic, was posted in the specified place.

Such an obliging attitude on the part of the regime is remarkable. But Peteese was not just any embalmer, he was also the *"archentaphiastes* (chief embalmer) of the gods Apis and Mnevis," that is to say, he had the honor of carrying out the embalming of the sacred bulls of Memphis and Heliopolis, the two most highly venerated living gods of Egypt, and he did not fail to stress the importance of his office in his petition. The Lagide sovereigns could not underestimate a person who played such a key role in one of the most intense moments in the religious life of the entire land, the burial of Apis. It is thus all the more painful to note that this royal protection was soon violated by the very Greek officials who were supposedly charged with enforcing it! Several months later, in the summer of 98, another subordinate of the *strategos* named Noumenios forced his way into Peteese's home and made off with some of his property. Peteese was then obliged to write a second petition to the king requesting that the new *strategos* Ariston respect the measures that had been taken. Finally, an unfortunately fragmentary letter indicates that Peteese attempted to make use of possible connections at the royal court through a linen merchant who made business trips between Memphis and Alexandria, with the goal of once again obtaining a direct intervention on his behalf from the sovereigns. We do not know the final outcome of the affair, whose ins and outs escape us, though we can guess that the ambition and arrogance of the embalmer, on the one hand, and the jealousy and scorn of the Greek bureaucrats, on the other, were the driving forces behind this sorry drama.

Our rich documentation regarding the Theban *choachytai* and the Memphite *entaphiastai* informs us only of their problems, both personal and professional. Though their mental world, whether cultural or psychological, is barely intelligible to us, we can see that they were fairly well educated and that they could read and write Demotic and, in all likelihood, the old sacred language in both its forms, hieratic and hieroglyphic. As priests, rather than scholars associated with great temples, they were nevertheless more open, and because of the private and quasi-commercial nature of their activities, they displayed an ability to adapt that was made necessary by the general context of their times. Thus, they knew how to make use of the resources of the Ptolemaic administration and the Greek system of law to resist pressure from those who saw them as easy prey, and they did not hesitate to use the Greek language and appeal to the highest authorities when they felt that their basic interests were threatened. As relatively well-to-do and envied subjects of the Ptolemies, they could serenely ignore the scorn their profession must have inspired in the defenders of Hellenism and thus view the latter as nothing more than future clients.

7 SOLDIERS AND PEASANTS

A MILITARY STATE

A "land conquered at lance point," [1] Egypt of the Ptolemies had to be controlled by an army that was sufficiently large and of unfailing loyalty. The land had a long military tradition that went back at least to the New Kingdom, as well as a long-standing tendency to resort to foreign mercenary troops. The latter, well Egyptianized, even became masters of the country during the "Libyan" dynasties (*ca.* 950–750 B.C.E.). In the Saite Period (664–525), the Egyptian pharaohs turned readily to Greek and Carian hoplites. Finally, the Persians planted Syrian and Jewish colonies, especially to guard the southern border of Egypt; a large number of Aramaic papyri revealing the history of this foreign community on Egyptian soil was found at Elephantine.[2] Parallel to the mercenaries, there had always been a native military caste, consisting mostly of the descendants of former Libyan mercenaries, culturally and socially integrated into the Egyptian population. The Saite pharaohs did not view them as reliable, however, seeing them as a potential support for possible rivals, while the Persian satraps rightly feared that they could be a source of nationalist revolts. Herodotus left a brief description of their division into two groups, Kalasirians and Hermotybians, who occupied different regions of the land.[3]

The arrival of Alexander changed the basic problem. When he left Egypt to conquer the heart of the Persian empire, he left behind an occupation force of twenty thousand men under the command of two of his lieutenants, Balakros and Peukestas.[4] We must imagine that only a small part of this force was drawn from the army participating in the campaign and that most of it was recruited on the spot. We cannot imagine that Alexander would have left Egypt to troops who were mostly Egyptian, so it is probable that these soldiers were recruited mainly from the Greek and Carian communities long since settled in the land; they could be easily assimilated into the Macedonian army, and they had everything to gain from the new power that was assuming control of the country. Among them, there were probably former mercenaries who had fought the Persians in the service of the last native kings and had not yet returned to their original homelands. Moreover, Alexander entrusted the administration of Egypt's finances to one of these Graeco-Egyptians, Kleomenes of Naukratis.[5] It is also possible that a certain number of Aramean and Jewish mercenaries passed, at least on an individual basis, into Macedonian military service. Thus was formed the core of the future Lagide army.

SOLDIERS IN THE COUNTRYSIDE

When Ptolemy son of Lagos took possession of Egypt while still satrap in 323 B.C.E., his first objective was to assure the security of his new territory against the pretensions of the other *diadochoi*. His first priority was thus to put together a powerful military organization. The inadequacy of the means at Ptolemy's disposal was made evident by Perdiccas' invasion in 321. Ptolemy owed his salvation only to tactical errors on the part of an adversary whose armed forces were incommensurate with his. Only the treacherous terrain of the Nile, where Perdiccas' troops found themselves bogged down in the mud outside Memphis, spared the city a fatal assault and Ptolemy a certain defeat.[6] Afterward, the fight against Antigonos the One-Eyed and his son Demetrios Poliorketes demanded huge numbers of soldiers, ships, and arms, raising the cost of recruiting mercenaries and obliging Ptolemy to draw on the treasure amassed by Kleomenes of Naukratis. After the defeat of Perdiccas, Ptolemy was fortunate enough to be able to recruit a portion of the soldiers in the defeated army. Later, after defeating Demetrios Poliorketes at the battle of Gaza in 312, he settled eight thousand prisoners in Egypt; following a well-established custom, they did not hesitate to enter his service.[7]

For the king to maintain such an army, however indispensable to his independence and prestige, was both very costly and potentially dangerous. Hellenistic mercenaries demanded payment partly in coins and partly in kind; since there was never a permanent state of war, they had either to remain inactive or to be released from duty and sent back to their native lands, in which case they would be lost to the service of the king. To address these inconveniences, Ptolemy had recourse to a system of settling soldiers in the Egyptian countryside. Instead of regular pay, each soldier was offered full use of a plot of cultivable land, assigned by means of a drawing and called a *kleros* in Greek; the recipient of the fields was called a *klerouchos* (cleruch). Thus was begun the process of forming a veritable reserve armed force that could be called up at any time if needed, free of the hazards of supply and demand on the market that had formed in the Peloponnesus, on Cape Tainaron. There was also a considerable savings for the regime, because there was no risk of mercenaries returning home to Greece or elsewhere with their cash instead of spending it in Egypt. This cleruchic system would be the basis of the military organization of Lagide Egypt down to the Roman conquest, and the cleruchs would become a privileged class that spread throughout the Egyptian *Chora*. The fields assigned to them had to be chosen with care. It would have been poor politics to expel the native small farmers or to appropriate the sacred lands of the temples. The king thus ceded for the most part cultivable fields that were not being exploited for one reason or another, most often because the inundation did not reach them. In such cases, the irrigation work had to be contracted out, and the cost was shared by the crown and the cleruch. The economic consequences of such a system were anything but negligible, because new fields previously left unsown were now cultivated, thus contributing to growth in the amount of land agriculturally exploited.

Though it was applied on a scale unprecedented in the Greek world, this system was not a Ptolemaic innovation. The military organization of Saite Egypt, as described by Herodotus,[8] had already included the assignment of a plot of twelve *aroura*s to each native soldier (*machimos*), whether or not he was in active service.[9] From the end of the sixth century on, Athens had employed the cleruchic system in the territories it controlled, though with some brutality, for the original occupants had to be systematically dispossessed of their lands. Ironically enough, the Athenian cleruchs settled on the island of Samos were expelled in 322 B.C.E., just as Ptolemy was beginning to recruit mercenaries.[10] It is not impossible that he took advantage of the situation to offer them the same position they had enjoyed on Samos and that they thus constituted the embryo of the cleruchic organization in Egypt.

This system quickly proved its merit, at least in the loyalty of the soldiers who benefited from it. In 307 B.C.E., when the army sent to Cyprus by Ptolemy was defeated by Demetrios Poliorketes, most of the prisoners defied custom by declining to enter the latter's service, explaining that they had left their means of subsistence in Egypt.[11] Most of the mercenaries came from agricultural regions in continental Greece that had been devastated by war; the prospect of once again having land to farm was undoubtedly more attractive to them than the advantages of pay and the joys of life in a garrison.

THE HAZARDS OF COHABITATION

From the Egyptian point of view, the most visible effect of the cleruchic system was the settlement of immigrants in the countryside. They were not just assigned to the garrisons scattered throughout the land, they were settled in most of the villages where fields could be assigned to them. This outcome was undoubtedly foreseen and desired by the regime; indeed, how better to establish a bond between the land and the Lagide dynasty? So as not to be rejected as a group of foreigners, it was necessary to occupy the land. The classic solution applied elsewhere by Greek imperialism had been to found cities peopled by colonists, but Egypt's terrain was already so filled with inhabitants that this was not practicable. Occupation thus had to occur on a smaller, more local level, with the Greek element scattered among the indigenous population and in the hope of beginning a long-term process of Hellenization.

This scattering of foreign soldiers throughout the towns and villages did not fail to provoke tensions with the local populace. First of all, it was necessary to house these men, and that led to requisitioning. It is significant that the oldest Greek papyrus found in Egypt is a placard forbidding the requisitioning of a lodging: "Order of Peukestas (the military governor left in Egypt by Alexander): It is forbidden for anyone to enter. It is the room of a priest." [12] In the third century B.C.E., the housing problem was the object of a stream of petitions addressed to the king by Egyptians infuriated with their enforced guests or sometimes by the soldiers themselves, who were disputing over the same lodgings. On a number of occasions, the kings were obliged to call for order regarding this thorny issue, as in this letter from Ptolemy II:

> King Ptolemy greets Antiochos. As for housing the soldiers, we have learned that acts of unjustified violence have been committed because they have not received their lodgings from the *oikonomoi,* but rather they are breaking into houses, chasing out those who live there, and settling themselves by force. Order that henceforth no more of this be done.[13]

The potential victims of such requisitions sometimes came up with ingenious methods of avoidance, such as setting up altars or chapels in front of their door, which made their houses inviolable.[14] The problem became less and less acute as immigration dried up and the newcomers became integrated into the population, yet as late as 118 B.C.E., in their great "philanthropic" edict, King Ptolemy VIII and his two wives found it necessary to mention all the categories of people exempt from the requisitioning of lodgings—essentially the priesthood and all those who worked for the revenues of the crown: royal peasants, weavers, pig and goose breeders, oil manufacturers, beekeepers, and brewers.[15]

INDEPENDENT INCOME FROM REAL ESTATE[16]

The parcels of land assigned to the cleruchs for their subsistence varied in size according to the rank of those who received them. They ranged from twenty to forty *arouras* (13.5–27 acres), according to rank, for infantrymen, and from 50 to 100 *arouras* (34–68.2 acres) for cavalrymen and bodyguards (*somatophylakeis*). These sizes were in fact theoretical. A cleruch who normally should have received 40 *arouras* could be assigned a much smaller parcel of land, and this happened more frequently as the cleruchic system progressively expanded and there was necessarily less and less available land. Though it is necessary to take into account the often considerable differences in the quality of the fields that comprised it, the size of a *kleros* was often large enough to feed more than one family, so much so that direct exploitation could lead to a surplus that could be sold or loaned at interest once the various taxes were paid. (The system of taxation of cleruchic lands was relatively favorable, however.) If a cleruch was not disposed to get his hands dirty, he could sublet his *kleros* to one or more native peasants and live with his family on the rents. This was generally the case with officers and cavalrymen with large parcels of land, though with regard to the latter, we must bear in mind the expense of maintaining a horse. Even after subtracting rent and the family's living expenses and current expenses, there was a remainder that could be invested. Thus, in the long run, a cleruchic bourgeoisie was able to form. In the beginning, these families must have lived close to the lands assigned to them; even in the smallest villages, they formed Greek communities that were well organized around a *gymnasion*, where Hellenic cultural traditions were perpetuated. This was especially the case in the Faiyum, where a massive colonization project was carried out in the reign of Philadelphos, enabling villages inhabited mostly by Greeks to be established everywhere.

Contrary to the initial expectations of the regime, the cleruchs tended to leave their rural homes to settle in the large centers, mostly the native cities that were the ancient nome capitals, and even in the capital city itself. The driving force behind this movement was a gradual change in the status of the lands that had been ceded to them; nominally the king's property, in theory these lands could be taken back from their recipients, for example, for leaving the king's service. Moreover, they could not be bequeathed or sold. But in practice, the concessions of cleruchic land quickly became permanent, and the cleruchs were able to transmit them to sons of an age to bear arms; at the same time, this simplified the problem of recruitment for the king. Soon, it became possible to bequeath them to sons who were minors and even to widows and daughters. The process culminated in the ability to sell the land to third parties, provided they belonged to the cleruchic class, a step that was taken only at the end of Lagide rule, in the course of the first century B.C.E.[17] At this time, and indeed from the middle of the second century on, the Greek cleruchs changed their designation to *katoikoi* (colonists), a more elevated term that distinguished them from Egyptians who had entered into the cleruchy around 218–217. The new native cleruchs, who held smaller parcels of land of only 5–30 *arouras*, constituted an intermediate class with a hybrid status. This measure, which had seemed to be the lesser evil in a time of crisis, had contradictory effects, the worst for the regime being the re-creation of an armed force capable of supporting Egyptian nationalistic demands, which were the principal cause of the lengthy secession of Upper Egypt from 205 to 187.

A SOLDIER-SPECULATOR: DIONYSIOS SON OF KEPHALAS[18]

Some miles north of the modern city of Minya but on the other side of the river, on the east bank, one can visit the picturesque ruins, clinging to the rocky escarpment, of ancient Akoris, also called Tenis (ancient Egyptian *T-dehene*, "the cliff," which survives in Arabic as Tihna). The remains stem mostly from the Roman period, but in the nineteenth century, excavators discovered a batch of Greek and Demotic documents dating to the end of the second century B.C.E., when the village was part of the Hermopolite nome, a strategically important region. Many soldiers were stationed there, both as reserves (cleruchs) and on active service. The archive in question belonged to a certain Dionysios son of Kephalas, two names that would testify to the Hellenism of their bearers were it not for the fact that Diony-sios, who was named after his paternal grandfather, was also called Plenis, a typically Egyptian name (*P-lyn*, "blacksmith"). Kephalas' mother also had an Egyptian name, Senobastis (daughter of the goddess Bastet), as did his brother Peteharpokrates (gift of the god Horus-the-Child). Like her son, Dionysios' mother had both a Greek name—Demetria, which was later changed to Sarapias—and an Egyptian name Senabellis (daughter of the god Abel).

This was thus a mixed Graeco-Egyptian family that demonstrated its af-filiation with the two cultures by its mixture of Greek and Egyptian names. Moreover, Dionysios was bilingual; he could compose documents in Greek, but he did not disdain to write Demotic on occasion. His occupations also revealed his involvement with the two worlds. On the one hand, he held a priestly office in an Egyptian chapel dedicated to an avatar of the god Thoth and to his sacred ibises, and on the other hand, around the age of thirty, he was inducted into the infantry as a "Macedonian." It is probable that his family was descended from a Macedonian soldier who entered the king's service during the third century and whose descendants married into the lo-cal population. His father Kephalas had the title *misthophoros,* that is, he was a paid soldier. Since his pay came directly from the crown, he was not one of the cleruchs. He was involved in other profit-making activities, how-ever, for in 154–153 B.C.E., he purchased 300 *chous* (about 870 liters) of wine for the sum of twenty-four bronze talents. Such a quantity could not have been just for home consumption, especially in an era when wine could scarcely be stored, so it is certain that Kephalas counted on making a profit from its sale. Though he did not have a *kleros,* a parcel of land granted by the king, it is probable that, like his son, he engaged in agricultural pur-suits. The latter in fact rented fields to farmers, undoubtedly "sacred" lands that he did not own himself but were in his charge in his capacity as priest of a chapel that had to feed its sacred ibises. Dionysios was also a "royal peasant" (*basilikos georgos*), that is, he farmed lands belonging to the king. He also had some parcels of land for the cultivation of which he bought or rented cows.

Most of Demetrios' documents, however, are concerned with loans of wheat. From 117 to 104 B.C.E., he borrowed varying amounts of wheat, sometimes large amounts, nearly every year, often along with his mother and his wife. While the use to which the wheat was put is never indicated, it is hardly likely that it was intended for household consumption or for sowing the fields Dionysios cultivated. The loans undoubtedly had to do with activity that was purely speculative in nature. He usually borrowed the wheat from other soldiers, usually higher in rank than he, cleruchs or otherwise, who had a grain surplus from their fields or their pay and who made a good investment by loaning it to Dionysios at the standard interest rate of 50 percent for in-kind loans. For his part, Dionysios must have sold the wheat on the open market, profiting from seasonal fluctuations in price, or loaned it in his own turn to down-and-out native peasants at exorbitant interest rates. It was undoubtedly at this level that Dionysios could best take advantage of his position between two worlds. As both a literate speaker of Greek and an Egyptian priest using the native language in his daily life, he was in a position to serve as an intermediary between his fellow soldiers, to whom he was a privileged companion, and the Egyptian peasants whose misery he exploited. Unfortunately, we know nothing of this second aspect of his activity, but we can fear the worst in view of the tortuous and clever expedients to which he resorted to postpone his payments without having to pay the designated penalties, often repaying his debts from one to five months late. We have the text of two petitions dated October 108 and addressed to the *strategos* and the secretaries of the nome (*basilikogrammateis*), by means of which he was able to avoid a possible imprisonment for debt threatened by a creditor, arguing that as a royal peasant, he could not be arrested during sowing season, so as not to harm the interests of the sovereigns. He succeeded in obtaining a postponement until December. This was undoubtedly not a case of bad faith but of a bad deal that had left him in difficulty. While short of pathetic, Dionysios' situation was certainly unstable, and the prospect of regular, steady pay must have led him to seek induction into the army.

A CURIOUS "PERSIAN" [19]

As the son of a soldier, Dionysios bore the curious designation "Persian by descent," though we can attribute no Persian ancestor to him. To understand how such a title could be commonly borne at this time by persons who had Greek and Egyptian names, it is necessary to recall that from at least as early as the New Kingdom, military professionals were recruited principally from foreign ethnic groups. The names of certain groups thus tended to designate a certain military class, such as the Meshwesh, the name of a Libyan people, which was usually abbreviated into Ma, during the Third Intermediate Period. After 525 B.C.E., during the Persian occupation, soldiers were naturally enough called "Persian," despite their diverse nationalities. With the arrival of the Greeks, this term was evidently not suitable for the new Graeco-Macedonian military caste, but it continued to designate soldiers, whether demobilized or not, from the former occupying army, as well as their descendants. As these blended into the Egyptian populace, the designation "Persian by descent" came to be applied, by way of a semantic shift, to all members of a family of military men, whether or not they were actually soldiers. The title was not as insignificant as it might appear at first glance, for it indicated a particular status consisting essentially of being able to be mobilized into the service of the king. In fact, since persons who were "Persian by descent" were susceptible of being called up for military service at any time, they did not have the possibility of claiming the right of asylum and taking refuge in a temple. Contrary to all expectations, this exclusion from the right of asylum became an advantage in that it made it easier to get loans, for the potential creditor was assured of being able to seize the person of the debtor in case of default. The condition of "Persian by descent" amounted to nothing other than an additional guarantee to a creditor granting a loan. This guarantee, which was at first reserved only for real descendants of soldiers, ended by being available to all who declared themselves "Persian," whatever their actual status otherwise. In contracts, moreover, we also find a number of women who bear the designation "Persian" (*persine*). The term survived well into the Roman period, down to the second century C.E., when the military connotation of the title had completely disappeared.

As for our Dionysios, his designation as "Persian by descent" corresponded to his actual status, since he was the son of a soldier in active service and entered into the career himself. But he seems to have used this status only to obtain loans more easily, and he continued to claim it even after he was enrolled in an infantry unit specifically designated by name, which theoretically should have entailed the loss of this particular status.

In 106 B.C.E., Dionysios ceased to be "Persian by descent" and became a "Macedonian," at first assigned to a unit of recruits under the command of a certain Demetrios and then the next year incorporated into an infantry regiment called *hegemonia,* under the *hegemon* (commandant) Artemidoros. Some years later, his older brother Paesis entered the cavalry as a "Libyan," a remarkable promotion given that Egyptians were normally allowed only in the infantry. We do not know what became of the two brothers. It seems that Dionysios himself had no children who survived him. It is striking that the long litany of grain loans ends abruptly in 103, when many regiments were mobilized for the war conducted by Cleopatra III in Syria against her brother Ptolemy IX Soter. It is quite possible that Dionysios disappeared not far from Mount Carmel or Damascus, having had some time to feel homesick, though a little too late, for the mountain of Akoris with its crocodiles and its sacred ibises.

A MILITARY COLONY IN THE SOUTH OF EGYPT: PATHYRIS

A little before 150 B.C.E., King Ptolemy VI Philometor decided to increase military colonization south of Thebes. He undoubtedly feared being taken by surprise by a possible insurrection in the old capital city of Upper Egypt when the death of the crown prince Eupator endangered the future of the dynasty, and when the confused situation in Seleucid Syria made it possible to envision Lagide intervention to recover the territories that had been lost half a century earlier. To hem in Thebes was the best way to avoid a repetition of the disturbances that had permitted the secession of the south of the country after the reign of his grandfather. For this redeployment of forces, he chose two localities on the west bank nineteen miles south of the Theban temples of Amun and their fanatical clergy. The more northerly was Krokodilopolis, which, as can easily be guessed, had a temple dedicated to the crocodile god Sobek, and nine miles to the south, Pathyris (meaning "the home of Hathor") has been located beneath the modern village of Gebelein (an Arabic word meaning "two mountains"). These two cities, which had lapsed into stagnation despite their ancient pharaonic past, now experienced a sudden prosperity and even an administrative promotion, for Pathyris became the capital of a specially created nome. Though the larger contingent was located there, Krokodilopolis has not left any identifiable traces. But the houses of Pathyris have yielded, in the course of both official and clandestine excavations, several lots of archives consisting of papyri and wooden tablets and that concern at least five different families who lived there between about 150 and 88 B.C.E.[20]

A CRETAN IN EGYPT: THE CAVALRYMAN DRYTON[21]

The most remarkable person revealed to us in these diverse archives is named Dryton son of Pamphilos. As a citizen of Ptolemais, the only Greek city founded in Upper Egypt, and enrolled in the *deme* Philotis, he enjoyed a privileged status that would have made him the envy of many of the Greeks settled in Egypt, who could boast only of their city or people of origin. But he did not forget his more distant roots, for he also presented himself as a Cretan. We can rightly distrust such a designation: in Ptolemaic

Egypt, to be a Cretan, a Boeotian, a Macedonian, and so forth was usually an administrative convenience, a fiction that enabled an individual to be inducted into a military unit. In this case, however, since Dryton and his son Esthladas bore typical Cretan names, there is scarcely room for doubt that this was indeed their origin. Following the Greek custom of endogamy, he first married a lady named Sarapias, another citizen of Ptolemais, who was also a Cretan, as we know from the name of her father, Esthladas. Their union produced a single child who reached the age of an adult. Named Esthladas after his maternal grandfather, he was born in 158 B.C.E., when Dryton was already nearly forty. By then, Dryton had a long military career behind him, one that had perhaps begun in the early 170s, when he had reached adult age. Enrolled in the cavalry, he first served in the garrison of his own city, Ptolemais, sometimes making stays at Thebes. We do not know whether he saw active duty in the sixth Syrian war of 170–168 or in the suppression of the nationalistic outbreak that followed it. In any case, he became an officer and was transferred to the fortress at Diospolis Parva, situated midway between Ptolemais and Thebes, 73 miles north of the latter. Around 150, the king sent him to the new military zone of Krokodilopolis-Pathyris, along with a mixed company of cavalry and infantry under the command of a certain Diodotos. His wife, Sarapias, had died in the meanwhile, and he at first settled with his son in the capital of the neighboring nome, Latopolis (Esna), about 19 miles south of Pathyris, undoubtedly because the latter was still just a vast construction site.

It was at Latopolis that he would marry on March 4, 150 B.C.E., the daughter of a soldier attached to the same company and whose family had been settled at Pathyris for several decades. His new wife, who was still an adolescent of thirteen years, had both the Greek name "Apollonia" and the Egyptian name "Senmonthis" (daughter of the god Montu). Since all her known relatives—her father, her grandfather, her great-grandfather, and her three sisters—also had two names, we might think that she belonged to a Hellenized Egyptian family. Apollonia, however, represented herself as a "Cyrenean," that is, theoretically as a citizen of the famous city of Cyrene, in Libya, which at that time was governed by the king's younger brother, Ptolemy Physkon. We cannot decide a priori whether one of her ancestors had actually immigrated to Egypt from Cyrene or whether this qualification was intended only to enroll her father and grandfather in a corps of "Cyreneans." Whatever the case, with this marriage, Dryton entered into a family whose status was inferior to his own—his father-in-law was only an infantryman—and one much more Egyptian in culture, as shown by the presence of a number of Demotic papyri in his archives. Dryton thus brought his wife and his new family a veritable social promotion and rather a lot of goods, which are enumerated in a testament he had drawn up on the occasion of his marriage, a precaution needed to avoid any conflict between his son, his young wife, and any children she might have. Despite the difference in their backgrounds, the marriage was a happy one and lasted more than twenty-five years, until the death of Dryton. Five daughters were born, all with both Greek and Egyptian names, showing how Dryton was Egyptianized by contact with his in-laws. At least three of Dryton's daughters were married, each to a soldier and one of them a cavalryman with the good Egyptian name Herienupis, but two of these marriages ended in divorce. A granddaughter of Dryton, born to his oldest daughter, also divorced in 99. All the documents regarding these divorces were written in Demotic, because in this area, Egyptian law was more favorable than Greek law. But while Dryton's daughters did not find happiness in their married lives, their relations with Esthladas, his son by his first marriage, were excellent, as shown by a very interesting letter he sent to Pathyris on January 15, 130.

At that time, Esthladas, who was about twenty-seven years of age and a cavalryman like his father, was somewhere in the north. Egypt was torn by civil war between the partisans of Queen Cleopatra II—the Greeks and Jews of Alexandria, and the native population of several large Egyptian cities—and those of Ptolemy VIII and Cleopatra III—the provincial administration, and most of the Greeks settled in the nomes. Esthaladas expresses himself thus:

> To his father and his mother, greetings and good health. Since I have already written you often to maintain a firm heart and to take care of yourselves until things settle down, I beg you again to encourage yourself and your people to be confident, for news has come that Paos (the new *epistrategos* appointed by Ptolemy VIII to pacify the Thebaid) will go up the Nile with numerous forces in the month of Tybi to subdue the mobs of Hermonthis and treat them like rebels. Take good care of my sisters [. . .]. Year 40, Choiak 23.[22]

Like the other Greeks in Pathyris and Krokodilopolis, Dryton and his family remained loyal to the king, at the risk of attack from the inhabitants of Thebes and nearby Hermonthis, who supported the opposing cause. Esthladas was justly concerned about his father's well-being, but he did not forget his stepmother and his half sisters. It seems astonishing that despite the isolation of the people of Pathyris caused by the participation of the Theban region in Cleopatra II's revolt, such a letter—containing military information!—could reach its addressees safely, a fact that implies control over and use of a network of desert roads.

A few years later, on June 29, 126 B.C.E., sensing his impending demise, Dryton had the Greek notary of Pathyris write a final testament taking into account the increase in his patrimony and descendants, for five daughters had been born to him since his testament of 150. He left his son Esthladas his cavalryman's horse and all his military gear, a chariot with its shaft, and a vineyard containing cisterns and a dovecote. The rest of his property, movable and immovable, was divided into two equal parts between Esthladas and his five half sisters. At that time, Dryton had four female domestic slaves, which is certainly indicative of his social level: two of them went to his son, and the other two to his daughters. The children were to pay a cash and in-kind pension to Dryton's widow, who for her part would keep her own property. We note that the older son, in accordance with both Greek and Egyptian custom, received the lion's share of his father's property, to the detriment of the other children. Shortly after the death of his father, however, Esthladas once again demonstrated his care for his sisters by ceding them half of the vineyard of which he had been the sole recipient, as attested in the text addressed by Dryton's five daughters to the *epistrategos* Phommous, between 115 and 110, against a Greek from Thebes who had illegally occupied their portion of the vineyard in question. Though he was still active in 103, Esthladas does not appear in this complaint, so we do not know whether he was able to come to the aid of his sisters on this occasion.

Since Dryton's family archive breaks off shortly after the turn of the century, we do not know exactly what happened to these people, except for two granddaughters. The process of Egyptianization must have continued, for despite the concentration of troops at Pathyris, the Egyptian element tended to dominate, at least numerically. One fact is significant in this regard: on June 29, 126 B.C.E., when five witnesses were sought to sign Dryton's last testament, the Greek notary could find only one person able to do so in Greek, a cavalryman named Ammonios. He thus had to resign himself to turning to four Egyptians who could write Demotic: three priests of Aphrodite-Hathor (the goddess of Pathyris) and Sobek (the god of Krokodilopolis) and an infantryman. Under their names, the notary added: "These four (witnesses) in the script of the land, because the equivalent number of Greeks is not here."[23] Even if we suspect that this shortage of Greeks was due to their mobilization in the military operations occasioned by the ongoing civil war, native Egyptians, little or not at all Hellenized, were necessarily more numerous, a fact that must have diverted the Greeks, if we suppose that such was their intention, from any inclination to live in material and cultural isolation.

THE SOLIDARITY OF AN EGYPTIAN FAMILY

In 95 B.C.E., one of Dryton's granddaughters, who had the good Egyptian name Tbokanoupis (the servant of the god Anubis) and the sister of the one who had divorced in 99, married a certain Phagonis. He belonged to one of the best-documented families of Pathyris, whose family tree can be established over five generations and whose most important personage was named Peteharsemtheus, Phagonis's older brother.[24] Without exception, the members of this family all had purely Egyptian names, though some of them were referred to as "Greeks born in Egypt." Their military status must have been relatively minor, for scarcely a single man per generation seems to have seen active service in the army. Phagonis himself is never called a soldier, and of his three brothers, only Petesouchos seems to have been involved in any military operations. Their father Panobkhounis, born in 163 B.C.E., had been a soldier between 125 and 123, at least, at the time of the civil war, and was assigned to the camp near Krokodilopolis. Horos, the latter's uncle, had been in the same company as Dryton the Cretan in 145 but as an infantryman receiving pay. Though the title "Persian," which we have already seen borne by Dionysios son of Kephalas, seems to have been hereditary in the family, most of their activities took place in the civilian realm.

These activities reveal a remarkable solidarity within the family group. Loans and acquisitions of land were often made in the name of several brothers of the same generation; thus, a document dated to 145 B.C.E. shows Totoes, the grandfather of our Phagonis, buying land together with his brother, Horos the soldier.[25] Phagonis himself often borrowed money and wheat jointly with his brothers. This solidarity even extended across the generations, as attested by the surprising affair of a cash loan made by Phagonis's great-grandfather, a certain Patous, on December 26, 138. Since he died in the meanwhile, this debt was repaid to the creditor's son-in-law only thirty years later, by Patous' grandchildren![26] One part was settled in 107 by Panobkhounis, the father of our Phagonis, who took over the share of his aunt Sennesis. In 104, it was the turn of his half brother Paous to settle the outstanding balance, though with exemption from the late fee, which was normally 50 percent! This is a good example of the sense of collective responsibility and honor exhibited by this Egyptian family so proud of its membership in a sort of local elite.

We see a keen sense of family in other, less expected areas as well, such as matrimonial ties. In his first marriage, around the age of eighteen, Totoes, one of the dominant figures of the family, married Tareesis, then about fifteen years old, the daughter of the impecunious Patous. It was from this union that Panobkhounis was born in 163 B.C.E. Fifteen years later, he divorced Tareesis to marry her younger sister Takmeis, who had been born only in 164 and was still just an adolescent. Tareesis was not abandoned, however, for she immediately married her brother-in-law, the soldier Horos, by whom she had a son. Such conjugal intrigue smacks of premeditated arrangement, even if we take into account the amorous passion that Takmeis' youth aroused in a Totoes who was nearly forty, already bald and pot-bellied. The two families of Patous and Totoes had a mutual interest in remaining allied, and it was impossible to allow Tareesis to take her own property into an unrelated family by way of a dowry. Besides satisfying Totoes' sexual appetite, the solution they adopted enabled his younger brother to end his celibacy and more closely joined the patrimonies of the two families. The latter were not negligible, to judge from the transactions that ensued down to 88. Their immovable property consisted of houses and of parcels of land planted with wheat, oleaginous plants (castor oil), or vines, some of them leased to farmers. The size of the parcels bought or sold, sometimes to guarantee loans, was generally modest, ranging from a quarter of an *aroura* (less than 840 square yards) to 3.5 *aroura*s (less than 2.5 acres). Since Phagonis and his brothers seem to have enjoyed a comfortable standard of living at the local level, their frequent borrowing should not be interpreted as a sign of ongoing lack of funds, but rather as part of a sound, well-managed investment activity.

The amount of the pay of the young soldier-brother would seem small in comparison, especially considering the discomfort and potential dangers of military life, as attested by three letters sent a few weeks apart by Petesouchos to his brothers during a peace-keeping operation in 95, perhaps in the region of Esna. On May 21, he and his comrades were safe, but he added:

Do not lament for those who have perished; they expected to be killed. As for us, he (no doubt the *strategos* mentioned in the following letters) has done us no harm, on the contrary, he has taken care of us.[27]

On June 30, he wrote,

I am in good health, along with the new recruits . . . . The *strategos* Ptolion is protecting us greatly, and we are enormously grateful to him."[28]

These two letters were written in Greek, but our soldier could also write Demotic in a missive that must be related to the same year 95, though the date has been lost, along with the end of the letter:

> Petesouchos greets his older brother Peteharsemtheus, as well as Phagonis. The *strategos* Ptolion has given a golden crown and a royal robe (*chiton*) to Horos. . . .[29]

Unfortunately, the text comes to an end, and we shall never know what great heroic deed or important promotion earned Horos, undoubtedly an Egyptian officer under the *strategos'* command, such exceptional honors. We sense pride bursting forth from under Petesouchos' pen, pride in serving such a general and a desire to impress his correspondents with his superior's display of beneficence and the lavishness of the rewards heaped on his comrades.

THE SUDDEN DISAPPEARANCE OF A GARRISON

Curiously, all the documentation regarding Pathyris and neighboring Krokodilopolis comes to a sudden end in 88 B.C.E. In that year, grave events once again threatened the domestic peace in Egypt. King Ptolemy X Alexander had just been driven from Alexandria by a revolt led by the garrison of the capital, who recalled his older brother, Ptolemy IX Soter II. The situation was unsettled, for Ptolemy X, who continued to have many partisans, attempted a return by force. On November 1, 88, the *epistrategos* in charge of the Thebaid, a certain Platon, wrote to the people of Pathyris:

> King Soter, the very great god, arrived at Memphis, and Hierax was appointed to subdue the Thebaid with considerable forces. So that this news might bolster your greater confidence, we have decided to inform you of it." [30]

Far from demonstrating loyalty to the dethroned king, the Thebans had taken advantage of the power vacuum to revolt, threatening the loyalists of Pathyris. This letter is unfortunately the last one in the collection, so that we may fear the worst regarding the events that followed. Pausanias mentions in passing that the revolt of Thebes was not put down until 85 B.C.E. Did the insurgents in the meanwhile succeed in seizing the two garrison towns, possibly massacring or deporting their people? Or did Hierax, the generalissimo of the royal troops noted by Platon, decide to transfer them to a more appropriate or less exposed locale? A single fact is certain: Pathyris and Krokodilopolis and their populations would disappear from the scene of history, their temples destroyed and their building materials reused in enlarging the nearby temples of Hermonthis and Tod. The Pathyrite nome itself would be eliminated and its place taken by the Hermonthite nome.[31]

THE END OF THE LAGIDE ARMY

In a way, the agony of the Pathyrite garrison in 88 B.C.E. prefigured that of the Lagide army less than sixty years later. As we have seen, the regional army reserves made up of cleruchs and *katoikoi* had developed into a privileged class whose social role eclipsed its military function. Moreover, dynastic conflicts and the suppression of local disturbances had decimated and exhausted the troops the sovereigns could still dispose of, while the international political context, dominated by Rome, no longer permitted their use in operations outside Egypt. Finally, in 55, there was an event of considerable importance for the military history of the land: King Ptolemy XII, who less than three years earlier had been driven from Alexandria and took refuge at Rome, had succeeded in bribing Aulus Gabinius, the governor of the Roman province of Syria, with the aim that the Roman army, under the latter's orders, would reestablish Ptolemy on the throne by force. For the first time, a Roman legion trod the soil of Egypt, easily defeating the local troops that had been hastily drawn together. A large part of the Roman force remained in Egypt, apparently at the disposition of the king, and they quickly vanished into the taverns and dives of Alexandria. A little later, these Roman soldiers would intervene massively at the time of the Alexandrian war, along with Achillas's Egyptian troops, against their compatriots in Julius Caesar's legions. Emerging victorious, Caesar in his turn left behind three legions, which Cleopatra got rid of after the death of the dictator. This de facto Roman occupation of 55–43 left material traces all the way through Upper Egypt, in the form of soldiers' graffiti at Abydos, the royal tombs of Thebes, and even on the walls of the temple of Isis at Philae.[32] Undoubtedly, it also led to a reorganization of the Lagides' Graeco-Egyptian army; in fact, in papyri from this period, we see the appearance of certain military terms of Roman origin, such as *speira*, which corresponds to "cohort."[33] Despite this start, and despite the evacuation of the Roman

FIGURE 39. Ring depicting Ptolemy IV. Walters Art Gallery 57.1699. Photo courtesy of The Walters Art Gallery, Baltimore.

army in 43, after its failure against Caesar at Alexandria in 47, Graeco-Egyptian soldiers played only a minor role, such as that of the last Lagide officer to bequeath his name to history, a certain Selaukos, who surrendered the fortress of Pelusium to Octavian in the year 30, perhaps with the consent of Cleopatra.[34]

Though there was now no question that what remained of the Lagide army could pit its strength against the Roman legions, there was one area in which Egypt was still able to distinguish itself: its navy.[35] The latter had had its hour of glory in the third century B.C.E., when Ptolemy II dominated the Mediterranean and the Red Sea with his 336 warships, the largest fleet of its day. The captains and the officers of these ships were Greek, but the many crewmen and the low-ranking noncommissioned officers were primarily recruited from the Egyptian population. His successors discontinued this costly effort, and the Rhodian fleet soon surpassed that of the Ptolemies, notwithstanding Ptolemy IV's (Figure 39) interest in shipbuilding, which led to the construction, as spectacular as it was useless, of a *tesserakonteres,* an ungovernable monstrosity more than 460 feet long and 79 feet high at the stern, theoretically propelled by 4,000 rowers and otherwise carrying 400 crewmen and 2,850 soldiers![36] In the second century, the abandonment of bases in the Mediterranean limited the Lagide fleet's sphere of operation outside Egypt to Cyrene and to Cyprus, whose *strategos* also held the office of grand admiral under Ptolemy VIII. The loss of the Syrian possessions also limited the possibility of obtaining timber for construction, and finally, Ptolemy V's agreement to cease recruiting oarsmen from temple domains undoubtedly provoked a crisis in recruitment. Nevertheless, Egyptian naval capability remained considerable and the object of envy, and it was an important issue in the war between Caesarians and republicans between 44 and 42. But it was the final battle that revealed, albeit in a negative way, the importance of the Lagide navy, which in fact supplied a quarter of the ships engaged at Actium. Antony had a large number of them burned to facilitate his maneuvers, but the sixty he spared, the largest and finest, constituted the reserve indispensable to his battle plan. It was their sudden flight by order of the queen that sealed the fate of the battle at a point when, as Plutarch states, "the battle was still equal and uncertain." [37]

8 TWO LANGUAGES, TWO CULTURES, THREE WRITING SYSTEMS

A MULTICULTURAL SOCIETY

A global assessment of Egypt in the reigns of the last Ptolemies would undoubtedly end by affirming that osmosis had proved impossible and that the precipice separating its two mutually incomprehensible cultures was crossed only by rare and fragile footbridges. The fracture line created by the massive arrival of Greeks in Egypt not only separated the two communities, it affected individuals to the point of sometimes provoking a veritable cultural schizophrenia. This sort of process was surely not unique. Similar causes have managed to engender similar situations elsewhere, and the intriguing phenomenon of acculturation is far from the most expected result of the encounter of two such different peoples. Yet ever since the nineteenth century, certain historians have wanted to celebrate in Hellenistic societies, and especially in Egyptian society under the Lagides, the birth of a mixed civilization enriched by the combined contribution of classical Hellenism and eastern—in this case pharaonic—traditions.[1]

This is an optimistic and naïve vision, and it has been opposed by one developed by a more conservative historiography, one that sees the inevitable decadence of a Hellenism spoiled by its deleterious contact with the obscurantism of oriental priests. Contemporary research, however, insists on a coexistence founded on relative and mutual ignorance, like two parallel universes developing almost autonomously, with few reciprocal effects.[2] Determining the extent and the nature of these influences evidently remains a subject of polemic for historians of Lagide Egypt.

With or without interaction, the two worlds that had to coexist in the Nile valley must each have had its vision of the other. It must be admitted that we have little knowledge of what Egyptians thought of Hellenism, and it is even likely that their perceptions were undecided and inconsistent. In this, they were at a disadvantage vis-à-vis the Greeks, who arrived in the land with definite preconceptions regarding their new neighbors.

Greek interest in Egypt was old, for the first contacts were as early as the seventh century, at the beginning of the Saite dynasty, when the Greeks were still in the Archaic phase of their civilization. This interest was not just commercial, and the first Greek communities who settled in Egypt learned the manners, the customs, and the mental universe of the people among whom they lived, albeit in the distorting mirror of their own prejudices. Thus developed a discourse about Egypt, beginning with Hekataios of Miletos around the end of the sixth century. Around the middle of the fifth century, Herodotus devoted the second book of his historical work to Egypt, laying out a coherent picture, based partly on his own experience, which served as the basis for the Greek vision of Egyptian civilization. At the time of Alexander's conquest, the Greeks thus already had their own idea of pharaonic culture, and as superficial and erroneous as it was, it nevertheless put them at an advantage over the Egyptians, who had no clear perception of Hellenism. Greek attitudes regarding Egypt were not necessarily negative or scornful, like those of white colonialists in Africa in the nineteenth century of our own era. In certain areas at least, Egyptians were invested with superiority in the eyes of their conquerors, or at least with an anteriority, which made them worthy partners for potential exchanges in matters of religion, divination, or medicine, for example. While the Greeks were thus able to borrow some elements from pharaonic civilization, they did not attempt a forced Hellenization of the land and its native inhabitants. The latter perpetuated and developed their own traditions untroubled by the clamor rising from the *gymnasia,* where the Greeks had re-created their cultural environment. Inevitably, however, by reason of ambition or necessity, certain individuals found themselves obliged to participate in both worlds and to find their own way to resolve the resulting contradiction.

THE NEW ATHENS[3]

Alexandria's early importance as the intellectual center of the Hellenistic world is well known. The reasons for this stunning success were purely temporary: the relative eclipse of Athens as the cultural capital of the Greek world at the end of the fourth century and the munificent patronage the first two Ptolemies lavished on the scholars and artists who came from all the horizons of Hellenism, and even from beyond them. The creation of the Museum and the Library, no doubt at the instigation of the Athenian Demetrios of Phaleron, was the means of their policy of prestige, which sought to give the new capital a luster that could be conferred far better by the grace of the Muses than by gold and marble.

The third century B.C.E. was thus Alexandria's golden age, and the contribution of Alexandria was the determining factor in many areas of Hellenistic intellectual history. This is not the place to describe all the facets of the activity in which the writers and scholars salaried by the king were engaged. The choice of the disciplines and genres pursued reveals both a certain orientation imposed by the central power and the major preoccupations of the time. Thus, philosophy, which had distinguished Athens in the preceding century, had almost no place at Alexandria. Though the Museum was created on an Aristotelian model, no Peripatetic philosopher settled in Alexandria, nor any representative of the great philosophical schools of the time—the Platonic Academy, the Stoics, the Epicureans, and the Cynics. It seems that the Lagide sovereigns' lack of interest in intellectual speculation was the main reason for this absence. Aside from some disciples of the Cyrenaic school, with its hedonistic and atheistic tendencies, which was already on the decline, the only famous Alexandrian writer classified as a philosopher was Eratosthenes, though he was in fact far better known for his works on geography and history.

It was at this time that Alexandrian science had its hour of glory. Medicine was distinguished by Herophilos of Chalcedon, Ptolemy II's physician, who made major discoveries in human anatomy. For mathematics, it suffices to cite Euclid, the father of geometry, and a contemporary of Ptolemy I. The astronomer Aristarchos of Samos was the first to try to measure the size of and the relative distances to the moon and the sun, and to place the latter in the center of the universe. Finally, physics was well represented by Strato of Lapsakos, author of a theory of the void, which enabled the engineer Ktesibios of Alexandria to design remarkable pneumatic and hydraulic devices.

In literature, lyric and elegiac poetry were principally represented by Kallimachos and Theokritos. The former was incontestably the greatest writer of his century, the author of a vast and varied oeuvre. In his fifteenth Idyl ("The Syracusans"), the latter gives us an extraordinary tableau of Alexandria in his day and age. Epic poetry was represented by little more than the famous *Argonautica* of Apollonios of Rhodes, who was otherwise director of the Library from 270 to 245 B.C.E.

The Alexandrian intellectuals did not expend the greater part of their energy on creative activity, though, but rather on the critical and grammatical study of classical works, especially those of Homer, and on lexicography and bibliography. Zenodotos of Ephesos, who was the first director of the Library and the tutor of Ptolemy II, was the first editor of Homer and Pindar. In addition to his purely literary works, Kallimachos composed the *Catalogues of the Authors Eminent in Various Disciplines* in 120 books. Eratosthenes worked out the chronological tables of his *Chronographia* for the benefit of historians, and he wrote a study on ancient comedy. Finally, Aristophanes of Byzantium and Aristarchos of Samothrace, who were successive directors of the Library, marked the apogee of Homeric and classical studies at Alexandria. This taste for hermeneutics, developed under the aegis of the Ptolemies, would have a long legacy, one that extended to cultural domains other than Hellenism. It was, in fact, at the invitation of Ptolemy II that Jewish scholars came to Alexandria to translate the sacred books of their people into Greek, thus enabling the Greek-speaking world to discover the Bible via the *Septuagint*.[4] The work of these Jewish scholars, which must have drawn on the techniques of textual criticism employed by the scholars of the Museum, inspired new reflection on the sacred texts and nourished the discipline of exegesis, which would so profoundly mark the development of both Judaism and Christianity.

DECLINE AND REBIRTH OF ALEXANDRIANISM

Though we do not know exactly why Ptolemy VIII conceived such hatred of the scholars and artists who graced his capital, his expulsion of them at the time of his second accession in 145 B.C.E. entailed dramatic consequences for the intellectual life of Alexandria. Aristarchos of Samothrace, the highly distinguished director of the Library, was replaced by an obscure military man, an officer of a company of lancers named Kydas. No renowned scholar would henceforth occupy this prestigious office. Without actually becoming a cultural wasteland, Alexandria nevertheless lost its position of superiority in the various branches of knowledge in which the scholars of the Museum had assured its reputation, to the benefit of Pergamon, its great intellectual rival, and of Rhodes, Antioch, and Athens. The effect was also disastrous for the image of Lagide Egypt in the Greek world. From his retreat at Athens, the historian and geographer Agatharchides of Knidos, one of the most famous victims of the persecution, violently denounced the tyranny of the Ptolemaic regime, in particular with his heart-wrenching description of the unfortunates condemned to forced labor in the gold mines of Nubia.[5]

Despite everything, by a curious turn of fortune, Alexandria would once again experience a brief but significant period of cultural flowering. It was occasioned by the Mithridatic war, which caused an exodus in the opposite direction from the one provoked by Physkon's wrath. Threatened by the military undertakings of the king of Pontos, Athens was emptied of its intellectuals, who took refuge at Rome and Alexandria, the only two cities that were safe. This time, philosophers were responsible for this veritable renaissance. During the second reign of Soter II, from 87 to 80 B.C.E., Antiochos of Ashkelon, who represented the dogmatic and Stoic tendencies of the New Academy, taught in the Lagide capital, where he launched polemics against the adherents of skeptical Platonism. The last two reigns of the dynasty, those of Auletes and Cleopatra, thus saw philosophical schools flourishing and carrying on their tumultuous controversies.

We must not, however, seek any originality in the thought of these authors, whose writings have almost entirely disappeared. Eclecticism was then in vogue, and most of the works whose titles we know were encyclopedias or manuals summarizing the opinions of the various schools, like those of the Alexandrian Eudoros, who in the 50s wrote the monumental *General Encyclopedia of Philosophy,* along with commentaries on Plato, Aristotle, and the Pythagoreans. At around the same time, another native of Alexandria, a certain Potamon, founded a new school whose sole aim was to make a synthesis of all doctrines and which was justly called the Eclectic school. More serious were the teachings of the Neopythagorean groups who rekindled interest in this old system of thought, and especially that of the Cretan Ainesidemos of Knossos, who founded the Neoskeptical school at Alexandria at the beginning of Cleopatra's reign, in healthy reaction to the prevailing eclecticism and dogmatism. He was undoubtedly the only original thinker in this whole period, and his relativistic theory of *tropoi,* which was taken up and developed by Sextus Empiricus, would influence philosophers down to the seventeenth and eighteenth centuries of our own era.

It should be noted that this sudden philosophical effervescence almost completely escaped the control of the sovereigns. Most of these intellectuals were in fact under the patronage of Romans, which was logical for persons who had fled the persecution of the Roman-hating Mithridates. Antiochos of Ashkelon was himself a member of Lucullus's following, and Ainesidemos dedicated his *Pyrrhonian Arguments* to a certain Lucius Aelius Tubero. Moreover, when certain of these theoreticians engaged in politics, they did so in a spirit of hostility toward the Lagide regime. This was the case with the philosopher Dio, a disciple of Antiochos, who sided with the Alexandrians in their revolt against Auletes, who was exiled at Rome, in 58 B.C.E.; sent to plead the Alexandrians' cause before the Senate, Dio was assassinated by the king's hirelings. More significant still was the attitude of Areios Didymos, a Stoic who was heavily influenced by Anthiochos. After arriving in Rome in 46, perhaps in Cleopatra's retinue, he became the philosophy teacher of the young Octavian, who was then seventeen, and he remained ever after a member of his circle of intimates. A representative of the eclectic trend, he wrote a summary of the principal doctrines for his illustrious pupil; it enjoyed a certain success in Rome and inspired a number of imitations. He returned to Alexandria in August, 30 B.C.E. along with the baggage of the conqueror of Actium, and he demonstrated his hostile or at least indifferent feelings toward the Lagide dynasty by urging Octavian not to spare Caesarion, while at the same time proving his affection for his native city and his compatriots by successfully pleading their cause with the Roman.

At the same time, the few philosophers whom Auletes and Cleopatra had succeeded in attracting into their entourage were mere buffoons or impostors, like Philostratos, an intimate of the queen and a smooth talker who obtained clemency thanks to Areios, despite Octavian's reservations and his false claim that he was a member of the Academy.

Other disciplines benefited from this intellectual renaissance in the final years of the dynasty. We may at least cite a historian, Timagenes, the son of an Alexandrian banker. His career in the Lagide city was quite brief, however, for he was implicated in the revolt against Auletes and taken prisoner to Rome by Gabinius in 55 B.C.E. There, he directed a school of rhetoric, and for a time, like his compatriot Areios, he was a counselor of Octavian before falling into disgrace. His lost work *On Kings,* which dealt with the dynastic history of the Hellenistic east, must have been violently critical of the Ptolemies, and especially of Auletes. He was one of the principal sources of the Gallic historian Pompeius Trogus, a summary of whom, written by Justinus, forms the basis of our knowledge of the internal history of the Hellenistic kingdoms.

The renewal of the philological sciences, which had made the reputation of Alexandria in the third century B.C.E., was undoubtedly done a disservice by a physical disaster whose exact magnitude still gives rise to discussion: the burning of the great Library in 47 B.C.E. Barring the hypothesis that the building destroyed was only an ordinary warehouse for copies of works destined for export, this loss would have deprived researchers of an incomparable resource, that is to say, all the monuments of erudition without which the critical research on classical texts undertaken under the first Ptolemies could scarcely have beeen continued. Nevertheless, during the reign of Cleopatra, a great scholar took up the torch left by Aristarchos of Samothrace a century earlier. This was Didymos, surnamed "Bronze Gut" (*Chalkenteros*) because of his incredible fecundity: no fewer than thirty-five hundred titles were attributed to him. Of very humble origin, the son of a fishmonger, he bears witness to the astonishing possibilities for promotion in Alexandrian society in the first century. His commentaries on the text of Homer were based on the earlier editions of Zenodotos and Aristarchos, but it seems clear from certain scholia on Homeric manuscripts reproducing his notes that he could not have had direct access to the works of his predecessors. Since we cannot doubt that the original papyri containing these works had been religiously kept in the Library, we can infer that they must have disappeared in the fire. His areas of interest were not confined to Homeric studies, however; he was also a great lexicographer, versed in the explication of rare, obscure, or dialectical terms in the writings of all the classical and Hellenistic authors. His commentary in three books on the *Philippics* of Demosthenes deserves mention, because we have a papyrus on which an important fragment is preserved, an isolated plank from the general shipwreck of a colossal work of critical erudition! This universal spirit extended his lexical curiosity to the medical texts of the Hippocratic corpus, which was at that time the object of intense research precisely at Alexandria.

MEDICINE IN THE REIGN OF CLEOPATRA

Medicine was the last flourishing area of intellectual activity in the Ptolemaic period. Quite unlike the renewal of philosophy, it is likely that in this instance the royal court played a determining role. In fact, at the end of the Hellenistic era, sovereigns nearly everywhere took an interest in medical discoveries, in particular toxic pharmacology, for its political applications seemed promising. Some of these studies were purely philological, consisting of commentaries on and glossaries of the Hippocratic texts, like those written by Dioskorides Phakas, one of the personal physicians of the great Cleopatra. But practical medicine was also well represented by the two schools that then occupied the field of research: the Herophilians and the empiricists, who respectively corresponded to the dogmatics and the skeptics in the domain of philosophy. Each of these groups distinguished itself in the areas of anatomy—by performing dissections—surgery and, of course, pharmacology. Among the many practitioners of these arts, we can cite Zopyros, an empirical pharmacologist who developed a famous prescription for an antidote for Mithridates, king of Pontos, and another one, aptly called "ambrosia," for his master Auletes.

It is quite certain that all this activity had little influence on practitioners outside the milieu of the royal court and the powerful families of Alexandria, who were in large part influenced by the old Egyptian medicine. With its many specialists, the latter enjoyed a solid reputation, even outside Egypt. Pharaonic medicine was far more ancient than the Hippocratic tradition, and the experience it had gained with the human body thanks to the procedures of the embalmers placed it well ahead of Greek medicine in many areas.

A curious papyrus from the second century B.C.E. illustrates the Greeks' interest in this Egyptian tradition. It is a letter addressed by a mother to her son:

> Learning that you are studying Egyptian writing, I am happy for you and for me, for now at least, on your return to town, you will go to Phaloubes, the specialist in enemas, to teach the boys, and thus you will provide for your old age.[6]

The addressee had left his mother, who lived in Alexandria, to study Egyptian, undoubtedly with native priests. His aim was to work as a teacher in a school where a certain Phaloubes taught a specialty of the Egyptian tradition, which was thus of necessity based on books in the hieratic or Demotic script, which had to be read, interpreted, and even translated into Greek. The "boys" (*paidaria*) were probably young slaves entrusted by their wealthy owners to a specialized teacher, either to become their personal physicians or to be sold as menial therapists in the service of the great foreign homes.

GREEK CULTURE IN THE COUNTRYSIDE

Passing through the gates of Alexandria, one entered a bicultural world. The Greeks who settled in the Egyptian *Chora* brought with them more than just their language, their preconceptions, and their economic interests. Above all, they attempted to maintain the cultural roots of their Hellenism, and to do that, they needed institutional frameworks. The ideal framework, of course, was the *polis*, the Greek city, but the kings did not wish to add more such political entities in Egypt after the unique creation of Ptolemais in Upper Egypt by Ptolemy I. In the various towns and villages where they were numerous, Greeks joined together in associations whose principal goal was the management of *gymnasia*. The *gymnasion* was the basic institution for preserving and developing Greek culture, where the young men of the community—the *epheboi*—received the intellectual and athletic training that distinguished a Greek from a barbarian. For adults, the *gymnasion* was also the community meetingplace and the center of their cultural and athletic activities. The associations collected contributions from their members, donations and perhaps endowments, to enable them to maintain the *gymnasion*. The institution was directed by a *gymnasiarches* elected by the members of the association, a position that was honorary but costly for its holder. He was assisted in his task by other officials, such as the *kosmetes*, who supervised the education of the *epheboi*.

Other, more specialized associations helped to keep Hellenic culture alive, such as those uniting the Dionysiac artists, that is, professionals in theater, poetry, and music. Patronized by the king himself, who maintained strict control over their membership, they were not confined to Alexandria but also extended to Ptolemais and to other cities whose Greek communities had the means to organize dramatic or musical performances. Even in the most remote areas of the countryside, troupes of itinerant actors and mimes must have served to rally a wavering Hellenism, even when they were no more than a band of castanet dancers.[7] Their success can be measured by the numerous terra cotta statuettes, found in rural houses and tombs, representing typical characters from the little plays these troupes performed.

POEMS IN THE MIDST OF ACCOUNTS

The best witnesses to the spread of Greek culture on Egyptian soil are the literary papyri that are sometimes preserved in private archives but were most often reused in mummy cartonnages or tossed onto rubbish heaps. These are sometimes meticulous copies stemming from the workshops of Alexandrian copyists and duly checked by a *diorthotes* (corrector). Such rolls, which were costly, had their place in the libraries of *gymnasia* or in the homes of well-to-do amateurs. More often, they are partial copies made by individuals at the local level, made from published copies as an exercise or simply as a diversion, or sometimes to be sent to isolated correspondents who had requested them. Finally, there are numerous school exercises, usually written in the maladroit handwriting of an *ephebos*.

The relative frequency of the various genres and authors serves to indicate the interests of these amateurs in belles-lettres isolated in the Egyptian countryside.[8] Thus, poetry decidedly outweighs prose. Since the Homeric epics constituted the basis of a Greek education, Homer was by far the most commonplace author, and the *Iliad* seems to have been more popular than the *Odyssey*. Running far behind are theatrical works, especially Euripides among the tragedians, followed by Menander and the New Comedy. It is noteworthy that Aeschylus and Sophocles were much less well appreciated, while Aristophanes was downright scorned. Certain scientific or technical texts must have been owned for professional use, such as medical texts, which one would expect to find in the home of a practitioner. In the same manner, the speeches of Demosthenes could have been used by a lawyer as models for his pleas.

Certain individual cases shed light on the prevailing cultural universe in a rather interesting manner. Among a group of receipts and accounting documents written on *ostraca* dating to the beginning of the second century B.C.E. and stored in the corner of a cellar at Philadelphia in the Faiyum were discovered five potsherds on which a single unknown hand had copied, as a schoolboy exercise, brief excerpts from classical authors (Homer, Hesiod, Euripides, etc.), along with an epigraph in distichs, a burlesque epitaph dedicated to the memory of a certain Kleitorios. This brief original poem, whose content is forthrightly pornographic, must have been written by the person who copied the other fragments, for Kleitorios, the object of the raillery, was a real person whose signature appears in the accounts from the same find.[9] We thus have an example of the learned amusements in which the young men who learned to write in a village in the Faiyum could indulge themselves.

Again in the Faiyum but at least three generations later, we unexpectedly find some literary extracts amid the abundant official documents left behind by the *komogrammateus* Menches. In fact, a papyrus with the text of a royal decree also contains a poetic anthology: a paradoxical lamentation by Helen over the infidelity of Menelaos, a description of nature, three amorous distichs, and a prose obscenity partly reproduced by the scribe on yet another papyrus. It is possible that Menches took advantage of a business trip to Arsinoe, the capital of the nome, to copy, in a library or the home of an individual, some texts that had caught his attention and today serve to inform us of his level of education, his tastes, and his interests.[10]

In a different setting, the archive of the recluses at the Serapeum presents an even more interesting case. Ptolemaios and Apollonios, the sons of Glaukias, did not have just mystical and material preoccupations, as our account of their adventures in an earlier chapter might have led the reader to believe. They were also aware of cultural pleasures, even if the exact nature of their curiosity can be debated. Among their papers was a beautiful copy of a treatise on astronomy, decorated with explanatory figures conveniently inserted in the text, making it the oldest illustrated book in Greek literature. This work, entitled the *Art of Eudoxos* (Figure 40), is a summary of the theories of Eudoxos of Knidos, the famous mathematician-astronomer and geographer of the fourth century B.C.E., perhaps compiled by a certain Leptines at the behest of one of the Ptolemaic monarchs. It contains the correspondences between the lunar and solar cycles, and the risings and settings of a certain number of stars and constellations. Pharaonic influence is

FIGURE 40. Portion of the *Art of Eudoxos*, Louvre N 2325. © Maurice and Pierre Chuzeville/Musée du Louvre. Photo courtesy of The Louvre.

evident in certain vignettes representing a mummified ibis and a solar scarab, as well as in the attention given to Egyptian calendrical usages.

It is probable that Ptolemaios owned this treatise because of the astrological implications he could draw from it and that must have been akin to his divinatory preoccupations. In this, he was following a trend that was at that time new among the Graeco-Egyptian population, whose infatuation with this new science would soon eclipse all other methods of predicting the future of an individual.[12]

On the verso of this papyrus were copies of several official and private texts whose subject matter and whose affected, verbose style seem to show that these are in fact models drawn from collections of sample letters.[13] Ptolemaios and his brother must have drawn on them for inspiration in writing their own correspondence and the numerous reports with which they inundated the authorities. All these texts were from the hand of professional scribes, and since they include a copy of a royal letter addressed to Dionysios, the *strategos* of Memphis, we can infer that it was the latter who had this disparate collection composed by his own people for the benefit of the sons of Glaukos, who were his protégés for a time. Their interest in acquiring such a compilation seems more utilitarian than cultural, and while the astronomical text could only have had a much more indirect practical application, the use of stylistic models demonstrates at least a social goal of passing for cultivated Hellenes.

It appears, however, that for our two brothers, culture was a means of rising above the sordid milieu into which they had sunk. If not, why would they have owned a philosophico-grammatical treatise on negations? This was scarcely an appealing text, but they must have appreciated the many citations from classical poets: Euripides, Sappho, Alkman, Anakreon, and so forth.[14] This interest in poetry is also revealed in the long extracts copied by both Ptolemaios and the adolescent Apollonios, sometimes after having learned them by heart. In this anthology of choice excerpts, we find an otherwise unknown play from the New Comedy, as well as Euripides' *Medea*, and *The Carians*, a lost tragedy by Aeschylus.[15]

As intriguing as that might seem, these extracts were more than just a selection from a popular anthology of their day, which they might have consulted. Curious correspondences between the narrative content of the citations and the actual life situation of the two copyists suggest that the latter deliberately chose these texts because they felt they saw in them an echo of their own condition. A single example suffices to show this. After having copied part of the prologue of Euripides' *Telephos,* a piece in which the hero, an Arcadian, laments his destiny as a Greek exiled among the barbarians of Mysia, Apollonios wrote: "Apollonios the Macedonian, a Macedonian, I say!"[16] It is clear that the young man viewed himself among the Egyptians as a latter-day Telephos among the barbarians. In this case, cultural appetite was born of a vague sense of rupture, of an impossible situation between two worlds, which led him to seek literary archetypes.

APOLLONIOS AND THE LAST PHARAOH

We should not conclude from this last notation that Apollonios had made a choice between two competing cultural models. Nothing is that simple. Apollonios did not disdain to copy, in his own faulty hand, a typical piece of pharaonic literature, the *Dream of Nectanebo,* a story about the last king of the last native dynasty. Asleep in a Memphite temple, the pharaoh dreamed of an appearance of the goddess Isis, enthroned in a barque of papyrus, in the midst of a divine assembly. The god Onuris—whom the author identifies with the Greek Ares—addressed Isis, complaining that Nectanebo had failed to complete the construction of his temple. Upon awakening, the king asked the priests for a report on the state of this sanctuary. Since it seemed that only the hieroglyphic texts had yet to be carved, a certain Peteese presented himself to complete the work in a very short time. Once paid in advance, however, he preferred to spend several days drinking and making merry. It was then that a very beautiful girl passed nearby. . . .[17]

The text copied in Greek by Apollonios breaks off at this point. Though we do not have the original version, the story, which belongs to a narrative genre held in great esteem in ancient Egypt, can only have been translated or adapted from Egyptian. Its interest to our recluses at the Serapeum, who were experts in oneiromancy, is obvious, and it even influenced Ptolemaios' own dreams, for one of them contains an invocation of Isis[18] which is an obvious, if inferior, version of that made by Onuris in the *Dream of Nectanebo.*

Thus, while vaunting themselves as representatives of Greek culture so as to lay claim to a social Hellenism, the sons of Glaukas also turned to Egyptian traditions in their quest for an intimate contact with the divine. But what real understanding did they have of these traditions? Though nearly all their papers were written in Greek, they were almost certainly bilingual; otherwise, we could not imagine how Ptolemaios was able to spend at least twenty years confined in an almost exclusively Egyptian environment. It is not impossible that Apollonios was able to write at least one account of his dreams in Demotic,[19] though he preferred to copy a Greek version of the *Dream of Nectanebo*, rather than one in Demotic. In addition, though we find Demotic literary texts in their archive, we may wonder whether the brothers actually used them or whether they had simply exchanged papyri with some of their Egyptian colleagues who had copied these works for themselves. The longest of these texts, in three columns, is a series of instructions supposedly addressed by a father to his son. This collection of practical aphorisms belongs to a traditional genre of Egyptian literature, of which it is in fact one of the poorest specimens in terms of its ethical level. There is scarcely anything in it other than truisms ("the wall of a city is its guardian," "do not associate with a bad man") and trivial advice ("do not let any affront by your wife pass, beat her"). Moreover, the text is an exceptionally poor copy, which is curiously evocative of the often-defective Greek of our two recluses. Ptolemaios reused the papyrus to write out one of his many accounts on the verso. Apart from that, nothing indicates that he or his brother ever took an interest in the content of this minor piece of Egyptian literature.[20]

THE NATIVE TEMPLES AS GUARDIANS OF RELIGIOUS CULTURE

The penetration of Greek culture into the cities and countryside of Egypt did not hinder the development of native culture. Quite the contrary, the latter experienced a veritable renaissance under the Ptolemies, coinciding with the renewed prosperity of the temples assured by the Lagide regime. The traditional guardians of this culture were the priests, who provided rigorous training in the writing systems, as well as instruction in sacred and secular literature, in the "houses of life," that is, the combined libraries and schools attached to the temples. The hieroglyphic writing system, along with its cursive equivalent, called hieratic, was a heritage from the past conveying a language dead for more than fifteen centuries—the classical Egyptian of the Middle Kingdom. Though they were used for sacred texts, this writing system and language were not rigid expressions of an obsolete and unchanging body of thought. Although the language was artificial because it was no longer spoken, the hieroglyphic writing system, which was both ideographic and phonetic, was open-ended, always offering the possibility of inventing new signs, new combinations, and new sound values. The temple scribes of the Ptolemaic period set themselves to exploring all the possibilities of this system, which until then had been subject to relatively

FIGURE 41. Enhanced photograph of a portion of a relief depicting the Khonsu Cosmogony. Temple of Khonsu at Karnak. Photo courtesy of Leonard H. Lesko.

rigid conventions. The hieroglyphic texts carved on temple walls in this period and sometimes on private stelae thus pose a certain difficulty for the modern translator, who must solve complex and learned word plays in order to read a commonplace invocation or an ordinary divine epithet.[21] Along with such intellectual diversions, we find an ostentatious erudition and an excessive purism that often confer an artificial archaism on the texts.

From Philae to Dendara, the temples erected in this period were overrun with texts, ranging from simple dedications and offering scene captions to detailed accounts of founding myths (Figure 41) or collections of pharmacological prescriptions. In this regard, the temples of the Ptolemaic period considerably expanded on the much more laconic information to be found on the walls of earlier temples. They constitute an irreplaceable corpus of texts for our knowledge of Egyptian religion, and not only in its latest form, for they include very ancient, scarcely altered rituals, along with catalogues of sacred geography, including cities and districts that had long since disappeared.

More so than the content of the texts, their location in the various parts of the temple, in relation to that of the innumerable scenes that were depicted, reveals the erudition of these priests, who conceived of each of these temples as a veritable microcosm—as the perfect illustration of an entire cosmogony. A Ptolemaic temple was a world unto itself and a totally closed world at that. But it was not a summary of all of Egyptian culture, which, happily enough, largely escaped its stifling framework.

DEMOTIC: LIVING LANGUAGE AND NEW LITERATURE

Parallel to their patient labors at learned exegesis of ancient myths and rituals, the same priests developed a much more lively and original literature. To do that, they abandoned the old language of the hieroglyphs for the vernacular, which was nearly as removed from the former as modern French is from Latin. The Egyptian spoken in this period was normally written down in Demotic, a cursive script derived from hieroglyphs but in which the latter were simplified and joined by ligatures to a point where the original signs were no longer recognizable. Demotic (the term denotes both a writing system and a stage of the language) originated in Lower Egypt, undoubtedly around the eighth century B.C.E. During Dynasty 26 (seventh and sixth centuries), it spread progressively through all of Egypt as the sole writing system for administrative and private documents. Later, it replaced hieratic in all but funerary and religious contexts. In the Ptolemaic period, Demotic and Greek were rivals at the lower levels of the bureaucracy and in the writing of private documents. But Demotic also gave literate Egyptians a new means of expression, one free of the constraints of the classical tradition.

Nevertheless, most of the genres developed in Demotic sprang from the heritage of the ancient pharaonic background. It is striking that the inevitable confrontation with Greek texts had so little effect on this nascent literature, as though literate Egyptians deliberately ignored this new source of inspiration, though there are many indications that they were at least superficially acquainted with it. It could be argued that a desire to affirm Egyptian cultural identity entailed an avoidance of any contamination stemming from the dominant culture. More simply, it is possible that the broad outlines of Demotic literature had already been established prior to the Macedonian invasion, though only later copies are known. In the choice of narrative themes developed in many of the Demotic stories, there is a manifest desire to revive past glory; these are often epic or fantastic adventures involving great historical figures. As we have already seen, Nectanebo II, the last native pharaoh, was the hero of an Egyptian story translated into Greek, and it is surely not irrelevant that this same Nectanebo later appears in the *Alexander Romance* in the role of the physical father of Alexander the Great. Though this incredible fiction was concocted in the Roman period, its evident goal was to appeal to Egyptian sentiments of nationalism by making the Macedonian conqueror into the heir of the ancient pharaonic dynasties.

EGYPTIAN STORIES AND ROMANCES

Not all the favorite heroes of Egyptian literature were as flattering to national pride, however. A notable case is the famous Khaemwese, a son of Ramesses II, whom the Demotic texts call Setne. The stories in which he figures undoubtedly stem from Memphis, home to the historical Khaemswese, who had been the high priest of Ptah. In a papyrus in the Cairo Museum dating to the second century b.c.e.,[22] he is presented as a sort of magician who explores the Memphite necropolis in search of the most powerful of all magical papyri, the Book of Thoth. He finally discovers it in the tomb of an ancient prince, but the ghost of the latter's wife makes an appearance to preserve the secrets of the precious papyrus. She tells him how her husband had stolen the book from the god Thoth, and how the latter took revenge by drowning his entire family. This warning does not dissuade Setne, who nevertheless must confront the mummy of the prince himself in a supernatural game of chess. Though he loses the first round, Setne succeeds in making off with the papyrus. He thus discovers the god's magic, but he is seduced by a woman named Tabubu, who does not consent to satisfying his desire until after she compels him to sacrifice all his goods and even the lives of his children! At the moment he beds her, she vanishes, and he finds himself completely naked in front of Pharaoh and his retinue. Realizing that he has been the victim of a dream sent by the gods by way of a reprimand, he consents to return the book to the tomb and pay homage to the deceased prince.

The structure of this episodic tale is typical of a genre meant only to entertain. Such stories might also have been intended to be read to an illiterate audience, like the fables of the *Thousand and One Nights,* which was undoubtedly the preferred means of transmission for popular culture. Equally popular was the mischief, or humor, in this earthy evocation of the wondrous tribulations of a person more to be scorned for his covetousness than praised for his talents as a magician. He appears in other adventures known from later papyri, wherein he is again confronted by redoubtable sorcerers and vengeful ghosts. In the course of one of them, his desire to know the post-mortem destiny reserved for the rich and the poor takes him to the netherworld, like an Egyptian Dante. There, he sees the damned suffering various punishments, among which we can recognize borrowings from Greek myths, such as those of Tantalos and Oknos.[23]

Other stories with recurrent characters are not without reminiscences of the Homeric poems, at least in certain details. In fact, we encounter both fierce single combats and general melees between opposing armies. The earliest papyrus of this sort recounts the struggle for the possession of the prebend of the high priest of Amun.[24] The episode takes place in the reign of a certain Pedubaste, a petty king of the delta who lived in the eighth or seventh century B.C.E. He strives to have his legitimacy recognized at Thebes, to the detriment of another pretender, a young priest who, along with twelve Asiatic mercenaries, makes off with the sacred barque of the god. The events are confused and the characters numerous, but the context and the themes invoked deal exclusively with the interests of the Egyptian priestly class.

It is not the same with other adventures whose chief protagonist is a certain Inaros.[25] The latter is made to battle both fabulous animals, such as a griffin who emerges from the Red Sea, and foreign invaders, specifically the Assyrians. After his death, an interminable war breaks out among various Egyptian princes over the possession of his breastplate. Other conflicts saw Egyptians contending with a race of female warriors, an allusion to the Amazons, or with the Babylonians. Nearly all these texts, which are varied in their subject matter but tedious in their treatments of it, are known to us from papyri of the Roman period. Though their settings and characters remain Egyptian, the psychology of the protagonists and the situations they confront are clearly influenced by the *Iliad* and the *Odyssey*.

WISDOM AND SATIRE

We have already mentioned a Demotic text belonging to the genre of wisdom literature. This was one of the most ancient of Egyptian literary traditions, undoubtedly going back to the Old Kingdom. Of the two principal works in this genre handed down in Demotic, the *Instruction of Ankhsheshonqy*[26] is very similar in style and content to the wisdom text on the papyrus from the Serapeum noted above, though it has a long introductory narrative relating the misadventures of its putative author. Imprisoned on the false accusation of plotting against the king, Ankhsheshonqy represents the archetype of the "just sufferer," like Job in the Bible or the Assyrian Ahiqar.[27]

By way of contrast, the second of these works, preserved on Papyrus Insinger,[28] is a highly original and cleverly organized text. Like older wisdom literature, it opposes the wise man, who maintains control over himself and respects divine law, to the fool, a slave to his instincts whose inevitable crimes must be punished by an immanent justice. But onto this classic schema, the author has superimposed another one, paradoxical and new in Egyptian thought, which exalts the transcendence of the plans of the divine; since all people are subject to a destiny that is in essence unpredictable, wisdom can just as well lead to misfortune as folly to prosperity. Thus, "it is not the wise man who saves who will enjoy a profit, or the fool who spends who will become poor,"[29] and "he who cares about tomorrow does not achieve his goal, while the one who does not care is protected by fate," for "fate and fortune go and come as the god commands."[30] This notion of an inscrutable divine will to which the wise can only submit without comprehension, is far removed from traditional Egyptian concepts regarding the relationship between the human and the divine, which was based on reciprocity and the immanence of retribution. A veritable treatise on theodicy, Papyrus Insinger is one of the most accomplished products of Egyptian thought and testifies to the intellectual and moral level of at least some of the native priests in the Ptolemaic period.

Many other texts bear witness to this prodigious intellectual activity, which continued into the Roman period, down to at least the second century of our own era, though we cannot assign precise dates to works that have come down to us in copies that are often much later than their composition. Some of these works belong to genres that were new in Egyptian literature, such as the satirical poem[31] denouncing the misdeeds of a drunken harpist, gluttonous and of questionable talent, who earns his pittance by going from village to village, livening up weddings and festivals while sowing disorder everywhere:

> He disputes with the party-goers, shouting, "I can't sing when I'm hungry, I can't hold my harp and recite without my fill of wine!" And he drinks wine like two people and eats the meat of three, the ration of five in all![32]

The style of the poem is difficult, and it abounds in rare words and inventive metaphors. Some have detected similarities with the Greek genre of invective, as illustrated, for example, by Archilochos and Hipponax, or with certain tirades of Aristophanes, yet the object of ridicule is a classic figure in pharaonic literature, and the many allusions to Egyptian deities (Mut, Horus, Seth, Harsaphes) argue for a purely native origin.

HELLENISM AT EDFU [33]

Egyptian and Hellenic culture thus coexisted like two completely partitioned worlds, two nearly incompatible modes of expression and thought that could by chance be practiced by the same individuals but could not really be blended together. At Edfu, far from Alexandria, we can observe what is perhaps the most striking example of this culture gap. Here, toward the end of the second century B.C.E., in the shadow of the magnificent temple (Figure 42) whose decoration was just being completed by Egyptian artists under the direction of the *hierogrammateis,* a certain Herodes composed epitaphs in Greek verse on behalf of the local military officers, who had Hellenic pretensions. His clients, who demanded Greek names in

FIGURE 42. Temple of Horus at Edfu. Photo © Michael S. Schreiber.

their metric epitaphs, reserved their Egyptian names for the hieroglyphic stelae that they also commissioned from native specialists. A certain Apollonios, whose father Ptolemaios had received the diadem distinguishing "relatives of the king" from the hand of Ptolemy VIII, was the same person as Pashu son of Pamenches, the "great general and commandant, unique friend, chief of the cavalry. . . ." In the Egyptian manner, he brandished all his civil and religious titles on his hieroglyphic stela, while his Greek epitaph simply evokes the deceased's career in the elegiac style:

> Yea, I am Apollonios, son of the famous Ptolemaios . . . whose loyalty in fact took him to the interior of lands and as far as the Ocean. That is why, as I contemplated the magnificent renown of my father, a desire was aroused in me to attain the same worth and to choose a troop worthy of my noble homeland, this sacred and lofty city of Phoibos, accompanying the friends of my father in their sailing . . . when the War of Scepters arose in Syria. I was devoted and . . . loyal, and I prevailed over all with my lance and my daring, but Fortune, who twists the threads of our days, crushed me—why must you learn it?—just when I was dreaming of a sweet return. I had not had my fill of life, however, nor had I satisfied my heart with the love of the children I had left at home.

From this poem, we understand that Apollonios, as the captain of a native detachment from Edfu ("sacred and lofty city of Phoibos"), left for Syria with queen Cleopatra III at the time of the Judaeo–Syro–Egyptian conflict of 103–101 B.C.E. (the "War of Scepters"), though he did not return alive; he was undoubtedly struck down by illness or the victim of an ordinary accident, rather than having died a glorious death in battle, which our versifier would certainly not have failed to mention.

Each of the memorials set up in his honor adheres so thoroughly to the conventions of its respective cultural environment that the points of contact between them seem practically nonexistent. Scarcely any biographical cliché in one of them finds an echo in the other. These families of military men, who were natives or perhaps of mixed origin, nevertheless felt a pressing need to advertise their double heritage, not through hybrid works but by means of monuments that were culturally pure, Egyptian inscriptions conforming to pharaonic tradition and Greek poems expressing a Hellenism that, albeit provincial, was intended to be elegant and refined.

CONCLUSION

The fears that gradually mounted among the citizenry of Alexandria during the month of July, 30 B.C.E., as Octavian's troops approached, were quickly dissipated when the Roman solemnly declared his intention to spare the city and its inhabitants, "in the first place for the sake of Alexander, their founder, secondly, out of admiration for the beauty and grandeur of the city, and third, to please his friend Areios."[1] Only certain relatives and associates of Antony and the queen fell victim to a persecution that was otherwise rather restrained. But the new master of Egypt was unfavorably disposed toward the land, for which he felt distrust and even hatred: of the previous dynasty, of cults he considered decadent and barbarous, and of the licentious atmosphere of the capital. But above and beyond these prejudices, fear that Egypt's riches could serve the interests of some politician who might compete with him for the empire prompted him to take various measures intended to ward off such a danger. Thus, he forbade all Roman senators and even high-ranking members of the equestrian order to enter the new province without his permission. Moreover, he did not entrust the province to a proconsul or a legate of senatorial rank, as was the custom with provinces of such importance, but to a simple knight with the title of prefect. However, the prefecture of Egypt was placed near the head of the equestrian *cursus,* just behind that of the praetor of Rome, and it was thus entrusted to experienced persons.[2]

The suspicions of Octavian—who would soon take the name Augustus (Figures 43 and 44)—were far from being unjustified, and he was obliged to dismiss the first prefect he named, Cornelius Gallus, for behaving more like an independent sovereign than a zealous

FIGURE 43. Marble statue head of Augustus Caesar (Octavian). Presumably made in Italy but reputedly found in Egypt. Walters Art Gallery 23.21. Photo courtesy of The Walters Art Gallery, Baltimore.

FIGURE 44. Augustus making an offering to Thoth, Shu, and Tefnut. Temple of el-Dakka in Nubia. After J.-F. Champollion, *Monuments de l'Égypte et de la Nubie,* Vol. I (Paris, 1835), Pl. LV *bis.*

functionary of the emperor.[3] A whole new bureaucracy was also set up at the top, around the prefect, and the positions were entrusted to Roman officials who were mostly members of the equestrian order. Only the local administration remained in the hands of Helleno-Egyptians but with its powers reduced; the *strategoi* became purely civilian governors, while their military responsibilities were assumed by the Roman army. The latter, three legions strong, was settled in various fortresses and garrisons, the most important of which were at Alexandria, Babylon (now Old Cairo) near Memphis, and Thebes. While the Ptolemaic system of cleruchies continued for some time, its beneficiaries became simple landowners relieved of any obligation to perform military service.

The changes brought about by the Roman occupation were not limited to the administration and the army. Augustus had economic and tax objectives for the new province, aimed at provisioning the city of Rome, which had by then become the world's largest metropolis, during at least a third of the year. As a result, there was a reorganization of the taxes on land and individuals. Their tax burden was now heavier, and the revenues were collected more efficiently, with less by way of tax relief or exemptions.

Every adult inhabitant of Egypt was obligated to pay a head tax that varied according to the location and status of the individual and that hit the native population in the countryside harder than the Greek citizens. This tighter fiscal control quickly led to revolts, like the one that once again broke out in the Thebaid and that Cornelius Gallus, the first prefect, had to suppress.[4]

In the same vein, a parallel administration assumed more and more importance, that of the "Special Account" (*Idios Logos*). Under the Ptolemies, it had managed the personal possessions of the sovereigns; now, the Special Account became an instrument for exploiting the land for the sole benefit of the emperor. To this end, this bureau henceforth took charge of all fields that were confiscated or unclaimed by heirs, as well as the sacred lands of the temples, which saw themselves deprived of ownership of all the agricultural domains they still possessed. Instead, they were obliged to choose between being paid a rent (*syntaxis*) by the state or the possibility of renting part of their former lands on favorable terms. From that time on, the temples lost what little economic independence the Ptolemies had allowed them, falling under a control that was later aggravated by the appointment of a "High Priest of Alexandria and all Egypt," who was in fact a Roman knight charged with overseeing the priests and the cults.[5]

One obsession of the Romans was to clarify the issue of the legal status of individuals. The distinction between citizens and noncitizens was a basic one to them, and they reinforced the barriers separating Egyptians and Greeks, which a long cohabitation had rendered rather permeable. In theory, Greeks had to live in the capitals of the nomes, and in the future, they alone would have access to the *gymnasia*. A whole series of regulations, curiously attached to the "Code of the Special Account" (the "*Gnomon* of the *Idios Logos*") defined how this veritable social segregation was to be applied. Three classes of free persons were clearly defined: Egyptians, the Hellenes of the nome capitals, and Roman citizens. Heavy fines and confiscation of property were inflicted on persons who attempted to cross these barriers in matters of inheritance, marriage, or otherwise. Candidates for the *gymnasion* had to submit themselves to a strict examination called an *epikrisis*, whose aim was to verify their status as Hellenes and which implacably barred any intrusion by persons of native origin, thus preventing social advancement.

A benefit of this policy was the rapid formation of a middle class jealous of its privileged status and that assumed, after a fashion, its responsibilities at the local level; in contrast, the Ptolemies had counted on the gradual Hellenization of the upper classes of native society, intentionally allowing the question of personal status to remain vague. The Romanization of Egypt thus took the form of a progressive standardization of the land, comparable to the other provinces of the empire, whose innumerable local communities were provided with a certain autonomy in managing their affairs and which in return contributed loyally to the general prosperity by accepting the necessary heavy responsibilities. But this process of leveling was much slower and more gradual than elsewhere, and for a rather long time, the emperors maintained a unique situation that in part allowed for the survival of the ancient pharaonic traditions but, more importantly and more prosaically, had to do with the predominant role of Egyptian wheat in the feeding of the Roman *plebs.*

Long a domain reserved for the emperor, who regarded it as a possession that was both reliable and of unequaled profitability, Egypt had to wait three centuries before it became, under Diocletian, a province like any other, with the elimination of its separate system of coinage and the last special features of its administration. This moment happened to coincide with the death throes of the old pharaonic civilization, as a new religion was in the process of sweeping it away, along with its ancient deities. It would be too deterministic a view of history to see the fall of the Lagides as the starting point of this destructive process that the evolution of Roman Egypt entailed. In any case, it was certainly not thus that the whole of Egyptian society, undoubtedly weary of a regime responsible for disorder and ruin, experienced this period of annexation, though the financial disadvantages of the new administration were soon sorely felt.

Nevertheless, it is possible that the annexation dealt a death blow to a change that had been occurring—a tendency toward a gradual fusion of the descendants of Greek immigrants in the *Chora* with the middle and upper classes of native Egyptian society. In essence, such a fusion could only have been the product of mixed marriages and a certain amount of cultural exchange. The former were heavily penalized by the new authorities. As for the latter, while the Roman administration neither could nor wished to hinder the Egyptianization of Greeks on the level of religious and funerary beliefs, it could considerably impede the Hellenization of Egyptians by the social segregation it imposed, which was especially manifest in its tight restrictions on admission to the *gymnasia.* It was perhaps by forcing native society into cultural withdrawal and an ossification of its traditions that the Romans spoiled the only Lagide legacy that held out promise to the land: the beginnings of a bicultural Graeco-Egyptian society. Otherwise, it is true that the annexation facilitated a more rapid spread of Egyptian cults throughout the Roman empire, but this extremely Hellenized and insipid reflection of pharaonic religion, whose popularity as far away as Britain was assured more by its exotic nature than by its actual content, was effectively cut off from its roots and deprived of any ties to the vitality of the culture that the priests of the Faiyum and the Thebais, in their confused sense of its inevitable end, were trying to preserve by means of one last, remarkable burst of intellectual effort.[6]

ABBREVIATIONS

Äg. Abh.	Ägyptologische Abhandlungen
Äg. Forsch.	Ägyptologische Forschungen
AIPHO	Annuaire de l'Institut de philologie et d'histoire orientales
AJA	*American Journal of Archaeology*
ALUB	Annales littéraires de l'Université de Besançon
APF	*Archiv für Papyrusforschung und verwandte Gebiete*
AS	*Ancient Society*
BASP	*Bulletin of the American Society of Papyrologists*
Bibl. d'Ét.	Biblothèque d'Étude
Bibl. Gén.	Bibliothèque Générale
BGU	*Ägyptische Urkunden aus den Staatlichen Museum zu Berlin, Griechische Urkunden* (Berlin, 1895)
BIFAO	*Bulletin de l'Institut français d'archéologie orientale du Caire*
BKP	Beiträge zur klassischen Philologie
BSFE	*Bulletin de la Société française d'égyptologie*
CdE	*Chronique d'Égypte*
Coll. Hell.	Collectanea Hellenistica
CP	The Carlsberg Papyri
CRIPEL	*Cahiers de recherches de l'Institut de papyrologie et d'égyptologie de Lille*
CST	Collection Signes des temps
DMAHA	Dutch Monographs on Ancient History and Archaeology
Dem. Stud.	Demotische Studien
EVO	*Egitto e Vicino Oriente*
GM	*Göttinger Miszellen*
JEA	*Journal of Egyptian Archaeology*
JJP	*Journal of Juristic Papyrology*
MÄS	Münchner ägyptologische Studien
MIFAO	Mémoires publiés par les membres de l'Institut français d'archéologie orientale du Caire
MPÖN	Mitteilungen aus der Papyrussammlung der österreichischen Nationalbibliothek (Papyrus Erherzog Rainer)
MU	Manuali universitari
OLA	Orientalia Lovaniensia Analecta
OLP	*Orientalia Lovaniensia Periodica*
Pap. Brux.	Papyrologica Bruxellensia
P. L. Bat.	Papyrologica Lugduno-Batava
P. Ent.	O. Guérard, *ENTEUXIS: Requêtes et plaintes addressées au roi d'Égypte au IIIe Siècle avant J.-C.* (Cairo, 1931–1932)

P. Grenf. II	B. P. Grenfell and A. S. Hunt, *New Classical Fragments and Other Greek and Latin Papyri* (Oxford, 1897)
P. Lips.	L. Mitteis, *Griechische Urkunden der Papyrussammlung zu Leipzig,* vol. I (Leipzig, 1906)
P. Ryl. Dem.	F. Ll. Griffith, *Catalogue of the Demotic Papyri in the J. Rylands Library,* 3 vols. (Manchester, 1909)
P. Tebt.	B. P. Grenfell, A. S. Hunt, J. G. Smyly, E. J. Goodspeed, and C. C. Edgar, *The Tebtunis Papyri,* 3 vols. (London, 1902–38)
RAPH	Recherches d'archéologie, de philologie et d'histoire
RdE	*Revue d'Égyptologie*
RdT	*Receuil de travaux relatifs à la philologie et à l'archéologie égyptiennes et assyriennes*
RGRW	Religions in the Graeco-Roman World
SAOC	Studies in Ancient Oriental Civilization
SB	F. Priesigke and F. Bilabel, *Sammelbuch Griechischer Urkunden aus Ägypten,* (Strassburg, 1915–)
SCO	*Studi classici e orientali*
SD	Studia Demotica
Select Pap.	A. S. Hunt and C. C. Edgar, *Select Papyri,* 2 vols. (rpr. Cambridge, Mass., 1970)
SH	Studia Hellenistica
SSA	Studi di storia antica
SO	Sources orientales
SSEAP	SSEA Publications
THF	Trierer historische Forschungen
UPZ	U. Wilcken, *Urkunden der Ptolemäerzeit (Ältere Funde),* 2 vols. (Berlin, 1927–57; rpr., Berlin, 1977)
Urk. II	K. Sethe, *Hieroglyphische Urkunden der griechisch-römischen Zeit* (Leipzig, 1904; rpr., Milan, 1977)
ZPE	*Zeitschrift für Papyrologie und Epigraphik*
ZSS	*Zeitschrift der Savigny-Stiftung*

NOTES

INTRODUCTION

1. Ilse Becher, *Das Bild der Kleopatra in der griechischen und lateinischen Literatur* (Berlin, 1966).
2. See especially Diodorus Siculus, *Library of History,* Book I, translated by E. Murphy as *Diodorus: On Egypt* (Jefferson, N.C., 1985). Strabo, *Geography,* Book XVII, translated by H. L. Jones under the title *The Geography of Strabo,* vol. VIII (London, 1982), stands out by reason of the precision of its description.
3. Among the many biographies of Cleopatra, we may cite H. Volkmann, *Kleopatra* (Munich, 1953) and M. Grant, *Cleopatra* (London, 1972).
4. See E. G. Turner, *Greek Papyri: An Introduction,* 2d ed. (Oxford, 1980); O. Montevecchi, *La Papirologia,* 2d ed. (Milan, 1988); P. W. Pestman, *The New Papyrological Primer,* 2d ed. (Leiden, 1994). A selection of Greek papyri translated into English can be found in A. S. Hunt and C. C. Edgar, *Select Papyri,* 2 vols. (London, 1932–34, with many reprintings). For the Demotic texts, see now M. Depauw, *A Companion to Demotic Studies* (Brussels, 1997).
5. Montevecchi, *La Papirologia,* p. 34.
6. Thus the excavations conducted since 1989 at the site of Tebtunis by the French Institute of Oriental Archaeology, Cairo, and the University of Milan under the direction of C. Gallazi.
7. See the list of sources in L. Ricketts, "The Administration of Ptolemaic Egypt under Cleopatra VII," Ph.D. diss. University of Minnesota, 1980, pp. 114–136; idem, "The Administration of Late Ptolemaic Egypt," in Janet H. Johnson, ed., *Life in a Multi-Cultural Society: Egypt from Cambyses to Constantine and Beyond,* SAOC 51 (Chicago, 1992), pp. 275–81.
8. P. W. Pestman, *Chronologie égyptienne d'après les textes démotiques* (P. L. Bat. 15) (Leiden, 1967), p. 72.
9. H. J. Thissen, *Die demotischen Graffiti von Medinet Habu* (Sommerhausen, 1989), p. 17.
10. C. Orrieux, *Les Papyrus de Zénon: L'Horizon d'un Grec en Égypte au IIIe siècle av. J.-C.* (Paris, 1983); idem, *Zénon de Caunos, parépidèmos et le destin grec* (Paris, 1985); W. Clarysse and K. Vandorpe, *Zénon: Un homme d'affaires grec à l'ombre des pyramides* (Louvain, 1995).

CHAPTER 1: HISTORICAL PERSPECTIVE

GENERAL SOURCES

A. Bouché-Leclercq. *Histoire des Lagides,* 4 vols. Paris, 1903–7.
E. Bevan. *A History of Egypt under the Ptolemaic Dynasty.* London, 1927.
G. Hölbl. *Geschichte des Ptolemäerreiches.* Darmstadt, 1994.
E. Will. *Histoire politique du monde hellénistique, 323–30 av. J.-C.* 2d ed. 2 vols. Nancy, 1979–82.
F. W. Walbank et al. *The Cambridge Ancient History.* 2d ed. Vol. VII, Pt. 1, *The Hellenistic World.* Cambridge, 1984.

1. F. Jacoby, *Die Fragmente der griechischen Historiker,* no. 234 (Berlin and Leiden, 1923–58).
2. A. Laronde, *Cyrène et la Libye hellénistique: Libykai Historiai* (Paris, 1987), pp. 445–46.
3. *BGU* 1762. Translation adapted from C. Préaux, "Esquisse d'une histoire des révolutions égyptiennes sous les Lagides," *CdE* 11, no. 22 (1936): 551–52.
4. H. Heinen, "Rom und Ägypten von 51 bis 47 v. Chr.," diss., University of Tübingen, 1966.
5. See M. Chauveau, "Ères nouvelles et corégences en Égypte ptolémaïque," *Akten des 21. Int. Papyrologenkongresses in Berlin 1995, APF* 43, no. 2 (1997): pp. 168–70.
6. *BGU* 1730 = A. S. Hunt and C. C. Edgar, *Select Papyri,* vol. 2, no. 209.
7. "Year 1 which is also year 3," see T. C. Skeat, *JEA* 48 (1962): 100–105.
8. H. J. Thissen, *Die demotischen Griffiti von Medinet Habu* (Sommerhausen, 1989), no. 44, pp. 18–20. Papyrus Cairo Dem. 30616 a and b; see Chauveau, "Ères nouvelles et corégences."
9. A. B. Brett, "A New Cleopatra Tetradrachm of Ascalon," *AJA* 41 (1937): 452–63. The coins are dated to 50/49 and 49/48 (?).
10. See the famous account by Plutarch in his "Life of Pompey," 83–86.
11. See Th. Schrapel, *Das Reich der Kleopatra* (Trier, 1996), pp. 225–34.

CHAPTER 2: GREEK PHARAOHS AND THEIR SUBJECTS

RECENT BIBLIOGRAPHY

H. Hauben. "Aspects du culte des souverains à l'époque des Lagides." In *Egitto e storia antica dall'ellenismo all'età araba (Atti Coll. int. Bologna 1987).* Bologna, 1989, pp. 441–67.
W. Huss. *Der makedonische König und die ägyptischen Priester.* Stuttgart, 1994.
L. Koenen. "Ägyptische Königsideologie am Ptolemäerhof." In *Egypt and the Hellenistic World (Proc. Int. Coll. Leuven).* Louvain, 1983, pp. 143–90.

S. Schloz. "Das Königtum der Ptolemäer—Grenzgänge der Ideologie." In *Aspekte Spätägyptische Kultur (Festschrift E. Winter)*. Mainz, 1994, pp. 227–34.

1. See R. A. Hazzard, *Ptolemaic Coins: An Introduction for Collectors* (Toronto, 1995), p. 3 and fig. 6.
2. Known from the famous description of Kallixenes of Rhodes preserved in Athenaios, *Deipnosophistai* V 197 c 203 c. For a French translation, see A. Bernand, *Alexandrie la Grande* (Paris, 1966; rpr. Paris, 1996), pp. 305–12.
3. Hazzard, *Ptoemaic Coins*, p. 4 and fig. 7.
4. See, e.g., R. S. Bianchi et al., *Cleopatra's Egypt: Age of the Ptolemies* (New York, 1988), p. 46, fig. 16, pp. 103–4 (no. 14), pp. 170–72 (no. 66).
5. See G. Hölbl, *Geschichte des Ptolemäerreiches* (Darmstadt, 1994), pp. 265–69.
6. J. Vercoutter, "Les statues du général Hor, gouverneur d'Héracléopolis, de Busiris et d'Héliopolis," *BIFAO* 49 (1950): 85–114.
7. For example, a great-nephew of Nektanebo I: *Urk.* II, pp. 24–26; see also J.-J. Clère, "Une Statuette du fils aîné du roi Nectanebô," *RdE* 6 (1951): 135–56.
8. D. Mendels, "The Polemical Character of Manetho's *Aegyptiaca*," in *Purposes of History (Proc. Int. Coll. Leuven 1988)* (Louvain, 1990), pp. 91–110.
9. Catalogue général of the Cairo Museum 22182 = *Urk.* II, pp. 11–22.
10. J. K. Winnicki, "Carrying Off and Bringing Home the Statues of the Gods," *JJP* 24 (1994): 149–90; D. Devauchelle, "Le Sentiment antiperse chez les anciens Égyptiens," *Transeuphratène* 9 (1995): 67–80.
11. W. Huss, "Die in ptolemäischer Zeit verfassten Synodal-Dekrete der ägyptischen Priester," *ZPE* 88 (1991): 189–208.
12. H. J. Thissen, *Studien zum Raphiadekret*, BKP 23 (Meisenheim, 1966).
13. S. Quirke and C. Andrews, *The Rosetta Stone* (London, 1988); D. Devauchelle, *La Pierre de Rosette* (Le Havre, 1990).
14. E. Bernand, *Receuil des inscriptions grecques du Fayoum,* vol. II (Cairo, 1981), pp. 30–40 (nos. 112–13).
15. *P. Tebt.* I 5 = *Select Pap.*, vol. II, no. 210, pp. 59–75.
16. D. Bonneau, "Le Souverain d'Égypte voyageait-il sur le Nil en crue?" *CdE* 36, no. 72 (1961): 377–85.
17. A. Bernard, *De Thèbes à Syène* (Paris, 1989), no. 244. See G. Dietze, "Der Streit um die Insel Pso," *AS* 26 (1995): 157–84. It is generally accepted that the second Cleopatra mentioned on this stela is the wife and not the grandmother of Ptolemy IX. The latter was evidently still alive, however, as seems to be proved by an unpublished hieroglyphic text from a chapel at Kalabsha undoubtedly decorated on the occasion of the royal visit.
18. Catalogue général of the Cairo Museum, stela 22181 = *Urk.* II, 28–54. For a translation, see H. de Meulenaere, *Mendès,* vol. II (Warminster, 1976), pp. 174–88.
19. Journal d'entrée of the Cairo Museum, 53147. See Cl. Traunecker, *Coptos: Hommes et Dieux sur le parvis de Geb* (Louvain, 1992), p. 317.

20. Athenaios, *Deipnosophistai* XII, 549 3, translation by H. Heinen, *Ktema* 3 (1978): 189–90.
21. Marcus Justinianus Justinus, *Epitome of the Philippic History of Pompeius Trogus,* XXXVIII 8, 10, translated by Heinen, in *Ktema* 3 (1978): 189–90.
22. H. Heinen, "Die Tryphè des Ptolemaios VIII. Euergetes II.," in *Althistorische Studien H. Bengtson* (Wiesbaden, 1983), pp. 116–28.
23. Plutarch, "Life of Antony," 28.
24. H. Gauthier, *Le Livre des rois d'Égypte,* vol. IV (Cairo, 1916), pp. 136–50.
25. J. von Beckerath, *Handbuch der ägyptischen Königsnamen,* MÄS 20 (Munich, 1984), p. 118.
26. Ibid., p. 119; see, most recently, C. G. Johnson, "Ptolemy V and the Rosetta Stone: The Egyptianisation of the Ptolemaic Kingship," *AS* 26 (1995): 145–55.
27. Harris Stela, lines 8–10. See E. A. E. Reymond, *From the Records of a Priestly Family from Memphis,* Äg. Abh. 38 (Wiesbaden, 1981), pp. 136–50.
28. J. D. Ray, *The Archive of Hor* (London, 1976).
29. Ibid., p. 11, text 1, lines 12–14.
30. Ibid., p. 18, text 2, recto, lines 7–10.
31. Ibid., pp. 18–19, text 2, verso, lines 4–12.
32. Ibid., p. 125.
33. See C. Préaux, "Esquisse d'une histoire des révolutions égyptiennes sous les Lagides," *CdE* 11/22 (1936): 522–52; L. Koenen, "Ein einheimischer Gegenkönig in Ägypten," *CdE* 34/68 (1959): 103–19; P. W. Pestman, "Haronnophris and Chaonnophris," in S. P. Vleeming, ed., *Hundred-Gated Thebes* (P. L. Bat. 27) (Leiden, 1995), pp. 101–37.
34. UPZ II, 199, 4 (*Théoïsin ekhthros*). See below, p. 84.
35. For a recent bibliography, see W. Huss, *Der Makedonische König und die ägyptischen Priester* (Stuttgart, 1994), pp. 165–79.
36. M. Chauveau, "Alexandrie et Rhakôtis: Le Point de vue des Égyptiens," in *Cahiers de la villa Kérylos (Beaulieu-sur-mer),* no. 9 (Paris, 1999).

CHAPTER 3: CITIES AND COUNTRYSIDE

1. P. G. P. Meyboom, *The Nile Mosaic of Palestrina: Early Evidence of Egyptian Religion in Italy,* RGRW 121 (Leiden, 1995).
2. G. Dietze, "Philae und die Dodekaschoinos in ptolemäischer Zeit," *AS* 25 (1994): 63–110.
3. Agatharchides of Knidos, *On the Erythraean Sea,* V, 23–29 = Diodorus Siculus, *Library of History,* III, 12–14.
4. See Th. Schrapel, *Das Reich der Kleopatra: Quellenkritische Untersuchungen zu den "Landschenkungen" Mark Antons,* THF 34 (Trier, 1996).
5. F. de Cenival, *Papyrus démotiques de Lille (III),* MIFAO 110 (Cairo, 1984), pp. 1–30 (no. 99). A new study of this papyrus, renamed P. Count 2–3, is being prepared by W. Clarysse and D. J. Thompson.

6. Diodorus Siculus, *Library of History*, I, 31, 8, though he notes that the population had at one time been as high as seven million.
7. Theokritos, *Idyls*, Idyl 17 (Praise of Ptolemy), 82–84.
8. Diodorus Siculus, *Library of History*, I, 31, 7: thirty thousand under Ptolemy I but only eighteen thousand under the ancient pharaohs.
9. Pliny the Elder, *Natural History*, V, 11: twenty thousand under Amasis (570–526 B.C.E.).
10. On Lagide Alexandria, see the fundamental work by P. M. Fraser, *Ptolemaic Alexandria*, 3 vols. (Oxford, 1972). Also to be consulted are A. Bernand, *Alexandrie la Grande*, CST 19 (Paris, 1966; rpr. Paris, 1996); idem, *Alexandrie des Ptolémées* (Paris, 1995); and the articles by various authors collected in C. Jacob and F. Polignac, eds., *Alexandrie IIIe siècle av. J.-C.*, Autrement, Série mémoires 19 (Paris, 1992).
11. See above, "Greek Pharaohs and Their Subjects," n. 36.
12. Pseudo-Kallisthenes, *The Life of Alexander of Macedon*, trans. and ed. E. H. Haight (New York, 1955).
13. See J.-Y. Empereur, "Fouilles et découvertes récentes," in *Alexandria: Lumière du monde antique = Les Dossiers d'archéologie* 201 (March, 1995), pp. 82–87, with a reproduction of a magnificent mosaic of the Ptolemaic period discovered in the palace quarter; and Fr. Goddio et al., *Alexandria: The Submerged Royal Quarters* (London, 1998).
14. Strabo, *Geography*, XVII, 1, 6–10.
15. See F. Daumas and B. Mathieu, "Le Phare d'Alexandrie et ses dieux: Un document inédit," *Academiae Analecta* 49/1 (Brussels, 1987), pp. 42–55.
16. "The Syracusans," or "The Women at the Adonis Festival" (Idyl 15).
17. L. Canfora, *La biblioteca scomparsa* (Palermo, 1987), translated into English by M. Ryle under the title *The Vanished Library: A Wonder of the Ancient World* (Berkeley, 1990), pp. 68–70.
18. See Empereur, "Fouilles et découvertes récentes," p. 86.
19. XVII, 52, 6.
20. See below, n. 31.
21. On Jews in Egypt in the Ptolemaic period, see J. Mélèze-Modrzejewski, *Les Juifs d'Égypte de Ramsès II à Hadrien* (Paris, 1991), pp. 43–130.
22. Strabo, *Geography*, XVII, 1, 17.
23. Fraser, *Ptolemaic Alexandria*, pp. 729–30 and 1021–26 (nn. 100–109).
24. These are the shepherds mentioned by a number of ancient novelists; see P. Grimal, *Romans grecs et latins* (Paris, 1958).
25. Thus, Ptolemy X Alexander in 103 B.C.E.; see Clarysse in E. Van't Dack et al., *The Judean–Syrian–Egyptian Conflict of 103–101 B.C.: A Multilingual Dossier Concerning a "War of Scepters,"* Coll. Hell. 1 (Brussels, 1989), pp. 83–84; or again Ptolemy XIII in 48.
26. Diodorus, *Library of History*, XXXIII, 28a, 1–2; Marcus Justinianus Justinus, *Epitome of the Philippic History of Pompeius Trogus*, XXXVIII, 8, 8–11.

27. For the definitive identification of Myos Hormos with present-day Qoseir, see A. Bülow-Jacobsen et al., *BIFAO* 94 (1994): 27–28.

28. S. M. Burstein in P. Green, ed., *Hellenistic History and Culture* (Berkeley, 1993), pp. 43–46.

29. L. Mooren, "The Date of *SB* V 8036 and the Development of the Ptolemaic Maritime Trade with India," *AS* 3 (1972): 127–33.

30. See D. J. Thompson, *Memphis under the Ptolemies* (Princeton, 1988), which has largely inspired our entire treatment of Lagide Memphis.

31. Thompson, ibid., p. 35, gives an estimate of between fifty thousand and two hundred thousand, but "probably at the lower end of the scale."

32. See the bibliography given earlier in the "Introduction," n. 10.

33. On Ptolemais, see A. Bernand, *Leçon de civilisation* (Paris, 1994), pp. 225–33.

34. On Graeco-Roman Thebes, see K. Vandorpe, "City of Many a Gate, Harbour for Many a Rebel," in S. P. Vleeming, ed., *Hundred-Gated Thebes: Acts of a Colloquium on Thebes and the Theban Area in the Graeco-Roman Period,* P. L. Bat. 27 (Leiden, 1995), pp. 203–39, and the other articles in this collaborative volume.

35. On domestic architecture, see M. Nowicka, *La Maison privée dans l'Égypte ptolémaïque* (Wroclaw, 1969), and G. Husson, *Oikia* (Paris, 1983). Since 1989, the Franco-Italian excavations at Tebtunis have brought to light a number of private and public buildings contemporary with the Lagides; see the annual reports in *BIFAO*.

CHAPTER 4: ECONOMY AND SOCIETY

THE FOLLOWING GENERAL WORKS ARE TO BE CONSULTED:

C. Préaux. *Le Monde hellénistique.* Paris, 1978. 3d ed., 1989–92, especially vol. I, pp. 358–88, vol. II, pp. 474–88, and the new addendum to the bibliography, pp. 723–26.

E. G. Turner. "Ptolemaic Egypt." In F. W. Walbank, ed. *The Cambridge Ancient History,* 2d. ed., vol. VII, pt. I. Cambridge, 1984, pp. 133–67.

1. H. Bengtson, *Die Strategie in der hellenistischen Zeit,* 2d ed., vol. III (Munich, 1967); N. Hohlwein, *Le Stratège du nome,* Pap. Brux. 9 (Brussels, 1969); L. Mooren, "On the Jurisdiction of the Nome Strategoi in Ptolemaic Egypt," in *Atti del XVII Congresso internazionale di paprologia,* vol. III (Naples, 1984), pp. 1217–25.

2. See S. Héral, "Deux équivalents démotiques du titre *nomarchès,*" *CdE* 65/130 (1990): 304–20.

3. E. Van't Dack, *Ptolemaica Selecta: Études sur l'armée et l'administration lagides,* SH 29 (Louvain, 1988), pp. 329–85.

4. Ibid., pp. 247–71 and 288–313.

5. E. Bresciani, *SCO* 9 (1960): 119–21. The date of stela Cairo Journal d'entrée 55941 should be corrected: 32 instead of 161.

6. R. S. Bianchi et al., *Cleopatra's Egypt: Age of the Ptolemies* (New York, 1988), pp. 126–27 (no. 32).

7. H. J. Thissen, "Zur Familie des Strategen Monkores," *ZPE* 27 (1977): 181–91. The date of the graffito Medinet Habu no. 44 should be corrected from 77 to 48.

8. See, most recently, L. M. Ricketts, "The Epistrategos Kallimachos and a Coptite Inscription: *SB* V 8036 Reconsidered," *AS* 13/14 (1982/83): 161–65.

9. See N. Lewis, *Greeks in Ptolemaic Egypt* (Oxford, 1986), pp. 56–68.

10. See, most recently, J. F. Oates, *The Ptolemaic Basilikos Grammateus, BASP* Supplement 8 (Atlanta, 1995).

11. L. Criscuolo, "Ricerche sul *Komogrammateus* nell'Egitto tolemaico," *Aegyptus* 58 (1978): 3–101.

12. P. W. Pestman, "The Official Archive of the Village Scribes of Kerkeosiris," in *Papyrus Erherzog Rainer (P. Rainer Cent.): Festschrift zum 100-Jährigen Bestehen der Papyrussammlung der österreichischen Nationalbibliothek* (Vienna, 1983), pp. 127–34; N. Lewis, *Greeks in Ptolemaic Egypt*, pp. 104–23.

13. *P. Tebt.* I 9–10; see D. J. Thompson, in H. Maehler and M. Strocka, eds., *Das ptolemäische Ägypten: Akten des internationalen Symposions, 27.–29. September 1977 in Berlin* (Mainz, 1978), p. 201.

14. *P. Tebt.* I 43; see N. Lewis, *Greeks in Ptolemaic Egypt*, pp. 116–17.

15. J. Bingen, *Les Papyrus Revenue Laws: Tradition grecque et adaptation hellénistique* (Opladen, 1978).

16. *P. Tebt.* I 38; see N. Lewis, *Greeks in Ptolemaic Egypt*, pp. 119–20.

17. *P. Tebt.* I 40.

18. The earliest mention of the Athenian *stater* in Egypt occurs in a Demotic text dated to 410; see M. Chauveau, *BSFE* 137 (1996): 38.

19. R. A. Hazzard, *Ptolemaic Coins: An Introduction for Collectors* (Toronto, 1995), pp. 71–75.

20. On the Ptolemaic banking system, see R. Bogaert, "Les Banques affermées ptolémaïques," *Historia* 33 (1984): 181–98; N. Lewis, *Greeks in Ptolemaic Egypt*, pp. 46–55.

21. R. Bogaert, "Un cas de faux en écriture à la Banque royale thébaine en 131 av. J.-C.," *CdE* 63/125 (1988): 145–54.

22. T. Reekmans, "The Ptolemaic Copper Inflation," *SH* 7 (1951): 61–119; W. Clarysse and E. Lanciers, "Currency and Dating of Demotic and Greek Papyri from the Ptolemaic Period," *AS* 20 (1989): 117–32; R. A. Hazzard, *Patlemaic Coins*, pp. 82–90.

23. Hazzard, *Ptolemaic Coins*, pp. 51–55.

24. J. Bingen, "Grecs et Égyptiens d'après PSI 502," in *Proceedings of the 12th International Congress of Papyrology* (Toronto, 1970), pp. 35–40.

25. See K. D. White, in P. Green, ed., *Hellenistic History and Culture* (Berkeley, 1993), pp. 214–15 and fig. 36.

26. P. Vidal-Naquet, *Le Bordereau d'ensemencement dans l'Égypte ptolémaïque,* Pap. Brux. 5 (Brussels, 1967).

27. H. Cuvigny, *L'Arpentage par espèces dans l'Égypte ptolémaïque d'après les papyrus grecs,* Pap. Brux. 20 (Brussels, 1985).

28. *P. Tebt.* I 61 b; see Vidal-Naquet, *Le Bordereau d'ensemencement,* pp. 39–40.

29. D. J. Crawford, *Kerkeosiris: An Egyptian Village in the Ptolemaic Period* (Cambridge, 1971); J. Bingen, "Kerkéosiris et ses Grecs au IIᵉ s. av. notre ère," *Actes du XVᵉ Congrès international de papyrologie* (Brussels, 1979), pp. 87–94.

30. See J. Bingen, "Économie grecque et société égyptienne," in *Das ptolemä-ische Ägypten (Akt. int. Symp. Berlin)* (Mainz, 1978), pp. 214–15.

31. D. J. Thompson, *Memphis under the Ptolemies* (Princeton, 1988), pp. 46–59.

32. Ibid., pp. 65–70.

33. H. Hauben, "Le transport fluvial en Égypte ptolémaïque: Les Bateaux du roi et de la reine," *Actes du XVᵉ Congrès international de papyrologie* (Brussels, 1979), pp. 68–77.

34. Thompson, *Memphis under the Ptolemies,* p. 61.

35. Of the abundant bibliography, we may cite here E. Seidl, *Ptolemäische Rechtsgeschichte,* Äg. Forsch. 22 (Hamburg, 1962); H. J. Wolff, *Das Justizwe-sen der Ptolemäer,* 2d ed. (Munich, 1970). On the question of ethnic defini-tion, see K. Goudriaan, *Ethnicity in Ptolemaic Egypt* (Amsterdam, 1988).

36. M. Chauveau, "P. Carlsberg 301: Le Manuel juridique de Tebtunis," in P. J. Frandsen, ed., *Demotic Texts from the Collection,* CP 1 (Copenhagen, 1991), pp. 103–27.

37. *P. Tebt.* I 5, pp. 207–20; see Mélèze-Modrzejewski, "Chrématistes et lao-crites," in J. Bingen, G. Cambier, and G. Nachtergel, eds., *Le Monde grec: Pensée, littérature, histoire, documents: Hommages à Claire Préaux* (Brussels, 1975), pp. 699–708.

38. See below, pp. 145–149.

39. There is an abundant bibliography; we may cite here I. Biezunska-Malowist, *L'Esclavage dans l'Égypte gréco-romaine,* pt. 1: *Période ptolémaïque* (War-saw, 1974); H. Heinen, "Zur Terminologie der Sklaverei im ptolemäischen Ägypten," *Atti del XVII Congresso internazionale di papirologia,* vol. III (Naples, 1984), pp. 1287–95; R. Scholl, "Zur Sklaverei am Hof der Ptole-mäer," in *Egitto e storia antica* (Bologna, 1989), pp. 671–81.

40. *UPZ* I 121 = *Select Pap.* II 234.

41. See below, pp. 131–134.

CHAPTER 5: PRIESTS AND TEMPLES

1. Herodotus, *Histories,* II, 37.

2. See J. Mélèze-Modrzejewski, *Les Juifs d'Égypte: De Ramsès II à Hadrien* (Paris, 1991), pp. 35–40.

3. S. Cauville, *Edfou*, Bibl. Gén. 6 (Cairo, 1984).

4. S. Cauville, *Le Temple de Dendéra: Guide archéologique*, Bibl. Gén. 12 (Cairo, 1990).

5. J. Quaegebeur, "Cléopâtre VII et le temple de Dendara," *GM* 120 (1991): 49–72, esp. 66–68.

6. S. Sauneron, *Les Fêtes religieuses d'Esna* (Cairo, 1962). The calendar of the festivals of the temple of Esna would date to the reign of Domitian.

7. At the beginning of the reign of Hadrian; see A. K. Bowman, *Egypt after the Pharaohs 332 B.C.–A.D. 642: From Alexander to the Roman Conquest* (London, 1986), p. 183.

8. Diodorus Siculus, *Library of History*, I, 83, pp. 8–9.

9. Strabo, *Geography*, XVII, 1, 38. Note also the program of entertainments provided for the visit of the senator Lucius Memmius in the Faiyum in 112 B.C.E.: *P. Tebt.* I 33 = *Select Pap.* II 416.

10. *P. Ox. Griffith* 27 = E. Bresciani, *L'Archivio demotico del tempio di Soknopaiou Nesos* (Milan, 1975), pp. 32–33.

11. *BGU* VI 1211 = M.-Th. Lenger, *Corpus des ordonnances des Ptolémés*, 2d ed. (Brussels, 1980), no. 29.

12. *SB* V 7835 (reign of Ptolemy XII).

13. See F. de Cenival, *Les Associations religieuses en Égypte d'après les textes démotiques* (Cairo, 1972).

14. D. J. Crawford, *Kerkeosiris: An Egyptian Village in the Ptolemaic Period* (Cambridge, 1971), p. 86 (Zeus, Dioskouroi), *P. Ox. Griffith* 16, Bresciani, *L'Archivio demotico*, pp. 16–17 (Demeter).

15. W. Clarysse et al., *The Eponymous Priests of Ptolemaic Egypt*, P. L. Bat. 24 (Leiden, 1983).

16. Demotic stela British Museum 1325, published by A. Farid, *Fünf demotische Stelen aus Berlin, Chicago, Durham, London und Oxford, mit zwei demotischen Türinschriften aus Paris und einer Bibliographie der demotischen Inschriften* (Berlin, 1995); the date should be corrected from September 21, 31 B.C.E. to January 19, 30 B.C.E.

17. J. Quaegebeur, "La Justice à la porte des temples et le toponyme Premit," in Chr. Cannuyer and J.-M. Kruchten, eds., *Individu, société et spiritualité dans l'Égypte pharaonique et copte: Mélanges égyptologiques offerts à Professeur Aristide Théodoridès* (Brussels, 1993), pp. 201–20.

18. E. Seidl, "Die Verwendung des Eides im Prozess nach den demotischen Quellen," *ZSS* 91 (1974): 41–53.

19. M. Chauveau, "Un contrat de hiérodule: Le P. dém. Fouad 2," *BIFAO* 91 (1991): 119–27.

20. D. J. Thompson, *Memphis under the Ptolemies* (Princeton, 1988), pp. 190–211.

21. N. Lewis, *Greeks in Ptolemaic Egypt* (Oxford, 1986), pp. 69–87; Thompson, *Memphis under the Ptolemies*, pp. 212–65.

22. S. Sauneron, "Les Songes et leur interprétation dans l'Égypte ancienne," in

S. Sauneron et al., *Les Songes et leur interprétation: Égypte ancienne, Baby-lone, Hittites, Canaan, Israël, Islam, peuples altaïques, Persans, Kurdes, Inde, Cambodge, Chine, Japon* SO 2 (Paris, 1959), pp. 19–61.

23. *UPZ* I 77, col. II, 22–30.
24. Ibid., col. I, 16–19.
25. Ibid., col. II, 4–17.
26. *UPZ* I 78, 1–28.
27. This is the interpretation of U. Wilcken, *UPZ* I, p. 118, which has in the meanwhile been generally accepted. But it would rather seem to be a ceremony involving cutting the fiancée's hair before the wedding ceremony, according to a suggestion of J. Mélèze-Modrzejewski in his seminar at the École Pratique des Hautes Études.
28. *UPZ* I 6a, but the attribution of the document, which was long ago restored incorrectly, is dubious; see W. Clarysse, *Enchoria* 14 (1986): 43–49.
29. See K. Goudriaan, *Ethnicity in Ptolemaic Egypt* (Amsterdam, 1988), pp. 42–57.
30. E.g., in *P. Ryl. Dem.* 9 (around 510 B.C.E.); see M. Chauveau, "Violence et répression dans la 'Chronique de Pétiésé,'" *Méditerranées* 6, no. 7 (1996): 233–46.
31. *P. Bologne Dem.* 3173, 8–12; see E. Bresciani et al., *EVO* 1 (1978): 95–99. The translation is uncertain, and other interpretations of this difficult text have been proposed elsewhere.
32. *P. Bologne Dem.*, 3173, 1–7.
33. The incompetence of the Ptolemaic bureaucracy is indeed patent in the details of this affair; see Lewis, *Greeks in Ptolemaic Egypt*, pp. 78–79.
34. See, e.g., the notice concerning two fugitive slaves cited above, p. 99.
35. *UPZ* I 70.
36. *UPZ* I 71.

CHAPTER 6: LIVING ON THE DEATH OF OTHERS

1. J.-C. Goyon, "La littérature funéraire tardive," in *Textes et langages de l'Égypte pharaonique, cent cinquante années de recherches, 1822–1972: Hommage à Jean-François Champollion*, Bibl. d'Ét. 64, vol. III (Cairo, 1972), pp. 73–81.
2. Herodotus, *Histories*, II, 86–88. This division of mummification into three classes was still in existence at the end of the Ptolemaic period, according to Diodorus Siculus, *Library of History*, I, 91, 2.
3. Sarcophagus Leiden 1383; see P. W. Pestman, in L. Criscuolo and G. Geraci, eds., *Egitto e storia antica dall'ellenismo all'età araba, bilancio di un confonto: Atti del Colloquio internazionale, Bologna, 3 agosto–2 settembre 1987* (Bologna, 1989), p. 139 and n. 7.
4. See, most recently, P. Gallo and O. Masson, "Stèle 'hellénomemphite' de l'ancienne coll. Nahman," *BIFAO* 93 (1993): 265–76.

5. P. Perdrizet, "Le Mort qui sentait bon," *Mélanges Bidez,* AIPHO 2 (Brussels, 1934), pp. 719–27 = E. Bernand, *Inscriptions métriques de l'Égypte gréco-romaine* (Besançon, 1969), no. 97, pp. 377–86.

6. See, most recently, P. W. Pestman, *The Archive of the Theban Choachytes (P. Survey),* SD 2 (Louvain, 1993).

7. D. J. Thompson, *Memphis under the Ptolemies* (Princeton, 1988), pp. 155–89.

8. Diodorus Siculus, *Library of History,* I, 91, 4–5.

9. For the most recent bibliography, see J. Quaegebeuer, "Books of Thoth Belonging to Owners of Portraits?" in M. L. Bierbrier, ed., *Portraits and Masks: Burial Customs in Roman Egypt* (London, 1997), pp. 72–77.

10. F.-R. Herbin, *Le Livre de parcourir l'éternité,* OLA 58 (Louvain, 1994).

11. P. Louvre Dem. 3452, dated to Berenike IV; published by G. Legrain, *Le Livre de Transformations: Papyrus démotique 3452 du Louvre* (Paris, 1890).

12. See, most recently, S. P. Vleeming, "The Office of a Choachyte in the Theban Area," in S. P. Vleeming, ed., *Hundred-Gated Thebes: Acts of a Colloquium on Thebes and the Theban Area in the Graeco-Roman Period,* P. L. Bat. 27 (Leiden, 1995), pp. 241–55.

13. B. Borg, "The Dead as a Guest at Table? Continuity and Change in the Egyptian Cult of the Dead," in Bierbrier, ed., *Portraits and Masks,* pp. 26–32.

14. A. Bataille, *Les Memnonia: Recherches de papyrologie et d'épigraphie grecques sur la nécropole de la Thèbes d'Égypte aux époques hellénistiques et romaine,* RAPH 23 (Cairo, 1952), pp. 224–25.

15. Ibid., pp. 271–77.

16. UPZ II 162, col. 8, 16–22 = P. W. Pestman, *Il processo di Hermias (P. Tor. Choachiti)* (Turin, 1992), pp. 194–95.

17. P. Berlin dem. 3115, published by F. de Cenival, *Les Associations religieuses en Égypte d'après les documents démotiques* (Cairo, 1972), pp. 103–35 = Pestman, *The Archive of the Theban Choachytes,* p. 61.

18. J. Quaegebeur, "Les 'Saints' égyptiens préchrétiens," OLP 8 (1977): 129–43.

19. P. W. Pestman, *Archive of the Theban Choachytes,* p. 23.

20. P. W. Pestman, *L'archivio di Amenothes figlio di Horos (P. Tor. Amenothes)* (Turin, 1981), pp. 52–75 (nos. 5–8).

21. P. Innsbruck dem., first published by W. Spiegelberg, "Ein demotischer Papyrus in Innsbruck," RdT 25 (1903): 103. See Thompson, *Memphis under the Ptolemies,* pp. 174–78.

22. Pestman, *Il processo di Hermias,* pp. 123–97 (nos. 11–12) = Pestman, *Archive of the Theban Choachytes,* pp. 42, 44, 48.

23. Pestman, *Il processo di Hermias,* pp. 182–83.

24. UPZ I 106–9; see Thompson, *Memphis under the Ptolemies,* pp. 186–88.

CHAPTER 7: SOLDIERS AND PEASANTS

1. Diodorus Siculus, *Library of History,* XVIII, 39, 5, and 43, 1.

2. See P. Grelot, *Documents araméens d'Égypte* (Paris, 1972).

3. Herodotus, *Histories,* II, 164–66. For the etymology of *Hermotybies,* see H. J. Thissen, "Varia Onomastica," *GM* 141 (1994): 89–91.

4. Arrian, *Anabasis,* III, 5, 5.

5. Between 331 and 323 B.C.E., Kleomenes was promoted to the rank of satrap. The oppressiveness of his administration is illustrated by anecdotes from the second book of a treatise on economy falsely attributed to Aristotle (1352, a, 17–b, 26). See also J. Seibert, *Chiron* 2 (1972): 99–102.

6. See D. J. Thompson, *Memphis under the Ptolemies* (Princeton, 1988), p. 12.

7. Diodorus siculus, *Library of History,* XIX, 85, 3–4. Cf. the attitude of the soldiers of Ptolemy captured by Demetrios in 307 B.C.E., *infra* n. 11.

8. Herodotus, *Histories,* II, 165–68.

9. R. Bagnall, *BASP* 21 (1984): 7–21.

10. E. G. Turner, "Ptolemaic Egypt," in F. W. Walbank, ed., *The Cambridge Ancient History,* 2d ed., vol. VII, pt. 1 (Cambridge, 1984), p. 124 and n. 13.

11. Diodorus Siculus, *Library of History,* XX, 47, 4.

12. E. G. Turner, "A Commander-in-Chief's Order from Saqqâra," *JEA* 60 (1974): 239–42.

13. *Select Pap.* II, 207. See N. Lewis, *Greeks in Ptolemaic Egypt,* pp. 22–23.

14. *P. Ent.* 11. See Lewis, *Greeks in Ptolemaic Egypt,* p. 23.

15. *P. Tebt.* I 5, 168–177.

16. See E. Van't Dack, *Ptolemaica Selecta: Études sur l'armée et l'administration lagides,* SH 29 (Louvain, 1988), pp. 7–16, 35–39. There is a good summary of the question in Lewis, *Greeks in Ptolemaic Egypt,* pp. 24–36.

17. See, most recently, J. F. Oates, "Cessions of Katoitic Land in the Late Ptolemaic Period," *JJP* 25 (1995): 153–61.

18. E. Boswinkel and P. W. Pestman, *Les Archives privées de Dionysios, fils de Kephalas,* P. L. Bat. 22 (Leiden, 1982). See Lewis, *Greeks in Ptolemaic Egypt,* pp. 124–39.

19. There is an abundant bibliography. See K. Goudriaan, *Ethnicity in Ptolemaic Egypt,* DMAHA 5 (Amsterdam, 1988), pp. 16–21.

20. See K. Vandorpe, "Museum Archaeology or How to Reconstruct Pathyris Archives," in *Acta Demotica: Acts of the Fifth International Conference for Demotists (Pisa, 4th-8th September, 1993),* EVO 7 (Pisa, 1994), pp. 289–300.

21. See N. Lewis, *Greeks in Ptolemaic Egypt,* pp. 88–103, complemented by W. Clarysse, *CdE* 61/121 (1986): 99–103; R. Scholl, *CdE* 63/125 (1988): 141–44; and J. K. Winnicki, in A. Bülow-Jacobsen, ed., *Proceedings of the 20th International Congress of Papyrologists, Copenhagen, 23rd-29th August 1992* (Copenhagen, 1994), pp. 600–603.

22. *Select Pap.* I, 101.

23. Lewis, *Greeks in Ptolemaic Egypt,* pp. 99–100.

24. P. L. Pestman, in E. Boswinkel et al., *Studia Papyrologica Varia,* P. L. Bat. 14, (Leiden, 1965), pp. 47–105; Lewis, *Greeks in Ptolemaic Egypt,* pp. 139–52; see also *supra,* n. 20.

25. P. Strassb. dem. 21 = Pestman, op. cit., pp. 58–59 (doc. 1).

26. *P. Lips.* 7 and *P. Grenf. II* 31 = Pestman, op. cit., pp. 65 (doc. 25), 67 (doc. 36).

27. *Select Pap.* I 103 = Pestman, op. cit., p. 71 (doc. 59).

28. *P. Lips.* 104 = Pestman, loc. cit, (doc. 60). Translation furnished by J.-L. Fournet.

29. *P. Claude dem.* 2 (unpublished).

30. *Select Pap.* II 418. See K. Vandorpe, in S. P. Vleeming, ed., *Hundred-Gated Thebes: Acts of a Colloquium on Thebes and the Theban Area in the Graeco-Roman Period,* P. L. Bat. 27 (Leiden, 1995), pp. 234–35.

31. D. Devauchelle and J.-C. Grenier, *BIFAO* 82 (1982): 157–69.

32. Van't Dack, *Ptolemaica Selecta,* p. 194.

33. Ibid., p. 222.

34. Plutarch, "Life of Antony," 74.

35. See Van't Dack, *Ptolemaica Selecta,* pp. 22–32, 43–45.

36. Plutarch, "Life of Demetrios," 43.

37. Plutarch, "Life of Antony," 66.

CHAPTER 8: TWO LANGUAGES, TWO CULTURES, THREE WRITING SYSTEMS

1. See especially J. G. Droysen, *Geschichte des Hellenismus* (Gotha, 1877).

2. For a clear synthesis of the question, see H. Heinen, "L'Égypte dans l'historiographie moderne du monde hellénistique," in L. Criscuolo and G. Garaci, eds., *Egitto e storia antica dall'ellenismo all'età araba, bilancio di un confronto: Atti del Colloquio internazionale, Bologna 31 agosto–2 settembre 1987* (Bologna, 1989), pp. 105–35.

3. For this and the following sections, see P. M. Fraser, *Ptolemaic Alexandria* (Oxford, 1972), vol. I, pt. II, "The Achievement."

4. See J. Mélèze-Modrzejewski, *Les Juifs d'Égypte de Ramsès II à Hadrien* (Paris, 1991), pp. 84–88.

5. See above, "Cities and Countryside," n. 3.

6. R. Rémondon, "Problèmes de bilinguisme dans l'Égypte lagide (*UPZ* I 148)," *CdE* 39/77–78 (1964): 126–46.

7. See A. K. Bowman, *Egypt after the Pharaohs* (London, 1986), p. 145.

8. See the table of finds of Greek literary papyri arranged according to authors and periods in O. Montevecchi, *La Papirologia,* MU 1 (Turin, 1973), pp. 360–63.

9. See W. Clarysse, "Literary Papyri in Documentary 'Archives,'" in E. Van't Dack, P. van Dessel, and W. van Gucht, *Egypt and the Hellenistic World: Proceedings of the International Colloquium, Leuven, 24–26 May 1982,* SH 27 (Leuven, 1983), p. 48.

10. Ibid., p. 51. See also N. Lewis, *Greeks in Ptolemaic Egypt: Case Studies in the Social History of the Hellenistic World* (Oxford, 1986), pp. 122–23. This

might also have been a successor of Menches in the position of *komogramma-teus* of Kerkeosiris.

11. See Clarysse, "Literary Payri in Documentary 'Archives,'" pp. 57–60; D. J. Thompson, *Memphis under the Ptolemies* (Princeton, 1988), pp. 252–65.

12. Though the manuscripts we have today are from the Roman period, most of the Egyptian astrological treatises seem to have been written in the Ptolemaic era. See F. Cumont, *L'Égypte des astrologues* (Brussels, 1937; rpr., 1982), and M. Chauveau, "Un traité d'astrologie en écriture démotique," *CRIPEL* 14 (1992): 101–5.

13. *UPZ* I 110–11, 144–45.

14. P. Louvre 2373.

15. P. Didot.

16. P. Med. II 15; See Thompson, *Memphis under the Ptolemies,* p. 261.

17. *UPZ* I 81; See L. Koenen, "The Dream of Nektanebos," *BASP* 22 (1985): 171–94.

18. The dream is translated above, pp. 128–29.

19. See the dreams translated above, p. 132.

20. P. Louvre Dem. N 2414; see G. R. Hughes, "The Blunders of an Inept Scribe," in G. E. Kadish and G. E. Freeman, eds., *Studies in Philology in Honour of Ronald James Williams: A Festschrift,* SSEAP 3 (Toronto, 1982), pp. 51–67.

21. See J.-C. Goyon, "L'Écriture 'ptolémaique,'" in *Alexandrie: Lumière du monde antique, Les Dossiers d'archéologie,* no. 201, (March 1995), pp. 22–25.

22. P. Cairo Dem. 30646; for a translation, see M. Lichtheim, *Ancient Egyptian Literature,* vol. III: *The Late Period* (Berkeley, 1980), pp. 127–38.

23. P. British Museum Dem. 604 verso; translated ibid., pp. 138–51.

24. For a bibliography, see M. Depauw, *A Companion of Demotic Studies* (Brussels, 1997), p. 88.

25. For a bibliography, see ibid., pp. 88–89; see also F. Hoffmann, *Der Kampf um den Panzer des Inaros: Studien zum P. Kroll und seiner Stellung innerhalb des Inaros-Petubastis-Zyklus,* MPÖN, n.s. 26 (Vienna, 1996).

26. P. British Museum Dem. 10508; for a translation, see Lichtheim, *Ancient Egyptian Literature,* vol. III, pp. 161–84.

27. See P. Grelot, *Documents araméens d'Égypte: Introduction, traduction, présentation* (Paris, 1972), pp. 427–52. Some fragments of a Demotic version of Ahiqar have been identified; see K.-Th. Zauzich, in H. Franke, W. Heissig, and W. Treue, eds., *Folia Rara: Wolfgang Voigt LXV. diem natalem celebranti ab amicis et catalogorum codicum orientalium conscribendorum collegis dedicata* (Wiesbaden, 1976), pp. 180–85.

28. For a bibliography, see Depauw, *Companion of Demotic Studies,* p. 100; for a translation, see Lichtheim, *Ancient Egyptian Literature,* vol. III, pp. 186–217.

29. P. Insinger, col. 7, ll. 15–16.

30. P. Insinger, col. 21, ll. 3–4, 6.

31. P. Vienna KM Dem. 3877; See. H. J. Thissen, *Der verkommene Harfen-spieler: Ein altägyptische Invektive (P. KM 3877),* Dem. Stud. 11 (Sommer-hausen, 1992).

32. Col. 4, ll. 2–4.
33. See J. Yoyotte, "Bakhthis: Religion égyptienne et culture grecque à Edfou," in *Religions en Égypte hellénistique et romaine (Colloque de Strasbourg)* (Paris, 1969), pp. 127–41. The epitaph of Apollonios has been published by E. Bernand, *Inscriptions métriques de l'Égypte gréco-romaine: Recherches sur la poésie epigrammatique des Grecs en Égypte,* ALUB 98 (Paris, 1969), no. 5; see also W. Clarysse, in E. Van't Dack et al., *The Judean–Syrian–Egyptian Conflict of 103–101 B.C.: A Multilingual Dossier Concerning a "War of Scepters,"* Coll. Hell. 1 (Brussels, 1989), pp. 84–88.

CONCLUSION

1. Plutarch, "Life of Antony," 80.
2. On Egypt as a Roman province, see G. Geraci, *Genesi della provincia romane d'Egitto,* SSA 9 (Bologna, 1983).
3. Dio Cassius, *Roman History,* LIII, 23, 5–6; See K. Vandorpe, in S. P. Vleeming, ed., *Hundred-Gated Thebes: Acts of a Colloquium on Thebes and the Theban Area in the Graeco-Roman Period,* P. L. Bat. 27 (Leiden, 1995), p. 236, n. 248.
4. Dio Cassius, *Roman History,* LI, 17, 4; See Vandorpe, in Vleeming, ed., *Hundred-Gated Thebes,* p. 236, n. 249.
5. See A. K. Bowman, *Egypt after the Pharaohs, 332 B.C.–A.D. 642: From Alexander to the Arab Conquest* (Berkeley, 1986), pp. 179–80.
6. On the diffusion of Egyptian cults, see the numerous studies in the series *Études préliminaires aux religions orientales dans l'Empire romain* (Leiden: Brill, 1962–95).

GLOSSARY

Antigonids. Family that ruled over various regions of the Macedonian east from 306 to 286 B.C.E., and over Macedonia itself from 277 to 168.

Antigrapheus. Clerk charged with checking documents, generally an assistant to the *oikonomos* of a nome.

Apomoïra. Tax on vineyards and orchards amounting to one sixth of their net produce, paid to the temples for the maintenance of the cult of Arsinoe Philadelphos.

Aroura. Surface area equivalent to one hundred square cubits, or .681 acre.

Arsinoe. Name of three queens of the Lagide dynasty. After Arsinoe III Philopator, it was borne only by the sister of the last Cleopatra, Arsinoe IV, who died in 40 B.C.E.

Artaba. Unit of measure, originally Persian, employed for dry materials. Of varying capacity according to what was being measured, it corresponded to 8–10.5 gallons.

Basileus. Greek for "king."

Basilikogrammateus. Literally, "royal scribe"; chief secretary of a nome.

Berenike. Name of several Lagide queens and princesses. Berenike III and IV also had the name Cleopatra.

Choachytes, pl. choachytai. Literally, "water pourer"; minor priest attached to the cults of the dead.

Chora. Originally, the rural territory of a Greek city. In Graeco-Roman Egypt, *Chora* designated all the native towns and countryside outside the territories of the Greek cities of Alexandria, Naukratis, and Ptolemais.

Chrematistes, pl. chrematistai. Name given to the three judges of the tribunals that heard cases according to Greek law.

Cleopatra. Name of most of the Lagide queens and princesses after the marriage of Ptolemy V in 195 B.C.E. The numbering of the Cleopatras employed by historians is somewhat arbitrary and subject to fluctuation; our Cleopatra VII has also been designated Cleopatra VI or VIII.

Cleruch. Soldier who enjoyed the revenue of a field (*kleros*) granted by the king, which he exploited either personally or through a third party.

Cubit. Egyptian unit of length equivalent to about 20.6 inches.

Demotic. Name applied to the language spoken by the Egyptians in the Ptolemaic period, as well as to its cursive writing system, which was derived from hieratic.

Diadochos, pl. diadochoi. Literally, "successor." The designation usually given by historians to the generals of Alexander who competed for control over the lands he had conquered.

Epistates, pl. epistatai. Title of various officials with judicial and police powers.

There was an *espistates* acting as a *strategos* in any nome that did not have its own *strategos*. At a lower level, *epistatai* represented the central authority in the towns.

Epistrategos. Important official superior in rank to a *strategos*. There was an *epistrategos* of the *Chora*, a sort of minister of the interior whose powers extended over all the land outside Alexandria, and an *epistrategos* of the Thebaid, a sort of governor of Upper Egypt.

Eponyms. Priests and priestesses of the Greek dynastic cults at Alexandria and Ptolemais, who had the privilege of being named in the datings of documents. These were purely honorific offices and were held by members of influential families in the two cities, usually for one year, though sometimes permanently.

Hieratic. Cursive writing system derived from the hieroglyphs, used from the Old Kingdom to the Saite period. Under the Ptolemies, hieratic was scarcely used, except for the texts of funerary and religious rituals.

Hieroglyphs. The ancient Egyptian writing system, always in use for texts carved in stone. Hieroglyphs were used to write Middle Egyptian, which was a dead language from the New Kingdom on.

Katoikos, pl. katoikoi. Military colonist. Practically the same as *cleruch*, this title was appplied specifically to Greek cavalrymen who held large parcels of land, beginning in the second century B.C.E.

Komarchos. Official responsible for agricultural production at the village level.

Komogrammateus, pl. komogrammateis. Village scribe, a subordinate of the *basilikogrammateus* at the village level.

Lagides. Macedonian family whose name derives from Lagos, father of Ptolemy; the latter was satrap and then king of Egypt, and his descendants reigned until 30 B.C.E.

Laokritai. Designation of the judges of the native tribunals that passed judgment according to Egyptian law.

Machimoi. Greek designation of native Egyptian soldiers. Beginning with the reign of Ptolemy IV, they were beneficiaries of the cleruchic system.

Nomarch. Originally, the Greek designation of the governor of a nome. From the third century B.C.E. on, the *strategoi* assumed most of their functions. After that, the nomarchs were responsible only for supervising agriculture in their districts.

Nome. Principal administrative district in Egypt; under the Ptolemies, there were about forty.

Oikonomos. Official responsible for royal financial interests at the level of the nome. His importance declined after the third century B.C.E., as that of the *basilikogrammateus* increased.

Olyra. Type of grain most commonly grown for human consumption in Egypt before the Lagide domination.

Pastophoros. Minor priest who performed purely physical tasks.

Ptolemy. Name given to all the princes of the Lagide family. Their numbering is purely a matter of convention. Here, so as not to disrupt the system most commonly employed, we have preferred not to use the number VII, which cannot have applied to any sovereign who actually reigned. Each Ptolemy also had one or more cultic epithets by which he was usually known. Certain of them also received somewhat opprobrious popular epithets, such as Ptolemy VIII's "Fatty," and Ptolemy XII's "Flutist."

Pylon. Monumental gateway of an Egyptian temple, flanked by two trapezoidal towers.

Satrap. Governor of a province of the Persian empire. The title was also used for the Macedonian governors of the empire of Alexander the Great. It was borne by the first Ptolemy until he was proclaimed king in 305–304 B.C.E.

Seleucids. Macedonian family that reigned over the Asiatic provinces of the empire of Alexander the Great from 312 to 63 B.C.E.

Stater. Gold or silver coin. A silver *stater* was worth four drachmas.

Strategos. Originally, an army officer. From the third century B.C.E. on, the civil and military governor of one or more nomes.

Talent. Large denomination corresponding to six thousand drachmas. After 210 B.C.E., the silver talent was distinct from the copper talent, which was most commonly used within Egypt itself.

Tetradrachm. Coin worth four drachmas, the equivalent of a *stater*.

Topogrammateus, pl. topogrammateis. Scribe of a district (*topos*), whose rank fell between that of a *basilikogrammateus* and a *komogrammateus*.

INDEX

Illustrations are referenced in bold. Bold italics denote text and illustration on same page.

Achaemenids, 33
Achillas, 24, 167
Actium, battle of, 3, 28, 169
Actors, 178
Aeschylus, 179, 181
Afterlife, belief in. *See* Funerary customs
Agatharchides of Knidos, 173–174
Agathos Daimon, 51
Agriculture, 73, 74, 76, 116, 194; in Kerkeosiris, 89, 90–93; and peasants' living conditions, 87–90; and tax system, 78–80
Ainesidemos of Knossos, 174
Akhenaten, 56
Akoris, 156
Alexander Balas, 14
Alexander Helios, 27
Alexander Jannaeus, 17
Alexander Romance, 186
Alexander son of Alexander, 8, 37
Alexander the Great, 3, 6–8, 7, 8, 33; deification of, 35; in Egyptian literature, 186; occupying force of, 151–152; pharaonic coronation of, 37; royal titulary of, 45; tomb of, 61
Alexandria, 9, 11, 15, 35–36, 137; and the Delta, 65; Donations ceremony in, 27; founding of, 8, 56; as Greek city, 56–58, 71; Greek priests in, 115; as intellectual center, 59, 61, 171–176; monuments in, 58–61, 63; population of, 62–63; port of, 61–62; and "The Potter's Oracle," 50–51, 57
Alexandrian war, 24, 61, 70, 167
Amasis, 96
Amenemope, 142
Amenneus *(basilikogrammateus),* 81
Amenophis, 50
Amenothes son of Horos, 144
Amnesty decrees, 16, 41–43, 80, 91, 97
Amun, 43, 68, 141, 142, 187
Animals: domestic, 92–93; sacred, 105–108, 121–123

Ankhsheshonqy, 187–188
Ankhwennofre, 11, 50
Antigonos the One-Eyed, 33, 35, 152
Antiochos of Ashkelon, 174, 175
Antiochus II (Syria), 30
Antiochus III (Syria), 4, 11, 13, 31
Antiochus IV Epiphanes (Syria), 13, 14, 48–49, 62
Antony, Mark, 25–28, 45, 54, 61, 191; and battle of Actium, 28, 169
Apamea, peace of, 13
Aphrodite, 26, 37
Apiculture, 93
Apis bulls, 47, 66, 106, 121, 121–123; embalming of, 127, 150
Apollinopolis, 69
Apollodoros *(strategos),* 149
Apollonia (wife of Dryton), 161–162
Apollonios (minister of finance), 4, 66–67
Apollonios of Rhodes, 172
Apollonios son of Glaukias, 99, 131–134, 180–183
Apollonios son of Ptolemaios, 190
Apollonios (cavalry member), 146
Apomoïra, 36, 42, 116
Archelaos, 20–21, 26
Archimedean screw, 88
Architecture, 69–70
Areios Didymos, 175, 191
Argonautica (Apollonios of Rhodes), 172
Aristarchos of Samos, 172
Aristarchos of Samothrace, 173, 176
Ariston *(strategos),* 150
Aristophanes, 179
Aristophanes of Byzantium, 174
Armenia, 27
Arsinoe (Cleopatris), 65
Arsinoe (Krokodilopolis), 67, 69, 160, 166–167
Arsinoe I, 30
Arsinoe II Philadelphos, 4, *10,* 30–31, *36;* cult of, 35–36, 116; temple of, 63
Arsinoe III, *32*

Arsinoe IV, 25
Artisans, 80, 93
Art of Eudoxos, 180, 180–181
Asklepios, 125
Associations: of funerary professionals, 141–144; for management of *gymnasia*, 178; religious, 110–113
Astronomy, 172, 180–181
Aswan, 53, 69
Asylum, 18, 40–41, 99, 159
Athens, 153, 171, 174
Atum-Re, temple of, 125
Augustus Caesar. *See* Octavian
"Auletes." *See* Ptolemy XII Neos Dionysos
Aulus Gabinius, 21, 26, 167, 175

Balakros, 151
Banks, 83–84
Basilikogrammateis (royal scribes), 76, 81, 90. *See also* Scribes
Basilikos georgos (royal peasant), 88–89, 157. *See also* Peasants
Bastet, 107
Bedouins, 92
Behbeit el-Hagar, temple at, 65, 110, 113
Berenike (daughter of Ptolemy II), 30
Berenike I, 36
Berenike II, 4, *30, 63,* 109
Berenike III (Cleopatra-Berenike), 4, 17–18, 30, 32, 149
Berenike IV, 4, 20, 21
Bible, the, 173
Bilingualism, 76, 157, 158, 182–183
Black market, 80–81
Book of the Dead, 136, *139*
Book of Thoth, 186
Book of Transformation, 139
Book of Traversing Eternity, 139
Books of Breathing, 139
Brick, 69
Bronze, 82, 84, 86
Bubastis, 65
Buchis bulls, 43, 68
Bureaucracy, 72–73; and law, 96–98; during Roman era, 193; scribes, 72, 76–77, 80–81, 88, 90; *strategoi,* 73–76, 97, 193; and tax structure, 78–80
Burial. *See* Funerary customs
Buto, temple of, 38

Caesar, Julius, 19, 22, 23–24, 25, 26; and Alexandrian war, 24, 167
Caesarion. *See* Ptolemy XV Caesar
Canopus decree, 39–40, 109
Catalogues of the Authors Eminent in Various Disciplines (Kallimachos), 173
Cato the Younger, 20, 21
Cats, sacred, 106, 107
Catullus, 63
Cemeteries, 58–59, 137, 148. *See also* Funerary customs
Children, as slaves, 98
Choachytai ("libation pourers"), 137, 139–143; and Hermias, 145–149
Chora (provinces), 16, 74, 137; Hellenism in, 34, 115, 177–182; royal visits to, 40, 43, 130
Chrematistai, 96–97
Christianity, 135, 173
Chronographia (Eratosthenes), 173
Cities: cadavers in, 147–149; cleruchs in, 156; in the Delta, 65; and Hellenism, 56–58, 71, 73, 178; of Upper Egypt, 68–69. *See also specific cities*
Civil wars: and amnesty decrees, 16, 41–43, 91; under Cleopatra VII, 23–24; economic effects of, 16, 86, 91–92; between Ptolemy VI and Ptolemy VIII, 13–14, 29; between Ptolemy VIII and Cleopatra II, 15–16, 42–43, 84, 86, 91–92, 162–163; Roman, 23–24, 25–26, 27–28; between Soter II and Alexander, 17–18, 69, 159, 166. *See also* Rebellions
Class: of cleruchs, 155–156, 167; and mummification, 136; of priests, 108–109; during Roman era, 194–195
Cleopatra I, 4, 11, 13, 31, 46
Cleopatra II, 13, 15–17, 31, *85, 145;* and Alexandrian Jews, 62–63; civil war under, 15–16, 42–43, 84, 162–163; provincial visits by, 130, 133
Cleopatra III, 15–17, 31–32, 37, 190; civil war under, 15–16, 42–43, 159, 162–163
Cleopatra IV, 17, 32
Cleopatra V Selene, 17
Cleopatra VI Tryphaina, 19, 20
Cleopatra VII Philopator, 23, *47,* 61, 74, 102; accession of, 22–23; and Alexan-

drian intellectualism, 174, 176–177; and Antony, 25–28, 45, 54, 169; and battle of Actium, 28, 169; and Caesar, 23, 24, 25; currency under, 86–87; and Lagide army, 167, 168; perceptions of, 1–2, 26, 45; royal titulary of, 46; sources regarding, 24–25

Cleopatra-Berenike. See Berenike III

Cleopatra Selene (daughter of Cleopatra VII), 27

Cleopatra Thea, 14, 31

Cleopatris (Arsinoe), 65

Clergy. See Priests

Cleruchic system, 66, 89–90, 91–92, 152–154, 193; and class, 155–156, 167; and Graeco-Egyptian relations, 154–155. See also Dionysios son of Kephalas; Pathyris

Contraband, 80–81

Convict labor, 53

Copper, 86–87

Cornelius Gallus, 191, 193, 194

Corvée labor, 74

Craft industries, 93–95, 116

Crassus, 19

Cremation, 136, 137

Crete, 54

Crime, 22, 42, 83–84, 117. See also Law

Crocodiles, 106–108

Crops. See Agriculture

Cult objects, return of, 38

Currency, 22, 78, 82–84, 86–87, 93–94; illustrations of, 10, 23, 36, 61, 63, 83

Cybele, 110

Cyprus, 13, 18, 19, 54, 153; dynastic conflicts over, 14, 17, 29; Ptolemy VIII's exile to, 15–16; Roman occupation of, 20, 21

Cyrenaica, 13, 17, 18, 29, 30, 54

Darius, King, 65

Death. See Funerary customs

Debt, 42, 157–158, 159

Delta, the, 63–65

Demeter, 115

Demetrios I (Syria), 14

Demetrios II (Syria), 14

Demetrios of Phaleron, 172

Demetrios Poliorketes, 35, 152, 153

Demosthenes, 176, 179

Demotic language and writing, 2, 3, 50; legal documents in, 109; literature in, 182–183, 185–189; and medicine, 177

Dendara, temple of, 47, 102

Didymos ("Bronze Gut"), 176

Dio, 21, 175

Diocletian, 59, 195

Diodorus Siculus, 55, 56, 62, 106, 138

Diogenes (banker), 84

Dioiketes, 21, 66, 76, 79

Dionysiac artists, associations of, 178

Dionysios (strategos), 132, 181

Dionysios (vice-thebarch), 84

Dionysios son of Kephalas, 156–160

Dionysos (god), 44, 111, 114

"Dionysos, New God." See Ptolemy XII Neos Dionysos

Diophantos (police chief), 143

Dioskorides Phakas, 176

Dioskouroi, 115

Districts. See Nomes

Djamet, temple at, 140–141, 142

Dodekaschoinos, 53

Dolabella, 25

Doloaspis (nomarch), 8

Domestic animals, 92–93

Domitian, 61

Donations, ceremony of the, 27

Dovecotes, 93

Drainage, 66

Dream of Nectanebo, 182–183

Dreams, 48–49, 124–127, 132, 133–134

Drowning, 143

Dryton son of Pamphilos, 160–164

Dynastic wars. See Civil wars

Eclecticism, 174, 175

Economy, 16, 18, 21–22, 82–84; crafts and commerce, 93–95; and inflation, 84, 86–87; parallel, 80–81; and slave labor, 98–99; of temples, 115–116. See also Agriculture; Currency; Taxation

Edfu, temple at, 43, 102, 103, 105, 189–190

Education: in gymnasia, 69, 109, 137, 155, 178, 194; in temples, 109, 183

Egyptians: agricultural practices of, 87–88; attitude toward Alexandria, 50–51, 57–58; bilingualism of, 76;

Egyptians *(continued)*
   as cleruchs, 156; Greek attitudes to-
   ward, 171; occupations of, 74, 76, 141.
   See also Graeco-Egyptian relations;
   Rebellions; *and specific individuals*
Eirenaios, 49
El-Dakka, temple of, 145, 193
Elephantine, 101, 151
Embalmers *(taricheutai)*, 137–138, 143,
   147
Embezzlement, 22, 83–84
Empiricists, 176–177
Entaphiastai (gravediggers), 138, 144,
   149–150
Epiphanes, as epithet, 36. *See also*
   Ptolemy V Epiphanes
Epistates, 74
Epistrategoi, 74
Eratosthenes, 172, 173
Esthladas son of Dryton, 161, 162–163
Euclid, 172
Eudoros, 174
Eudoxos of Knidos, 180–181
Euergetes, as epithet, 36. *See also*
   Ptolemy III Euergetes; Ptolemy VIII
   Euergetes II
Eukharistos, as epithet, 36. *See also*
   Ptolemy V
Euripides, 179, 181–182

Faiyum, the, 53, 55, 66–67, 90, 179;
   agriculture in, 92; colonization of, 66,
   155–156. *See also* Kerkeosiris
Festivals, 105
Funerary customs, 135–136, 139–141;
   and animal burial, 106–108; of Greek
   colonists, 136–137, 148; legal dispute
   regarding, 145–150; and professional
   associations, 141–144

Gaius Popilius Laenas, 13
Galaistes, 15
General Encyclopedia of Philosophy (Eu-
   doros), 174
Geography, 52–54; of the delta, 63–65;
   Memphis and the Faiyum, 65–66; Up-
   per Egypt, 67–69; and urban design,
   71. *See also* Alexandria
Glaukias (father of Ptolemaios and Apol-
   lonios), 133, 180
Gods: and dreams, 125–126, 133–134;

Greek, 31, 34–35, 101, 111, 113–115;
   Hellenic cults, 113–115; household,
   109–110; of Memphis, 118–123; and
   military expeditions, 38–39; Ptolemaic
   identification with, 30, 34–37, 38;
   slavery to, 117–118. *See also* Priests;
   Temples; *and specific gods*
Gold, 53, 95
Graeco-Egyptian relations, 4, 6, 9–10,
   170–171, 189–190; after Roman annexation, 194–196; and allegiance of
   clergy, 46–49, 50; and cleruchic system, 153, 154–155; and Lagides as
   pharaohs, 37–40; and law, 96–98;
   145–149, 162, 194; and religious associations, 110–111; and royal incest,
   31; and royal visits to provinces, 43,
   149–150. *See also* Rebellions
Gravediggers *(entaphiastai)*, 138, 144,
   149–150
Greek colonists: agricultural practices of,
   87–88; in Alexandria, 62; attitude toward kings, 33–34; bilingualism of,
   76, 182–183; in bureaucracy, 72; and
   cleruchic system, 66, 89, 91–92, 152–
   156, 167, 193; funerary practices of,
   136–137, 148; interest in Egypt, 171;
   Nile trade by, 95; religious beliefs of,
   34–35, 101, 110–111, 113–115. *See
   also* Graeco-Egyptian relations; Hellenism; *and specific individuals*
Grenfell, Bernard P., 2
Gymnasia, 69, 109, 137, 155, 178; during Roman era, 194

Haremphis *(strategos)*, 74
Harmais (recluse), 130–131
Harsiese (god), 38
Harsiese (rebel leader), 50, 84
Harwennofre (rebel leader), 50, 145, 146
Hekataios of Miletos, 171
Heliopolis, 65, 125, 127
Hellenism: Alexandria as intellectual center of, 59, 61, 171–176; associations
   promoting, 178; and cities, 56–58, 71,
   73, 178; in the countryside, 115, 177–
   182; decorative style in, 70; Egyptian
   coexistence with, 4, 170–171, 189–
   190; and *gymnasia*, 69, 109, 137, 155,
   178, 194; and kingship, 33–34; and
   law, 96–97, 148–149, 162; and medi-

cine, 172, 176–177; and religion, 31, 34–35, 101, 110–111, 113–115. *See also* Graeco-Egyptian relations; Greek colonists

Hera, 31

Hermaïskos, 20

Hermias son of Ptolemaios, 145–149

Hermonthis, 68, 69

Hermopolis, cemetery of, 137

Hermotybians, 151

Herodes, 189–190

Herodotus, 100, 151, 153, 171; on mummification, 136, 138

Heroes, 34–35

Herophilians, 176–177

Herophilos of Chalcedon, 172

Hieratic writing system, 177, 183

Hierax, 166–167

Hieroglyphics, 183–185

Homer, 136, 173, 176, 179, 187

Horos (brother of Totoes), 164, 165–166

Hor son of Harendotes, 48–49

Horus, 64, *110*, 112; temple of, at Edfu, 103, 105, 189–190

Housing: architecture of, 70; requisitioning of, 154–155

Hunt, Arthur S., 2

Iliad (Homer), 179, 187

Imhotep, 125, **126**

Immigration, 6, 62–63, 95. *See also* Greek colonists

Inaros, 187

Incest, 10, 30–31, 35

"Incisers" *(paraschistai)*, 138, 144

Inflation, 84, 86–87

Inscriptions, 3, 24–25, 183–185

Instruction of Ankhsheshonqy, 187–188

Inundation, the, 43, 52, 55, 64–65, 90–91. *See also* Nile River

Irrigation, 66, 74, 87, 88, 90–91; of cleruchic lands, 153

Isis, 64, 122, 127, 182; Lagide identification with, 26, 31, 37; temples of, 65, *110*, 113

Isolympic Games, 35

Jews, 14, 17, 62–63, 101, 173

Jonathan (Jewish leader), 14

Jouguet, Pierre, 2

Judaism, 101, 173

Judiciary, 74, 96–97, 109. *See also* Law

Justinus, 175

Kalasirians, 151

Kallimachos, 63, 74, 172, 173

Kanephoros, 35

Karnak, 69, **184**

Katoikoi, 91, 92, 156, 167

Kerkeosiris, 89, 90–93

Khaemwese, 186–187

Khery-heb, 138

Khonsu, temple of, **184**

Khonsu Cosmogony, **184**

Kingship, Greek conceptions of, 33–34

Kleomenes of Naukratis, 6, 8, 152

Kom el-Shuqafa, 58–59, 137

Komogrammateis (town scribes), 76–77, 80–81, 88, 90. *See also* Scribes

Kom Ombo, temple of, 102, **104**

Krokodilopolis, 67, 69, 160, 166–167

Ktesibios of Alexandria, 88, 172

Kydas (director of Alexandrian library), 173

Lagide dynasty: amnesty decrees and *philanthropa* under, 16, 41–43, 80, 91, 97; clergy's allegiance to, 46–49, 50; deification of, 34–37; extravagance of, 44–45; and Greek conception of kingship, 33–34; hostility toward, 49–51; importance of women in, 4, 30–32; as pharaohs, 37–40; provincial visits by, 40, 43, 130, 133, 149–150; and right of asylum, 18, 40–41; royal titularies of, 37, 45–46; succession in, 29–30; synods during, 39–40. *See also specific monarchs*

Laodicean War, 10

Laokritai, 96–97, 109

Latopolis, 69

Law, 74, 96–98, 109, 145–149; of divorce, 162; and oaths, 117; during Roman era, 194

Lepidus, 25

"Libation pourers." *See Choachytai*

Library at Alexandria, 57, 59, 61, 172, 175–176

Libyan dynasties, 151

Lighthouse at Alexandria, 59, **61**

Linen, 94, 138

Literature: classical Egyptian, 183–185; Demotic, 182–183, 185–189; Greek, 172, 178–182
Loans. See Debt
Lower Egypt, 64
Lower Nubia, 53
Lucullus, 26
Lykonpolis, siege of, 39
Lysimachos, 30

Macedonian conquest, 6–8, 151–152. See also Lagide dynasty
Magas, 30
Manetho (priest), 38
Marble, 70
Market places, 71
Mathematics, 172
Medicine, 172, 176–177
Medinet Habu, 69, 140
Mediterranean coast, 53
Memphis, 40, 51, 65–66, 144, 186; clergy in, 37, 47–48; decree of, 39, 46; deities of, 118–123; metalworking in, 94–95; Serapeum of, 122–123, 124, 130, 149, 180
"Memphites." See Ptolemy VII Theos Neos Philopater
Menander, 179
Menches (komogrammateus), 76–77, 80, 81, 90, 179
Mendes, 65
Mercenaries, 151, 152–154. See also Military
Merchants, 93–95
Meroe, 53
Metalworking, 94–95
Military, 11–13, 73–74, 151–152, 156–160; and cleruchic system, 89–90, 91–92, 152–156, 167, 193; decline of, 167–168; and Egyptian deities, 38–39; navy, 25, 28, 43, 168–169; Roman, 193. See also Pathyris
Mining, 53
Mithridates, 19, 20, 177
Mithridatic wars, 61, 174
Mnevis, 125–126, 127
Money. See Currency
Monkores (strategos), 74
Monopolies, 80–81, 140, 143–144
Mummies, status of, 143

Mummification, methods of, 136, 137–138. See also Funerary customs
Museum at Alexandria, 57, 59, 61, 172

Nabataeans, 19
Nabunun, tomb of, 142–143
Naukratis, 65
Navigation, 95
Navy, 25, 28, 43, 168–169
Nebwenenef, 142
Necho, Pharaoh, 65
Nectanebo II, Pharaoh, 182, 186
Nectanebos (pharaohs), 38
Nefertem, 119, 120
Nekrotaphoi, 140
Neoskeptical school, 174
Nephoris (mother of Taus and Thaues), 127, 129, 130
Nephthys, 127
"New God Dionysos." See Ptolemy XII Neos Dionysos
Nile mosaic, 53, 54
Nile River, 53, 54, 95, 143; delta of, 63–65; Inundation of, 43, 52, 55, 64–65, 90–91
Nomarchs, 73
Nomes, 72–76
Noumenios (strategos), 150
Nubia, 53, 145, 174, 193

Oaths, 117
Octavia, 27
Octavian, 3, 25, 27, 192, 193; annexation of Egypt by, 28, 191–193; and Areios Didymos, 175, 191; currency under, 87; propaganda of, 1, 26, 45; Selaukos's surrender to, 168
Odeon, the (Alexandria), 58
Odyssey (Homer), 179, 187
Oikonomos, 76, 79
Oils, 79–80, 81, 93, 116
Oinoparas, battle of, 14
Olive trees, 87
Ombos, 69
Onias IV, 62
On Kings (Timagenes), 175
Onuris, 182
Oracles, 117
Osiris, 31, 38, 108, 122, 127, 139
Osoeris son of Horos, 143

Osorapis, 123
Ostraca, 2–3, 48, 83, 179

Pachomios Hierax (strategos), 74, 75
Palestine, 17, 23, 54
Panobkhounis son of Totoes, 164, 165
Papyri, 2–3, 24, 50, 67, 90, 179; of choa-
chytai, 137; and oracles, 117
Papyrus, manufacture of, 93
Papyrus Harris I, 116
Papyrus Insinger, 188
Paraschistai ("incisers"), 138, 144
Pashu son of Pamenches, 190
Pastophoros. See Choachytai
Pathyris, 69, 160–164; disappearance
of, 166–167; Egyptian family life in,
164–166
Patous (father of Tareesis), 164, 165
Pausanias, 69
Peasants, 87–90, 91, 116, 157. See also
Agriculture
Pedubaste, 187
Pelusium, 64, 168
Perdiccas, 152
"Persian by descent," soldiers designated
as, 158–159
Persian occupation, 6, 38, 96, 151, 158
Persian Wars, 33
Peteese (Dream of Nectanebo), 182
Peteese (embalmer), 149–150
Peteharsemtheus son of Panobkhounis,
164
Petenephotes (paraschistes), 144
Petesouchos son of Panobkhounis, 165–
166
Petiese (nomarch), 8
Petrie, William Matthew Flinders, 2
Peukestas, 151, 154
Phagonis son of Panobkhounis, 164
Pharaonic culture. See Egyptians; Graeco-
Egyptian relations
Pharos, 59, 61
Philadelphia, 67, 71
Philadelphos, as epithet, 36–37. See also
Arsinoe II Philadelphos; Ptolemy II
Philae, temple at, 102, 110
Philanthropa, 42–43
Philip Arrhidaios, 37
Philippi, battles at, 25
Philippics (Demosthenes), 176

Philometor, as epithet, 36–37. See also
Ptolemy VI Philometor
Philopator, as epithet, 36–37. See also
Arsinoe III; Cleopatra VII Philopator;
Ptolemy III Philopator; Ptolemy IV
Philopator; Ptolemy XIV Philopator
Philadelphos
Philosophy, 172, 174–175
Physics, 172
"Physkon." See Ptolemy VIII Euer-
getes II
Pigeons, 93
Pindar, 173
Piracy, 98
Platon (epistrategos), 166
Pliny the Elder, 56
Plows, 88
Plutarch, 24, 45, 169
Poetry, 179, 181, 188–189
Pompeius Trogus, 175
Pompey, 19, 21, 22, 23–24, 26
"Pompey's pillar," 59, 60, 61
Population, 55–56; of Alexandria, 62–
63; of Memphis, 66
Potamon (philosopher), 174
Pothinos, 24
"Potter's Oracle, The," 50–51, 57
Pottery, 94
Poverty, 18, 80, 88–89
Priestesses, 35, 115
Priests, 38, 113, 115, 158; allegiance of,
46–49, 50; as guardians of culture,
183–185; as judges and lawyers, 96,
109; original literature of, 185–189;
prestige of, 108–109; and right of asy-
lum, 40–41; during Roman era, 194;
and royal titularies, 37, 45–46, 50;
and synods, 39–40. See also Funerary
customs; Temples
Provinces. See Chora
Psenptaïs, 48
Ptah, 95, 119, 121; priests of, 47–48,
186; temple of, 47, 66
Ptolemaic dynasty. See Lagide dynasty
Ptolemaic era, sources regarding, 2–3,
4–5, 24–25, 67; temple inscriptions,
3, 183–185. See also Menches; Papyri;
Stelae
Ptolemaieia, 35
Ptolemaios (father of Hermias), 145

Ptolemaios son of Glaukias, 99, 118, 123–127; and Apollonios, 131–134; reading material of, 180–183; and Tathemis and Harmais, 129–131; and the twins, 127–129

Ptolemais, 68, 71, 115

Ptolemy I Soter, 8–10, 9, 29, 30, 36; and Alexandria, 56, 61, 172; austerity of, 44; currency under, 22, 82; deification of, 35; military of, 152–154; as pharaoh, 37–38; royal titulary of, 45; and Sarapis, 123; as satrap, 33, 66

Ptolemy II, 4, 36, 53, 56, 88; and Alexandrian intellectualism, 172, 173; and cleruchic system, 66, 154, 156; currency under, 82–83; extravagance of, 44; incestuous marriage of, 10, 30–31, 35; laws under, 96; navy of, 168; provincial visits by, 43; religious cults established by, 10, 31, 35–36, 116; royal titulary of, 45

Ptolemy III Euergetes, 10, 30, 39, 55, 102; priests under, 39, 109; royal titulary of, 45

Ptolemy IV Philopator, 31, 43, 61, 111, 168; and battle of Raphia, 11, 39, 95

Ptolemy V Epiphanes, 3–4, 11–13, 12, 29, 145; amnesty decree under, 41–42; coronation of, 47; navy under, 168; royal titulary of, 46

Ptolemy VI Philometor, 13–15, 29, 31, 39, 96; and Alexandrian Jews, 62–63; currency stabilization under, 86; provincial visits by, 40, 43, 130, 133; royal titulary of, 46

Ptolemy VII Theos Neos Philopater ("Memphites"), 15–16

Ptolemy VIII Euergetes II ("Physkon"), 18, 31, 57, 145, 190; amnesty decree under, 16, 42–43, 91; civil war between Cleopatra II and, 15–16, 42–43, 84, 86, 91–92, 162–163; expulsion of scholars and artists by, 59, 61, 173–174; laws under, 96–97; navy under, 168; propaganda against, 50; provincial visits by, 43; and Ptolemy VI, 13–14, 29; on requisitioning of housing, 155; tryphe of, 44

Ptolemy IX Soter II, 16–18, 32, 43, 174; civil war under, 17–18, 69, 159, 166

Ptolemy X Alexander I, 4, 29, 149; civil

war under, 17–18, 69, 159, 166; and right of asylum, 18, 41

Ptolemy XI Alexander II, 18

Ptolemy XII Neos Dionysos ("Auletes"), 4, 19–22, 29–30, 74, 102; and Alexandrian intellectualism, 61, 174, 175; and clergy, 48; deification of, 37; inflation under, 86; rebellion against, 20–22, 32, 167, 175; royal titulary of, 46

Ptolemy XIII Philopator, 22, 23, 24

Ptolemy XIV Philopator Philadelphos, 24, 25

Ptolemy XV Caesar ("Caesarion"), 25, 27, 47, 102, 175; royal titulary of, 46

Ptolemy Apion, 18

Ptolemy Eupator, 14, 49

Ptolemy Keraunos, 29

Ptolemy of Cyrene. See Ptolemy VIII Euergetes II

Ptolemy Philadelphos (son of Cleopatra VII), 27

Public officials. See Bureaucracy

Public works, 61–62, 66. See also Irrigation

Pyramids, 59

Pyrrhonian Arguments (Ainesidemos of Knossos), 174

Rabirius Postumus, 21–22

Ramesses II, 56, 186

Ramesses III, 140

Raphia, battle of, 11, 39, 40, 95

Ra-qed, translated, 57. See also Alexandria

Rebellions: against Auletes, 20–22, 32, 167, 175; ideology of, 49–51; against Ptolemy V, 4, 11, 41–42, 145, 146; against Roman rule, 194; in Upper Egypt, 11, 68–69, 145, 146, 156, 166. See also Civil wars

Red Sea, 53, 65

Religion: and anti-Ptolemaic propaganda, 51; and biblical exegesis, 173; centrality of, 100–101; household, 109–110; oracles and oaths, 117; in professional and private associations, 110–111, 113; and sacred animals, 105–108, 121–123. See also Gods; Priests; Temples

Rents, agricultural, 88–89, 91, 116, 194

Requisitioning, 154–155

Rhakotis. *See* Alexandria
Ritual, daily cult, 104–105
Romances, 182–183, 186–187
Roman occupation, 3, 28, 191–196;
   Alexandria during, 58–59, 137; currency during, 87; temples during, 102
Rome: annexation of Cyprus by, 20, 54;
   and "Auletes," 19–20, 21; civil war in,
   23–24, 25–26, 27–28; Cleopatra VII's
   diplomacy with, 22, 24–28, 54; and
   decline of Lagide army, 167–168; Egypt
   as bequest to, 14, 18; intellectual patronage by, 174–175; and perceptions
   of Cleopatra VII, 1–2, 26, 45; population of, 62; and Ptolemaic extravagance, 44–45; and Syria, 13, 19
Rosetta Stone, 46
Royal peasant *(basilikos georgos),* 88–89,
   157. *See also* Peasants
Royal scribes *(basilikogrammateis),* 76,
   81, 90. *See also* Scribes
Royal titularies, 37, 45–46, 49–50

Sacred animals, 105–108, 121–123
Sais, 65
Saite Period, 151, 153, 171
Sakhmet, *119*
Salt tax, 55
Samos, 153
Sanctuary, 18, 40–41, 99, 148, 159
Sarapias (wife of Dryton), 161
Sarapis, 63, 66, 110, 122, 123; as inspira-
   tion for dreams, 128, 133
Satire, 188–189
"Satrap Stela," 38
Scipio Aemilianus, 44, 64
Scribes, 72, 76–77, 80–81, 88, 90
Sebennytos, 65
Selaukos, 168
Seleucid dynasty: dynastic wars of, 14; in-
   vasion of Egypt by, 13, 48–49; Lagide
   intermarriage with, 4, 11, 30, 31; perse-
   cution of Jews by, 14, 62; Roman defeat
   of, 19. *See also* Syria; Syrian wars
Sema, the, 61
Senamunis (daughter of Taynchis), 144
Septuagint, 173
Serapeum of Alexandria, 61
Serapeum of Memphis, 122–123, 124,
   130, 149, 180. *See also* Apollonios son
   of Glaukias; Ptolemaios son of Glaukias

Seth, 38, 50–51, 64
Setne, 186–187
Sextus Empiricus, 174
Shopkeepers, 93–95
Shu, 193
Silver, 82, 84, 86, 95
Slavery, 98–99; temple, 117–118
Sobek, 67, 106, 160
Soldiers. *See* Cleruchic system; Military
Sophocles, 179
Sostratos of Knidos, 59
Soter, as epithet, 36. *See also* Ptolemy I
   Soter; Ptolemy IX Soter II
Special Account, 194
Speculation, 157–158
Stater, 22
Stelae, 3, 37–38, 48, 184; commemorat-
   ing synods, 39–40; and right of asy-
   lum, 40–41
Stories, 182–183, 186–187
Strabo, 57, 59, 64, 68, 106
Strategoi, 73–76, 97, 193
Strato of Lapsakos, 172
Sulla, 18
Synods, 39–40
Syntaxis, 116, 194
"Syracusans, The" (Kallimachos), 172
Syria, 14, 54, 62, 64; invasion of Egypt
   by, 13, 48–49; Roman conquest of, 19;
   and War of Scepters, 17, 190. *See also*
   Seleucid dynasty
Syrian wars, 10, 11, 13, 35; and battle of
   Raphia, 11, 39, 40, 95; inflation dur-
   ing, 84

Tabubu, 186
Tanis, 65
Taposiris Magna, 63
Tareesis (daughter of Patous), 165
Taricheutai (embalmers), 137–138, 143,
   147
Tathemis, 129–130
Taus (recluse), 127–129
Taxation, 55, 72, 74, 76, 89; avoidance
   of, 80–82, 94; of cleruchic lands, 155;
   and inflation, 86; laws regarding, 96,
   97; oppressiveness of, 40, 51, 80, 89,
   193–194; during Roman era, 193–194;
   system of, 78–80; and temples, 36, 40,
   42, 116
Tax farming, 40, 78–80, 89

Taynchis (mother of Senamunis), 144
Tbokanoupis (wife of Phagonis), 164
Tefnut, 193
Telephos (Euripides), 181–182
Temples, 102–105; agriculture of, 116; in
  Alexandria, 61, 62–63; animals of, 92,
  105–108, 121–123; asylum in, 18, 40–
  41, 99, 159; in the delta, 65; economy
  of, 115–116; and education, 109, 183;
  Greek, 115; inscriptions on, 3, 183–
  185; Jewish, 62–63, 101; linen produc-
  tion by, 94; and oracles and oaths, 117;
  and philanthropa, 42–43; during Ro-
  man era, 194; slavery to, 117–118; and
  taxation, 36, 40, 42, 116; in Thebes,
  68; and urban design, 71; violence in,
  131. See also Gods; Priests; Ptolemaios
  son of Glaukias; and specific temples
Tenis. See Akoris
Tesserakonteres, 43, 168
Tetradrachm, 22
Textiles, 94, 116
Thaues (recluse), 127–129, 132
Thebes, 43, 68–69, 140–143, 144, 166
Theogenes (dioiketes), 84
Theokritos, 56, 172
Thiasoi, 111
Thoth, 186, 193
Thynabounoun, 142–143
Tigranes, tomb of, 137
Timagenes (historian), 175
Timonikos (assistant to strategos Apollo-
  doros), 149
Titularies, royal, 37, 45–46, 49–50
Tombs, 137, 140, 142–143, 148. See also
  Funerary customs

Totoes (father of Panobkhounis), 164,
  165
Towns, 64–65, 67–68, 71. See also Cities
Town scribes (komogrammateis), 76–77,
  80–81, 88, 90. See also Scribes
Trade, 11, 95
Tryphe, 44–45
Tuthmosis IV, 124–125

Upper Egypt, 66, 67–69, 167; rebellions
  in, 11, 68–69, 145, 146, 156, 166.
  See also Thebes
Urban design, 71
Urbanization. See Cities

Villages: life in, 90–93; number of, 56.
  See also Agriculture; Peasants

Wadi Allaqi, 53
Wah-Mu. See Choachytai
War of Scepters, 17, 190
Water wheel, 88
Weapons, manufacture of, 95
Wenenper. See Choachytai
Wheat, 78, 87, 92, 157–158
Wisdom literature, 183, 187–188
Women, status of, 4, 30–32, 97
Wool, 94
Writing systems, 2, 183–186. See also De-
  motic language and writing; Literature

Zenodotos of Ephesos, 173, 176
Zenon of Kaunos, 4–5, 67
Zeus, 31, 59, 68, 111, 113, 115
Zopyros (pharmacologist), 177